Non-Jewish Zionism

Regina S. Sharif

GW00713228

Non-Jewish Zionism

Its Roots in Western History

Regina S. Sharif

Zed Press, 57 Caledonian Road, London N1 9DN.

Non-Jewish Zionism was first published by Zed Press, 57 Caledonian Road, London N1 9DN in 1983.

Copyright © Regina Sharif, 1983

Copyedited by Bev Brown
Typeset by Kate Macpherson
Proofread by Mark Gourlay
Cover design by Jacque Solomons
Printed by The Pitman Press, Bath, U.K.

All rights reserved

British Library Cataloguing in Publication Data

Sharif, Regina
Non-Jewish Zionism.
1. Zionism—History
I. Title
956.94'001   DS149

ISBN 0-86232-151-4
ISBN 0-86232-152-2 Pbk

Contents

Preface

The purpose of this book is to give an account of a phenomenon which I chose to call 'non-Jewish Zionism'. In so short a book about so complex a subject there will inevitably be omissions and over-simplifications which will catch the eye of the professional historians. Their criticisms, which I doubtlessly deserve, will be gratefully accepted. But my primary objective has been to present a broad outline of the phenomenon of non-Jewish Zionism in order to stir the general reader's interest and awareness of the phenomenon's relevance to the problem of Palestine today. I realize that I am dealing here with a most controversial subject and one which is far from being closed. But within the context of my own background and persuasion I have conscientiously tried to be as objective as possible.

I would like to express my sincere appreciation to all those who have assisted me in the planning, writing and the final preparation of this work.

I owe special thanks to Dr Hassan al-Ebraheem and Dr Anis Kassim for the generous support they accorded and thereby helped to make this work possible.

I am most grateful to Dr Elmer Berger and Dr John Lapp who read the manuscript and subsequently gave valuable counsel, guidance and suggestions.

Thanks should also be expressed to the many kind people who assisted me in obtaining access to the literature needed for the research, especially the staff of the libraries of the Palestine Research Center and the Institute for Palestine Studies in Beirut, as well as the staff members of the Library of Congress in Washington, D.C.

Most of all, I owe an irredeemable debt to my husband Walid – without whose help and constant encouragement it is unlikely that this project would have been completed – and to our children Khalid, Tania and Qais, who have accepted many hours of my preoccupation with the problems of Zionism rather than their own. I sincerely hope that once grown up they will be convinced that the result justified their patience and forbearance.

Kuwait, December 1982.

1. Introduction

The question of the intrinsic nature of Zionism again moved into the foreground of international attention when the United Nations General Assembly, on 10 November 1975, in Resolution 3379 (XXX) determined 'that Zionism is a form of racism and racial discrimination'.[1] The adoption of this resolution was the first time the majority in the community of nations openly rejected the traditional presentation of the Zionist movement as the national liberation movement of and for the Jewish people.[2]

Much has been written about Zionism since it first made its appearance as an organized political movement among Jews at the end of the 19th Century in Western Europe. Yet, most studies on Zionism remain limited in their scope and content, highly subjective and generally written by committed Zionists themselves. Frequently subsidized by Zionist organizations, the purpose of these publications is either to justify the Zionist position before world Jewry or to mobilize world public opinion among non-Jews for the Zionist cause.[3]

Any valid and comprehensive study of Zionism must do more than merely trace the emergence of the Zionist idea among Jews in the late 19th and early 20th Centuries. The present study makes no further attempt to examine the history of the Zionist idea among Jews. Rather, we propose to deal extensively and solely with a hitherto neglected portion of the history of Zionism, namely the phenomenon of non-Jewish Zionism on the international scene.

Non-Jewish Zionism as a Distinct Phenomenon

The birth of Jewish political Zionism as the ideological instrument for mobilizing international support for an exclusively Jewish state in Palestine dates from the publication of Herzl's *Der Judenstaat* in 1896. Political Zionism was strengthened when the 1st Zionist Congress, convened by Theodor Herzl in 1897, accepted the Basle Platform calling for a 'publicly secured and legally assured homeland for the Jews in Palestine'.[4]

Herzl may indeed be the founder of political Zionism, but this does not mean that his ideas were original. His predecessors are many and various, and include both Jews and non-Jews.[5] But, whereas most Jewish Zionist writings appeared during the second half of the 19th Century, non-Jews had already developed the ideas and programme basic to what would become the Jewish political Zionism. Indeed, non-Jews had begun to promote the Zionist idea of a Jewish national consciousness directed towards Palestine three centuries before the 1st Zionist Congress.

It is our contention that the evolution of Zionist ideas and prejudices among non-Jews deserves to be viewed as an independent historical phenomenon and studied in its own right. It usually figures only in the margins of the general run of Zionist histories, with the acknowledgement of a few incidental and idealistic pre-Herzlian schemes designed by non-Jews for Jewish settlement in Palestine – theories supposedly totally removed from the prevailing reality. Some attention has also been paid to what Zionists prefer to call 'Gentile' or 'Christian' Zionism.[6] These are studies dealing with the theological aspects of the so-called Christian interests in Jewish Zionism. More often, though, non-Jewish Zionism is relegated to the background, too insignificant to warrant more than perhaps an introductory mention of those Christians who supported Jews in their Zionist endeavours. Yet, as an account of the motivations of these Christian protagonists of Zionism, such treatment is hardly adequate if it is to function as an integral part of Western social and political history. By contrast, the history of anti-Semitism, often portrayed as the norm in the non-Jew's relation to the Jew throughout history, finds vivid expression in Western histories.

There is of course a major problem in deciding exactly what Zionism is and determining who should be classified as Zionist. Zionism is generally understood to be a complex of beliefs aimed at the practical realization of the 1897 Basle Platform. Zionists are those who perceive the community known as Jews as a separate national people to be resettled as a sovereign political entity in Palestine in order to establish there an exclusively Jewish nation-state.

For the purposes of our study, non-Jewish Zionism is defined as a complex of beliefs among non-Jews aimed at the promotion of a Jewish nation-state in Palestine by right and in accordance with the Basle Programme. Therefore, non-Jewish Zionists are those who are favourably disposed towards the aims of Zionism and actively promote them either openly or covertly.

The traditional terms 'Gentile' or 'Christian' Zionism are misleading since they now suggest a Christian enthusiasm for Zionism motivated essentially by Biblical or theological reasoning. But it is the political motivations of non-Jewish protagonists of Zionism which have above all today come to make up an integral part of the non-Jewish Zionist matrix. Many non-Jewish people of public stature have consistently expressed their own faith in the Zionist idea and have often given eloquent expression to their own personal Zionist predispositions. It is precisely this unique phenomenon of non-Jewish Zionism that we propose to analyse here.

In our study, emphasis will be placed on what non-Jewish Zionism has meant historically for non-Jews, how it interacted with different governmental policies as well as social moods, and how it is maintained today in Western political culture as a force bolstering Jewish Zionism and Israeli policies. We shall document and analyse the building of Jewish Zionist strength from the reservoir of latent but potential non-Jewish support.

Our argument thus runs counter to the usual representation: most historians and political analysts attribute the success story of Zionism – its triumphant consummation in the Jewish state of Israel – to the political and diplomatic skills of Zionist Jews, like Chaim Weizmann, Louis Brandeis or Nahum Sokolow, who tirelessly influenced non-Jewish public figures. Most credit for the Balfour Declaration usually goes to Weizmann and his unbounded energy, determination and singleness of purpose. Similarly, the present-day pro-Israeli American policy is attributed to the all-too-powerful Zionist lobby in Washington.

The success story of Zionism is hardly ever attributed to non-Jews. Our study will reveal that such interpretations of Zionist strength are far too simple. Weizmann's skills in international diplomacy and persuasion, however great, would have remained fruitless had not the seeds of Zionism been sown and cultivated by non-Jews long before the appearance of Herzl's *Der Judenstaat* in 1896. By the same token the Zionist lobby in the United States would never achieve its level of influence were it not for the simple fact that it operates today within a political environment that is most conducive to Zionist ideas.

As for the existing studies on Zionism, we do not intend to challenge or contradict any of them. Our object is basically to add what we regard as the missing link in the study of Zionism. Most scholarly studies, apart from works of pure propaganda, are indeed based on historical facts, although the facts are often taken out of their general historical context. Jewish historians tend to view Jewish history simply as the national history of the Jews; Zionism is examined only in its relation to insular Jewish interests rather than in connection with the history of the different countries in which the Jews lived. Thus, the Balfour Declaration is seen as nothing more than the fruit of Weizmann's skills in the art of persuasion and the science of industrial chemistry. Little is said about Balfour's political motivations in finally succumbing to Zionist pressure. Nor is it often asked why, among all the world's countries, it was England and subsequently the United States that were to make possible the realization of the Zionist dream in Palestine.

In this book we attempt to rewrite the history of Zionism from a less ethnocentric standpoint. Non-Jewish Zionism will be shown as an integral element in Western religious, social and political history, forming a parallel and not an annex to the history of Jewish Zionism. We will thus attempt to bring together in one place authentic historical material which would otherwise remain scattered over that immense literary canvas known, all too tellingly, as the Judaeo-Christian tradition. The present study traces the development of non-Jewish Zionism from post-Reformation Europe up to its present insidious intrication in Western culture. Consequently, the intrinsic character of present-day Zionism, as practised by the Zionist state of Israel, will be made visible as one face of Western imperialism. It will also be obvious that current Western attempts to find a solution to the Palestine problem will remain futile as long as the West does not come to grips with its own inherent Zionist prejudices embedded in its past and present.

'A Form of Racism': From Protestantism to Practical Politics

The socio-political roots of non-Jewish Zionism first appeared in the religious sphere prevailing in the Protestant Anglo-Saxon countries. The evolution of these views over the centuries has made them a deeply engrained part of Western culture, although it was not until the 19th Century that Zionism finally forsook the realm of religion and mysticism for practical politics. As a nationalist doctrine, it operated in active concert with prevailing imperialist power politics.

By portraying the non-Jewish element of Zionism at the time of 20th Century colonialism and overseas expansion, we shall necessarily expose the collusion of Zionism with such reactionary forces as colonialism, imperialism and anti-Semitism. This history substantiates the charges embodied in the UN Resolution cited at the beginning of this chapter, designating Zionism as a form of racism.

Zionism and Anti-Semitism

The many influential non-Jews who advocated Zionism were certainly not all moved by simple philo-Semitism, i.e. love for the Jews. We shall show that non-Jewish Zionists often felt, and for that matter still feel today, the same prejudices as their anti-Semitic contemporaries, promoting Jewish Zionism not as a means to safeguarding the Jews, but to justify deporting them to 'where they belonged', or refusing them entry.

Some even saw the existing world-order as necessarily involving racial antagonism. Like their Jewish Zionist friends, they did not consider anti-Semitism abnormal, absurd or perverse, but took it as a fact of nature and the norm in the relationship of non-Jew to Jew.

Richard Meinertzhagen, General Allenby's political officer, and one of the most active and revered British non-Jewish Zionists of the Mandate era, is by no means unique in confessing that his Zionism was based on his 'anti-Semitic instinct . . . invariably modified by personal contact.'[7] Countless other similar quotations, by both Jewish and non-Jewish Zionists, can be produced to show the common theoretical point of departure of Zionism and anti-Semitism.[8] 'The point of view of the Zionists is similar to that of anti-Semites . . . Just like anti-Semitism, Zionism expresses itself in disharmony, in strong intolerance, in injustice, and in lack of understanding of the opponent.'[9] Thus Zionism cannot be regarded as the Jewish reaction *to* anti-Semitism but more its spiritual counterpart – 'the natural and abiding ally of anti-Semitism and its most powerful justification.'[10]

Finally, even where not attached to anti-Semitism as such, many Zionist claims were founded on the inherent racism which allocates everything from personality characteristics to rights over national terrorism on the basis of the so-called unities of race and racial origin.

Zionism and Nazism

In the more recent past, new documentary evidence even justifies one in speaking of the Nazi-Zionist alliance during the Third Reich and to rank certain Nazi figures among the non-Jewish Zionists.[11] The introduction to the infamous racist Nuremberg Laws of 15 September 1935 included the following paragraph with regard to Jewish Zionism and its justification:

> If the Jews had a state of their own in which the bulk of their people were at home, the Jewish question could already be considered solved today, even for the Jews themselves. The ardent Zionists of all people have objected least of all to the basic ideas of the Nuremberg Laws, because they know that these laws are the only correct solution for the Jewish people.[12]

And Haim Cohen, one-time judge of the Israeli Supreme Court, noted:

> The bitter irony of fate has decreed that the same biological and racist arguments extended by the Nazis, and which inspired the inflammatory laws of Nuremberg, serve as the basis for the official definition of Jewishness in the bosom of the State of Israel.[13]

Recent studies have clearly brought to light the frequent collaboration between Nazis and Zionists.[14] Jewish emigration from Germany to Palestine served the cause of both the Nazi anti-Semitic élite who wanted to free Germany from its 'Jewish yoke' and the Zionists who were in need of increased Jewish immigration in order to consolidate their position in Palestine and to create their Jewish state.[15]

On the theoretical as well as on the practical level, the Nazis and the Zionists saw eye to eye. Both were working towards the same goal: to uproot world Jewry from its established environment in order to transplant the Jews into the new Jewish ghetto of Palestine, a land already harbouring a recalcitrant indigenous Arab population. The cornerstone of Zionist theory, namely that anti-Semitism 'is the visa to the Jews' passport into the world of modernity' found its ultimate justification in the Nazi theories of racial supremacy.

Therefore, one must reject the modern-day Israeli equation, anti-Zionism=anti-Semitism, used in the endless Zionist polemics against their non- or anti-Zionist adversaries and critics.[16]

In this light, the present 'unholy alliance' between Israel and South Africa is not arbitrary nor is it sheer coincidence that South Africa's leaders and advocates of apartheid consider themselves 'friends' of Israel. The ideological affinity and practical collaboration between Israeli Zionism and South African apartheid have now become the subject of various reports and resolutions of the United Nations and other international organizations.[18]

Zionism and the Palestinian People

Finally, we shall examine the way non-Jewish Zionism today affects the Palestine problem by blocking any possible solution. Ignorance of the historic cause of Zionism is one reason for the many misunderstandings which afflict the Palestinian cause in the West. An understanding of the phenomenon of non-Jewish Zionism exposes Zionism as a movement organically linked to Western imperialism, embracing the same imperialist racist perception.

To set the record straight, we shall show how the subterranean stream of Western history and culture has become muddied with the whole effluvium of Zionist myths, both secular and religious, making Zionism the invisible yet most forceful link between Israel and the West. Zionist Israel and the West are bound together in a community of ideology and affinity from which the Arab world is necessarily excluded. The United Nations only rarely deviates from the general trend prevailing among Western countries in their steadfast support for the Jewish state and its policies. Third World and socialist countries, on the other hand, are far less inhibited in their condemnation of Israel's aggressive policies and Zionist racism.

The Myth of the Mighty Jewish Lobby

It is often argued that within the United States the Zionist lobby represents the most effective and often an invincible instrument of political and diplomatic pressure. Recent studies tend to reinforce this image of Zionism as a striking example of a successful interest group able to influence American foreign policy.[19] These studies concentrate their analysis on the organization and the methods the Zionist lobby uses to exert its pressures on the decision-making process of the United States government. They do not examine the way pro-Zionist attitudes pervade American culture, conditioning the American policy to be receptive to Zionist demands. Our study of non-Jewish Zionism helps the reader to understand more fully just why Americans generally, and American politicians in particular, have become so susceptible to the pressures of Israel and its lobby.

At present the United States represents the most clear-cut example of the tradition of non-Jewish Zionism. The broad concepts of Zionism have become a pervasive theme in American thought and policy towards the Middle East and Palestine since the very beginning of the American Republic, a trend which continues today. General policies on the Palestine problem tend to symbolize the United States' acknowledgement of Jewish 'rights' to Palestine.

It is highly unlikely that any proposed 'solution' to the problem of Palestine coming from the West will ever do justice to the Palestinian or Arab cause until the West faces up to the intrinsic nature of Zionism and frees itself from its deeply entrenched Zionist prejudices. Nothing less than a major re-orientation is required.

Notes

1. United Nations, *Resolutions adopted by the General Assembly during its Thirtieth Session* (6 September–17 December 1975), Supplement No. 34 (A/10034), pp. 83–4.
2. See, for example, Bernard Lewis, 'The Anti-Zionist Resolution', *Foreign Affairs*, Vol. 55, No. 1, October 1976, pp. 54–64.
3. There are many examples of such literature: Leonard J. Stein, *Zionism* (London, 1925); Israel Cohen, *The Zionist Movement* (New York, 1946); Joseph E. Heller, *The Zionist Idea* (London, 1947); Arthur Hertzberg (ed.), *The Zionist Idea: A Historical Analysis and Reader* (New York, 1969); Walter Z. Laqueur, *A History of Zionism* (London, 1972); Howard M. Sacher, *A History of Israel: From the Rise of Zionism to Our Time* (New York, 1976); Robert C. Goldston, *Next Year in Jerusalem* (Boston, 1978).
4. Minutes of the 1st Zionist Congress in Basle, Switzerland, 29–31 August 1897: see *Protokoll des ersten Zionisten Kongresses in Basel* (Vienna, 1898). For the basic demands of the Basle Programme, see *Erster Zionisten Kongress Basle* (Vienna, 1897) pp. 114–15 or Chapter Five of the present book. More recently, the Zionist Congress meeting in Jerusalem in 1968 redefined the aims of Zionism as follows: 1) the unity of the Jewish people and the centrality of Israel in Jewish life; 2) the in-gathering of the Jewish people in its historic homeland, *Eretz Israel*: 3) the strengthening of the State of Israel; 4) the preservation of the identity of the Jewish people; and 5) the protection of Jewish rights.
5. The term 'Zionism' is said to have been first coined in 1890 by Nathan Birnbaum. Israel Cohen (op. cit.) maintains that Herzl was totally ignorant of the works of his predecessors, for example, Moses Hess, Zebi Hirsch Kalisher, and Leon Pinsker.
6. Two early Zionist accounts of 'Gentile Zionism' are Nahum Sokolow, *History of Zionism* (London, 1919) and N. M. Gelber, *Vorgeschichte des Zionismus* (Berlin, 1917). Both studies stress the tradition of Biblical Zionism in Great Britain prior to the Balfour Declaration. They particularly focus on the history of the so-called Restoration idea and treat non-Jewish advocates of the Restoration as the forerunners of modern Zionism. Albert M. Hyamson, *British Projects for the Restoration of the Jews* (London, 1917) falls into the same category. A more recent study, yet very short, and limited in its analysis

to theological implications, is Franz Kobler, *The Vision Was There* (London, 1956). A Zionist historian inquiring into the nature of Christian Zionism is Barbara Tuchmann, *Bible and Sword: England and Palestine from the Bronze Age to Balfour* (London, 1956); she stresses the Puritan era in England. Two further studies discussing the political activities and roles played by British non-Jewish Zionists are Christopher Sykes, *Two Studies in Virtue* (London, 1953) and N. A. Rose, *The Gentile Zionists* (London, 1973).

7. Richard Meinertzhagen, *Middle East Diary, 1917–1956* (London, 1960), p. 49.
8. See, for example, Moshe Machover and Mario Offenberg, 'Zionism and its Scarecrows', *Khamsin*, No. 6, 1978, pp. 34–8. The authors clearly expose the Zionist-anti-Semite alliance. For the most vulgar descriptions of the 'Jewish race' by 19th Century Zionists see Moses Hess, *Rome and Jerusalem: A Study in Jewish Nationalism*, translated by Meyer Waxman (New York, 1918) and Leo Pinsker, *Auto-Emancipation*, edited by A. S. Eben (London, 1932). See also Chapter Seven of this book.
9. Antizionistisches Komitee, *Schriften zur Aufklaerung ueber den Zionismus*, No. 2 (Berlin, n.d.).
10. Lucien Wolf, 'The Zionist Peril', *Jewish Quarterly Review*, Vol. 17, October 1904, pp. 22–3.
11. Jon and David Kimche, *The Secret Roads: The Illegal Migration of People, 1938–1948* (London, 1954).
12. *Die Nuernberger Gesetze*, 5th edition (Berlin, 1939), pp. 13–14.
13. Quoted in Joseph Badi, *Fundamental Laws of the State of Israel* (New York, 1960), p. 156.
14. See Eliahu Ben Elissar, *La Diplomatie du IIIe Reich et les Juifs* (Paris, 1969) and Klaus Polkehn, 'Secret Contacts: Zionism and Nazi Germany, 1933–1941', *Journal of Palestine Studies*, Vol. 5, Nos. 3–4, pp. 54–82.
15. Ben Elissar, op. cit., p. 86.
16. See, for example, Shlomo Avineri, 'The Re-emergence of Anti-Semitism', *Congress Monthly*, Vol. 43, No. 1, pp. 14–16.
17. Morris S. Cohen, 'Zionism: Tribalism or Liberalism?', *New Republic*, 8 March 1919, p. 183.
18. Paul Giniewski, *Two Faces of Apartheid* (Chicago, 1965); see also *Report on the Relations Between Israel and South Africa*, adopted by the UN Special Committee against Apartheid, 19 August 1976. There is a longer discussion of this theme in Chapter Seven of this book.
19. See Earl D. Huff, 'A Study of a Successful Interest Group: The American Zionist Movement', *Western Political Science Quarterly*, Vol. 25, March 1972, pp. 109–124; also Morrell Heald and Lawrence S. Kaplan, *Culture and Diplomacy* (New York, 1978).

2. The Genesis of Non-Jewish Zionism

The Founding of a Mythology

Zionism as a systematic secular political ideology, as well as a modern organized political movement, first appeared on Europe's political stage towards the end of the 19th Century. Yet Zionism as an idea pre-dates both the 19th Century and Jewish Zionism. The major Zionist presupposition, including their underlying mythology, did not stem from this era at all, but can be traced back 300 years prior to the 1st Zionist Congress in Basle in 1897 when a select group of European Jews for the first time publicly rallied behind the Zionist banner.[1] The tapestry of Zionism took shape during four centuries of European religious, social, intellectual and political history through the interweaving of many different strands of Western culture, but first and foremost religious ones. The non-Jewish Zionist tradition is thus based on a whole constellation of Zionist myths which managed to creep into Western history most noticeably via the Protestant Reformation of the 16th Century.

The Zionist myths which began to be cultivated at that early stage within the non-Jewish environment were very much in line with those that eventually came to make up the inner logic of Jewish political Zionism, namely the myth of the Chosen People, the myth of the covenant and the myth of the Second Coming of the Messiah. The myth of the Chosen People set the Jews up as a nation and one favoured above all others. The myth of the covenant centred upon the continuous and indissoluble connection, as promised by God, between the Chosen People and the Holy Land, thus giving Palestine to the Jewish nation as its predestined territory. Finally the myth of messianic expectancy guaranteed that the Chosen People would in due time finally set an end to its exile and return to Palestine in order to establish there their national existence once and for all.

We use the term 'myth' in the sociological sense as outlined by Talcott Parsons,[2] meaning sanctified or hallowed belief patterns accepted by society at large as having both cognitive and evaluative elements and related to religion, history or politics. As such, myths become fused into complex ideological belief systems generally and often subconsciously accepted by the members of a community. The peculiarity of Zionist myths consisted in the close fusion of national, historical and religious elements referring primarily to the interconnecting relationship between three elements: the Bible (Old Testament), the Holy Land, and the Chosen People.[3]

Non-Jewish Zionism began to take on a recognizable form in the early 16th Century when Renaissance and Reformation combined to lay the foundation of modern European history. The revived interest in Biblical literature and its exegesis awakened public interest in the Jews and their return to Palestine. Thus what came to constitute the 'Jewish Question' in the 16th Century was not Jewish emancipation – the granting of citizens' rights – but the role assigned to the Jews in such new doctrinal questions as the fulfilment of Biblical prophecies, the Latter Times and the Second Coming of Christ the Messiah. There may have been philo-Semitism prior to the 16th Century, but there is no record of it.

Hence, by opening up the question of Jewish national revival and the Jews' collective return to Palestine, the Protestant Reformation initiated a continuous non-Jewish Zionist record as an important element in Protestant theology and eschatology. (Eschatology is that area of theology dealing with 'last things', such as death, immortality, the end of the world or the Last Judgement.)

The Reformation of Bible Reading

Medieval Christian Palestine

Prior to the Reformation, traditional Catholic thought had no place for the possibility of a Jewish return to Palestine nor any such concept as the existence of a Jewish nation. The early Church Fathers generally avoided literal interpretation of the Bible in favour of other modes of theological reading, especially allegorical exegesis which became the official mode of Biblical interpretation as set by the Roman Catholic Church.

Biblical passages, particularly found in the Old Testament, referring to the Jews' returning to their Homeland were held to apply not to the Jews as such but metaphorically to the Christian Church. As for the Jews themselves, according to official Catholic doctrine, they had sinned and consequently God had banished them from Palestine into Babylonian exile. When they finally rejected Jesus as the Messiah, God exiled them once more and, with this second dispersion, the existence of what could have been called 'a Jewish nation' had come to an end forever. For the Jews there was thus no collective national future left. On the other hand, Jews as individuals could still find salvation through their personal conversion to Christianity.

Equally, the prophecies regarding Jewish Restoration were read as applying to the return of the Israelites from exile in Babylon; they had thus already been fulfilled in the 6th Century BC when Cyrus allowed the

Jews back into Palestine. The other prophetic passages predicting a glorious future for Israel were interpreted to apply to the 'new Israel' i.e. the Christian Church, which was regarded as the 'true' Israel and the direct heir to the Hebrew religion.

This was precisely the theme of St. Augustine's *De Civitate Dei*, the *magnum opus* of early Catholic theology. Writing in the 5th Century, the Church Father Augustine had created the doctrine according to which the Church itself already embodied the millenial kingdom of God. This view was universally accepted until the 16th Century as the traditional Christian opinion on the subject of the Jews. As a result the medieval period tended to dissociate contemporary Jews from the ancient Hebrews.[4]

Palestine was considered primarily as the Holy Land of Jesus, as inherited by the Christians. Jerusalem was not described as the Jewish Zion, but as the Holy City of the New Testament. The importance of Jerusalem as the Holy City had in any case tended to decline after AD 590 when the papal throne of Pope Gregory the Great became the seat of Christian authority, and Rome took precedence over Jerusalem. The Bishop of Jerusalem, although recognized as the legitimate ecclesiastical successor of St. James, the brother of Jesus, was ranked only fifth in the newly classified Catholic hierarchy.[5]

Yet Palestine as the Holy Land continued to permeate the lives and imagination of medieval Christians. A trip to the Holy Land remained a cherished ambition for every Christian, with the additional lure of adventure and sometimes even economic gain. Every pilgrim returning from Palestine brought back stories of wonderful sights and aroused the desire of others to go there. Without these mass pilgrimages, interest in the Holy Land would most likely have completely subsided.

Not until the 11th Century did Palestine and Jerusalem again become the focus of attention for the medieval Christian polity, with the Turkish Muslim conquest of the land of Palestine. The papacy and nobility joined together in the Crusades to retake the Holy Land from the infidel, whether Muslim or Jew.

As the Zionist historian Barbara Tuchmann points out, popular hatred of the Jews in Europe was most profound during the time of the Crusades, and prior to that had not been a particularly active sentiment.[6] Other historians also indicate that pogroms against the Jews were initiated by Christian Crusade warriors *en route* to Palestine.[7] The time of the Crusades also saw the beginning of the ghetto system and thus the isolation of the Jews from their Christian surroundings.

Pre-Reformation Europe did not look upon the Jews as the Chosen People destined to return to the Holy Land; the Jew, if chosen for anything, had been chosen for damnation. The Jews were generally regarded as heretics, often branded as the murderers of Christ. There was no strain of romantic affection for the ancient glory of the Hebrew race or any ray of hope for the Jews' spiritual or national regeneration. The earlier Jewish possession of Palestine hardly entered into medieval thinking. Non-Jewish Zionism was completely absent from the Europe of the Middle Ages, while 'Israel' was regarded merely as the name of a religion and an inferior one at that. There was no idea that 'Israel' might also include national qualities.[8]

The Reformation and the Hebrew Ethos

In the history of Christian-Jewish relationships, the Protestant tradition set in motion by the Reformation of the 16th Century stood in sharp contrast to the previous Catholic tradition. Indeed this Reformation is often characterized as a 'Hebraising' or 'Judaizing' revival, engendering a new view of the Jewish past and present and particularly its future. The Protestant Reformation was intensely preoccupied with the world to come, and life was viewed against the backdrop of eternity. Belief in messianism and millenarianism, both features of the Judaic tradition, also became prevalent.[9]

Although Christianity was in great measure an outgrowth of Judaism and always contained some strong Jewish elements it was only with the theological shifts of the Reformation that the concept of the Jews as a nation set apart, or the emphasis on their physical return to the land of Palestine, gained currency. Before that, a sharp distinction had been made between the Hebrew people of the Old Testament, often idealized, and contemporary Jewry which was generally disdained. During the Reformation era the Biblical Hebrews came to be associated with their modern co-religionists. At the same time it became popular belief among Protestant adherents that the Jews scattered in their present dispersion would be regathered in Palestine in order to prepare for the Second Coming of Christ.

The new religious climate of the 16th Century, reinforced by a series of political upheavals, contributed to the emergence of such Zionist precepts. They arose in an environment saturated with the spirit of the Old Testament and often controlled by specific legislation. Under the motto 'Return to the Scripture', a new interest developed in the Bible as God's very own word. The Bible came to constitute the supreme authority of belief as well as conduct. Instead of the infallible Church as represented by the Pope in Rome, there came now the infallible word of God, as revealed in the Bible, now translated into the languages of ordinary people. 'The faithful were summoned to return to the Bible itself as the source of true, pure Christianity, and to understand the text in its simple, evident sense.'[10]

Protestantism came up with the idea of basing religious truth upon personal authority, imposing no limitations on Biblical interpretation. Every Protestant was free to search the Bible and judge individually the meaning of Biblical texts, thus opening the door for innovations in Christian theology. Simple, literal interpretation now became the new mode of exegesis, as the traditional symbolic and allegorical methods of Biblical exegesis were abandoned by Protestant reformers.

The 'Judaizing'[11] strain of the Protestant Reformation was further stimulated and enhanced by the rediscovery of the Old Testament so central to the Reformation, for: 'if it is doubtful whether Protestantism could have arisen without the knowledge of the Old Testament, it is certain that without it the Reformed Church could not have assumed the shape it took.'[12] The so-called Old Testament not only constitutes the largest part of the Christian Bible, but is known as the Jewish or Hebrew Bible. As such, it is the only record of the history of the ancient Jewish state, made up of a collection of myths, legends, historical narratives, poems, prophetic and apocalyptic pronouncements. It is because of this common heritage that Ben-Gurion referred to the Christian Bible as the 'Jews' sacrosanct title-deed to Palestine . . . with a genealogy of 3,500 years'.[13]

With the translation of the Bible into the vernacular, the Old Testament in particular served to familiarize the Western mind with the history, traditions and laws of the Hebrews and the land of Palestine which they controlled for less than 1,000 years. The Old Testament stories and characters became as familiar as bread and many Protestants could recite passages by heart. Jesus himself became known and thought of not so much as the son of Mary but as one of a long line of Hebrew prophets. Old Testament heroes like Abraham, Isaac, and Jacob came to replace the Catholic saints.

The expiatory, or cleansing, virtue of the pilgrimage to Jerusalem was rejected along with the intercession of saints and the veneration of their relics. Yet the Holy Land was not totally forgotten. On the contrary, it assumed a new significance with almost exclusively Zionist connotations. As the land of the Chosen People, Palestine was constantly present in the Protestant imagination, and their own identification with the land and people of the Book received expression in Protestant liturgy, rituals and even in the given names of their children.[14] To the Christian mind in Protestant Europe, Palestine became the Jewish land. The Jews became the Palestinian people who were foreign to Europe, absent from their Homeland, but in due time were to be returned to Palestine.

As it became part of regular rituals of church services and readings the non-Jewish Zionist tradition acquired a fixed form and a fixed place in the national consciousness of Europe.

> Every Sunday called to his mind the ancient history and lost prosperity of the 'glory of all lands', while the existing ruin and desolation of the country gave testimony to the truth of the Bible and the certainty of the promised blessings . . . the biblical descriptions of the Holy Land contribute no less to the propagation of which which we may call the Zionist idea.[15]

The Old Testament not only became the most popular literature for the Protestant laity, but also the source book for general historical knowledge. This is the moment when a process of historical manipulation began. The present-day Zionist falsification of history which claims 'historical right' to Palestine found its Christian precursor in Protestant Biblicism. The total history of Palestine was gradually reduced to those episodes concerning only the Jewish presence. People in Europe became conditioned to believing that nothing had happened in Palestine except the legends, historical narratives and myths recorded in the Old Testament. Only they were not regarded as such, but accepted as true history.

Since education for most people consisted mainly in reading Biblical literature, generations yet to come could not help but look at Palestine as the Jewish Homeland. Only the migration of Abraham, among many other migrations, was remembered; only the Davidic kingdom, among so many others before and after, seemed to have existed; and only the revolt of the Maccabees, among so many others, was noted. Peoples other than the Hebrews who settled and lived in Palestine, and most of them for much longer periods, seemed not to have existed at all. This historical manipulation was truly an innovation of the Reformation era. The Jews' thousand-year possession of Palestine had hardly entered the mind of the pilgrim of the Middle Ages.[16]

Hebraism and Western Culture

Of major importance for the post-Reformation development of Christian Zionism was the great weight the Reformation gave to the Hebrew language as the Holy Tongue (*Leshon Ha-Kodesh*), the language in which God had revealed himself to his People.[17]

Up until that time, the Catholic Church had preserved the knowledge of Latin as a living tongue. The Latin Vulgate translation of the Bible, dating back to Jerome's translation of the 3rd Century, was still considered sacred. In traditional Catholic circles the study of Hebrew, or even of Greek, was often regarded as the pastime of heretics and Hebrew learning was styled by many as a 'Jewish heresy'.[18] Vigorous steps were often undertaken to uproot the study of Hebrew during the era of medieval scholasticism. In the Middle Ages the *trilinguis homo* spoke Latin, French and English. But, beginning with the Renaissance, the scholar knew Latin, Greek and Hebrew, and knowledge of Hebrew soon became a recognized part of general European secular culture. The Reformation gave it a specifically religious sanction and made it a standard part of the theological curriculum.

The Reformation's interest in the Hebrew language was stimulated by its strict Biblicism. In order to understand correctly the infallible word of God as revealed in the sacred scriptures, a knowledge of the original language was now deemed indispensable and scholars and reformers were thus impelled to become acquainted with the substance of the Old Testament in its original tongue.

Already before the close of the 16th Century, Hebrew typefaces were employed in printing. This new knowledge of Hebrew was by no means confined to the books of the Biblical canon, i.e. the books of the Old Testament. Rabbinical literature was also studied deeply by others than rabbis, and by the Christian laity as well as the clergy. Hebrew became

> a matter of erudition as well as of religion; and familiarity, or at least partial acquaintance with Jewish literature, passed rapidly on from perusal of an incorrect and frequently incoherent translation of the Old Testament Canon to a knowledge of these books in their original tongue, and an extended survey of hitherto unexplored realms of Hebrew thought.[19]

Among the many other Hebrew texts that were diligently studied during the Renaissance and Reformation, the Cabala ranks above all. The Cabala is a theosophical collection of writings, including commentaries on the Old Testament, stemming from the mystical side of Judaism. Cabalistic literature was generally regarded as a collection of the treasures of ancient wisdom. The mysticism of the Cabala represented a drastic change from the dry, arid scholastic theological system of the late Middle Ages. Johann Reuchlin's *De Arte Cabalistica* (1517) ranked as a best-seller and most of the European intelligentsia, religious as well as secular, referred to it in their works. Many Protestant reformers, particularly in the various mystical movements and pietist sects, were attracted to its messianism and attempted to apply it to their own eschatological teachings.[20]

Among many Protestant groups and sects, this new appreciation for Hebrew as a language very often combined with an appreciation of Jewish traditions and values. The best example of this was Puritan England, a topic we shall discuss later in this chapter. General appreciation of the Jewish past led to respect for contemporary Jewry, often resulting in greater degrees of toleration in territories under the political influence of Protestantism. The Protestant Netherlands, under the ruling House of Nassau-Orange, was a case in point. During the 16th and the 17th Centuries, Amsterdam was known among Europe's Jews as the new Jerusalem.[21] Hugo Grotius, the well known Hebraist, philosopher, theologian and lawyer, and frequently cited today as the founder of public international law, established the common sources of Christianity and Judaism in his treatise *Ueber die Wahrheit der Christlichen Religion* (The Truth about the Christian Religion). He strongly objected to traditional Christendom's degradation of Judaism as an inferior religion.

The new Hebraic spirit penetrated the arts and literature as well, leaving an eternal imprint on European civilization. Rembrandt and his artist contemporaries now drew, etched or painted scenes from the Bible, notably the Old Testament. Meanwhile, in the field of literature, the miracle plays popular during medieval times, were being superseded by a new kind of scriptural drama based on Old Testament narratives and commentaries. The lives of Old Testament figures like Absalom, Queen Esther, Jonah, Josephus and figures from the Apocrypha were represented as moral examples for the public. Emphasis was placed on the Old Testament now as a source of ethical teaching rather than for dogma or theology.

It is still not clearly recognized how the influence of Judaism and Hebraism in those early days of the Reformation have deeply affected the mind of modern Europe.[22] Though the facts are available to all, none has attempted to put them together in one place and show that they combined to form the beginnings of a philo-Judaic tradition in Europe that was later to result in what we call the phenomenon of non-Jewish Zionism.

Jewish Restoration and Christian Millennarianism

One of the most definite effects of the Protestant Reformation was the emerging interest in the fulfilment of Biblical prophecies concerning the End of Time. The core of millenarianism was the belief in the Second Coming of Christ whose return would establish God's kingdom on earth, which was to last for 1,000 years (that is, a millennium). Millenarians regarded the future of the Jewish people as an important element in the events to precede the End of Time. In fact, the literal interpretation of the apocalyptic writings in the Bible[23] led them to conclude that the Millennium was to be heralded by the physical Restoration of the Jews as a nation (Israel) to Palestine. However, the Jews' conversion to Christianity was an important element as well. Some sects insisted on Jewish conversion prior to their restoration; others believed that their conversion would take place after their return to Palestine.

Eschatological belief in the speedy return of Christ had persisted in various forms throughout the history of the Christian Church. It was common during the 1st Century AD and often surfaced again during times of political and social unrest. But generally it must be remembered that the very concept of the End of the Age was subversive and regarded as a threat to the security of such a great and powerful established institution as the medieval Church.[24]

After Christianity became the official religion of the Roman Empire in AD 380, the early Church Fathers, such as Origen and Augustine, were determined to wipe out millenarian ideas and expectations. Augustine in his *City of God* seemed to have settled this problem, at least until the 16th Century. Using the allegorical methodology, Augustine interpreted the Millennium as a spiritual state into which the Church collectively had already entered at the time of Pentecost, i.e. just after the death and resurrection of Christ. Pre-Reformation semi-sectarian minority movements expressing millenarian yearnings had to remain underground. They were persecuted and suppressed by the Church in Rome and their teachings were branded as heresies.[25]

The national revival of the Jewish people usually did not figure profoundly in the teachings of these early movements, which more often awaited the speedy conversion of the Jews.[26] Although millenarianism never became dominant even in the Protestant main denominations (both Luther and Calvin, for example, continued to adhere to the Augustinian teachings in this regard), it did maintain a certain presence and its ideas percolated down to the masses. It continued to find followers in every period of history after the Reformation and finally culminated in 20th Century American fundamentalism which insists that the state of Israel presents the literal fulfilment of prophecy in modern history.

Reformation Millenarianism

The Reformation produced a mentality which saw itself caught up in this vivid history. The Reformation itself was thought to have been an apocalyptic turning point, indicating the imminence of the End of Time. The continent of Europe, tormented as it had been for decades by devastating wars, proved fertile ground for such eschatological prognostications. The severe persecution suffered by many Protestant sects at the hands of the official Church was interpreted by them as another sign that the End of Time was indeed near. In this context the many Biblical prophecies about Israel's future took on a keen significance and many sects were convinced that the fulfillment of the prophecies would involve contemporary Jews in one way or another.

The first printed literature on millenarian speculation and Jewish Restoration appeared towards the end of the 16th Century. It spread on the Continent, but even more so in the British Isles where the Reformation had gained a very firm footing since Henry VIII's complete break with Rome. On the Continent messianic hopes were voiced by minority sects such as the Anabaptists and Frankists; but Lutheran and Calvinist official churches ruthlessly persecuted them as disruptive heretical forces. Michael Servetus (1509–53) was burned alive as a 'anti-Trinitarian Judaizer'. In England, Francis Kett suffered the same fate in 1589. Both Servetus and Kett were Unitarians and wrote about a Restoration of the Jews. For both, the ingathering of God's Chosen People was understood literally to mean the nation of the Jewish people.

In Holland and Switzerland, a few messianic sects survived at the price of adopting a certain measure of conformity. In Germany, they were stamped out when Lutheranism had achieved a position of equality with Catholicism to form an alliance with the established order. In Anglican England, the idea of Jewish Restoration was not as easily suppressed. Athough still vehemently suppressed by both secular and religious authorities of the time, the new belief soon gained a certain respectability in English religious circles.

Less than a decade after Kett's unfortunate end as a millenarian heretic, Thomas Brightman (1562–1607), an esteemed theologian, took up the same topic, elaborating further what Kett had often only hinted at. In his *Apocalypsis Apocalypseos* Brightman addressed himself directly to the problem of Jewish Restoration. He stated that the Jews as a nation shall return again to Palestine, as the land of their early Fathers 'not for religion's sake, as if God could not elsewhere be worshipped, . . . but not to strive any longer as strangers and inmates with forraine nations'.[27]

Brightman, the father of the British doctrine of the Restoration of the Jews, had many contemporary followers, including Members of Parliament. One of them, Sir Henry Finch, the most eminent legal authority of his time, accepted Brightman's exposition in *Apocalypsis Apocalypseos* and in 1621 published his own controversial *The World's Great Restoration or the Calling of the Jews, and (with them) of all the Nations and Kingdoms of the Earth, to the Faith of Christ*. In it he wrote:

> Where Israel, Judah, Zion and Jerusalem are named [in the Bible] the Holy Ghost meant not the spiritual Israel, or the Church of God collected of the Gentiles or of the Jews and Gentiles both . . . but Israel properly descended out of Jacob's loynes. The same judgement is to be made of their returning to their land and ancient seats, the conquest of their foes . . . the glorious church they shall erect in the land itself of Judah . . . These and such like are not allegories, setting forth in terrene similitudes or deliverance through Christ (whereof those were types and figures), but meant really and literally the Jews . . .[28]

Finch rejected outright the traditional Augustinian allegory. He insisted that, according to Biblical prophecy, God had indeed intended to restore the Jews collectively and nationally to their former homeland:

> Not . . . a few singled out here and there, but . . . the Nation in general . . . They shall repaire towards their own country . . . shall inhabit all the parts of the land, as before . . . shall live in safety . . . shall continue in it for ever.[29]

His forecast was unique in that it included also a description of the future Israel restored. 'What lent a distinctive character to Finch's prediction was the blend of religion and politics expressed by him in the vision of the restored Jewish Commonwealth. A perfect theocracy, the ideal of the epoch, is here visualized and projected into a redeemed land of Israel.'[30] Zionist phraseology was skillfully employed by Finch in order to attract both Jews and non-Jews to this great plan. Yet Finch's Zionism was still premature. His Jewish contemporaries saw no reason to adhere to his call and likewise he was unable to gain the general approval of his own co-religionists and countrymen.

King James I (1603–25), however, took such millenarian views seriously enough to regard them as a personal affront and an infringement of his own prerogatives as absolute sovereign. Finch was forced to retract and his teachings met criticism even in Parliament where some members warned of new Judaizing prophets laying claim to Jewish Restoration.[31] Yet, in spite of the general denunciation of these Zionist precepts at the beginning of the 17th Century, they had taken root in the spiritual life of England and were to re-emerge and find their Golden Age in the subsequent Puritan era.

These millenarian Zionist ideas were still in a very infantile and rudimentary stage. But the nucleus had already been created in an over-literal espousal of certain already over-literal ideas of the Protestant Reformation. Non-Jewish Zionism during the Reformation era remained confined to the realm of spiritual speculations and theological discourse. Yet the main elements of both philo- and anti-Semitism were there, including the strange blending of the two seemingly opposite trends.

Early Restorationists often expounded a love for God's Chosen People. But this was not out of concern for the Jews, but for their role in God's plan, as revealed by his promise to them. Jewish conversion to Christianity was still the ultimate aim.[32] Hence, Finch, in spite of his contemplation of a golden future for the Chosen People, saw it conducted along harsh Christian lines. In his Preface to *The World's Great Restoration*, he stated this very clearly:

> But the days of this thy sinfulness, God Winking at, doth now every where, and by all means, invite thee to repentance. Out of all the places of thy dispersion, East, West, North and South, his purpose is to bring thee home again, and to marry thee to himselfe by faith evermore.[33]

Non-Jewish Zionism was already fraught with certain anti-Semitic overtones which remained a characteristic component of the whole non-Jewish Zionist tradition.

Martin Luther and the Judaizing Spirit

Martin Luther's role needs further and more precise explication if only because of his pre-eminent position among all the Protestant reformers. because of his controversial and sometimes totally contradictory attitudes towards the Jews, he has been seen sometimes as a philo-Semite, and sometimes as an anti-Semite and precursor of German Nazi anti-Semitism.[34]

As the founder and leader of the Protestant Reformation, Martin Luther was greatly responsible for the emergence of the new religious and spiritual climate of the 16th Century that, as we have shown, had provided such a fertile breeding ground for early Zionist ideas. Luther's own Judaic inclination included his zeal for the study of the Hebrew language, his preference for simple Jewish dogmas in contrast to the complexities of Catholic theology, and most of all his emphasis on the centrality of the Bible in Christian life. Consequently, the Papist enemies of Luther lost no opportunity in branding him as a 'Jew' and a 'Jewish patron'. His doctrines, especially with reference to his polemics against idolatrous images and the worship of relics, won him the title of 'semi-Judaeus' or 'Half-Jew'.[35]

On the other hand, we also find Martin Luther hurling the charge of Judaizing at his own adversaries within the Reformation movement, particularly against the Anabaptists or the more liberal Hebraists at German universities who were critical of Luther's translations of the Hebrew Old Testament.[36] Luther's own writings concerning the Jews fall into two distinct periods, before and after 1537. In 1523 Luther wrote a pamphlet *Dass Jesus ein Geborner Jude Sei* (That Christ Was a Born Jew), republished seven times in the same year. In it he expounded very pro-Jewish attitudes, condemning their persecution over the ages by the Catholic Church and arguing that Christians and Jews came from the same stock:

> Through them alone the Holy Ghost wished to give all books of Holy Scripture to the world; they are the children and we are the guests and the strangers. Indeed like the Canaanite woman, we should be satisfied to be the dogs that eat the crumbs which fall from their master's table.[37]

But the closing paragraphs show indisputably that Luther's ultimate aim was Jewish conversion to Christianity, i.e. Protestantism:

> I would advise and beg everybody to deal kindly with the Jews and to instruct them in the Scripture; in such a case we could expect them to come over to us. If, however, we use brute force and slander them, saying that they need the blood of Christians to get rid of their stench, and other nonsense of that kind, and treat them like dogs, what good can we expect of them? Finally, how can we expect them to improve, if we prohibit them from working among us, and so force them into usury. If we wish to make them better, we must deal with them not according to the law of the Pope, but according to the law of Christian charity. We must receive them kindly and allow them to compete with us in earning a livelihood, so that they may have an opportunity to witness Christian life and doctrine; if some remain obstinate – what of it? Not every one of us is a good Christian.[38]

As an enthusiastic supporter of the apostle Paul, Luther also strongly believed in the fulfillment of the Biblical prophecy that all Israel, as a nation, should be saved. He blamed the papacy for perverting Christianity and thus repulsing Jews who would otherwise convert to Christianity.

But in the latter part of his life, Luther's attitude towards the Jews became embittered. He was particularly angered by the news that, far from converting, Jews were proselytizing for their own faith through the Sabbatarian movement in Moravia. Luther's *Concerning the Jews and their Lies*[39] was written in 1544 to confront these challenges to Lutheranism. In this treatise, Zionism and anti-Semitism were strangely (but, in the tradition of non-Jewish Zionism, not untypically) intermingled:

> Who prevents the Jews from returning to their land of Judea? Nobody. We shall provide them with all the supplies for their journey, only in order to get rid of them. They are a heavy burden for us, the calamity of our being . . .[40]

Luther's vulgar anti-Jewish outbursts are often quoted in studies on the history of anti-Semitism in which he figures as the true representative of what might be called medieval anti-Semitism.[41] But it is well known that Luther was never refined in his language, especially when attacking his enemies. His use of rude and even obscene expressions was characteristic of his unrefined style and personality. His vulgar anti-Jewish utterances were at least matched, if not outdone to a degree, by his vulgar outbursts against the 'Papists' and the other competing Protestant sects. He himself was not an example of religious tolerance, but of intolerance sometimes bordering on bigotry.

Nevertheless, the Reformation movement which he set in motion by his open defiance of the established ecclesiastical authority could not help but usher in a new age of toleration which had a positive influence upon Jewish life as well. Never again could the Catholic Church claim to be universal, and no longer were Jews cast as the only outsiders. For the first time the Jews had the experience of not being the most persecuted religious minority group, a fate now reserved at this time for small splinter groups like the Anabaptists or other Protestant sects. Finally, what reason and common sense could not bring about was ultimately decided on the battleground during the wars of religion. The Peace of Augsburg (1555), the Council of Trent (1547–63) and the Treaties of Westphalia (1648) all combined to bring about the progressive laicization of European society. Toleration had emerged as a result of political necessity.

The Tenets of Protestant Zionism

The main importance of the Reformation for non-Jewish Zionism lies more in what it achieved unintentionally and often unconsciously rather than in its direct goals and achievements. However, the principal tenet of Zionism was already established along clear-cut lines. The emphasis on the character of the Jews as a nation was very explicitly stated during the 16th Century; they were no longer a 'church' like other churches, nor were they regarded as a religious confession. The popularization of the Biblical texts in their original form, now unalloyed by official ecclesiastical interpretation, revolutionized Protestant Christian thinking and thus enabled certain Protestants to politicize the scriptures.

It is ironic that, during the same period, the Jews themselves were attempting to de-politicize them: the messianic idea among the Jews, firmly coupled with Restoration, was opposed to a human or earthly realization of the hope in political terms, and instead expected a divine intervention.[42]

The significance of the Reformation lies in the pioneering of the Zionist ideas of the Jewish nation, the Jewish Restoration, and Palestine as the Jewish Homeland, which were subsequently to acquire their enormous vogue and popularity. Through its religious tradition, non-Jewish Zionism took on a fixed form during the 16th Century when it became part of regular church rituals and hence spread through everyday cultural life. Non-Jewish Zionism had many notable representatives in every period of history after the Reformation. It grew from a theological doctrine into a political ideology of the contemporary West.

English Puritanism and the Revival of the Ancient Kingdom

The Hebraic revival, with its implicitly interwoven pro-Zionist themes, was to reach its highest stage during the Puritan Revolution in 17th Century England. Puritanism represented the most radical form of Protestantism and was a direct heir of Calvinism. As in Geneva under Calvinist rule, the Puritans in England developed a crude and strict 'bibliolatry' with a special preference for the Old Testament.

The Puritans combined a distinct benevolence towards Judaism with an image of the Jews as the successors to the ancient Hebrews. The Puritans' reverential regard for the Old Testament and its people grew entirely out of their own experience of persecution by the established Church. Puritans in England had little personal knowledge of Jewish life since officially, at least, Jews were expelled from England by the Crusader King Edward I in 1290.

Puritan knowledge and acquaintance with Jewish life was based solely on their conversance with the Hebrew Bible, and ultimately their own identification with God's people.

> In the bitter experiences of persecution and of civil war they found, in the Old Testament in particular, language and sentiments which exactly fitted their mood and suited their occasion . . . It was a very real experience of religious and political strife and persecution which gave point and verisimilitude to the Old Testament imagery and made them use its names and language as the fittest vehicle of their tumultuous thoughts.[43]

17th Century post-Elizabethan England was extremely well suited for the spread of Zionist ideas among non-Jews. Yet, when studying Puritanism's contribution to Zionism, we must not lose sight of the more general context in which English Puritan Zionism was able to grow. The Puritan Revolution was not an isolated event in English history, nor was it merely a link in the chain of a so-called typically English tradition, as some Zionist writers tend to present it.[44] Puritanism was the Protestant Reformation brought to its most logical conclusion. Even when Puritanism waned, with the restoration of Charles II in 1660, its ideals, including those favouring Zionism, continued to prevail in England as well as on the Continent and spread from there to the New World.

By the beginning of the 17th Century, the Protestant Reformation had gained its strongest footing in England, where the merry and passionate vivacity of Elizabethan culture gradually was replaced by a new era of spiritual and intellectual strife, generally referred to as the Puritan Revolution. The 16th Century rediscovery of the Bible had produced the English language of the renowned King James version. The wide access to Biblical literature had also resulted in a proliferation of controversial Biblical interpretations. The essence of the Puritan faith was precisely bound up with this right to individual interpretation, and England had been one of the first Reformation countries to discard the ecclesiastical and papal overlordship in this regard.

Hebraism in Everyday Life
Socially and culturally, Puritanism introduced to England the invasion of 'Hebraism' that had already swept the Continent. Now it came to be more deeply felt on the popular level and in the daily life of the nation. The Puritans found in the Old Testament 'a divine example of national government, a distinct indication of the laws which men were ordered to follow, with visible and immediate punishment attached to disobedience.'[45] Like the Calvinists on the Continent, they invoked the Old Testament in support of their political ideas. The Genevan Commonwealth of Saints now became the Puritan Republic of Saints.

The Old Testament became their one and only book. 'It was their sole literature, their intellectual and spiritual food, their guide, philosopher and friend, their justiciary warrant and their high court of appeal. Their thought was moulded to its form.'[46] Their ignorance of contemporary Jewish life even led them to follow Old Testament admonitions long discarded by the Jews themselves.[47] English speech came to be deeply permeated with Hebraic phrases, and there were some who even considered Hebrew to be the proper and only language for prayer and the reading of the Bible.

John Milton, Puritanism's outstanding literary figure, suggested in his essay on education that the study of Hebrew be introduced into the curriculum of general education in the grammar schools. Puritan preference for the Old Testament also showed up in the habits of the daily life: 'The general tendency of Puritanism was to discard Christian morality and to substitute Jewish habits in its stead.'[48] The Puritans 'followed the letter of an ancient code instead of trusting to the utterances of a divinely instructed consciousness . . . .'.[49] Demands that the Government declare the Torah[50] as the code for English law were made by the Levellers, an ultra-Republican group of Puritans. And after the Long Parliament had been dissolved by Cromwell in 1653, a Short Parliament was introduced, to be composed only of Saints, i.e. Puritans. The Council of State was to consist of 70 members, mimicking the number of the ancient Jewish Sanhedrim.

No longer were children baptized with the names of beloved Christian saints, but were given the names of Hebrew warriors or patriarchs. They 'turned the weekly festival by which the church had from primitive time commemorated the resurrection of her Lord, into the Jewish Sabbath.'[51] Some even went further and converted to Judaism, like John Traske and his entire group of followers as well as other important personalities such as the distinguished artist and miniaturist, Alexander Cooper.[52] Those who remained Christians were more common, but they began to look 'with ever-increasing sympathy on those whom they called the ancient people of God.'[53]

It was impossible so to steep oneself in the history of the Old Testament, to restore it as divine inspiration, to live with it as a daily guide, and not to consider the people responsible for all this. The concept of the chosen Jewish people thus came to play a special role in Puritan English thought and understanding of the existing order.

Jewish Restoration to Palestine

The idea that Palestine had to be restored to its Hebrew ancestors became an increasingly popular notion in England in the 1640s. Before that, Palestine had existed in the popular mind as the Christian Holy Land, whose Christian character had been defended by so many Englishmen in the Crusades against the Muslim infidels. Now shorn of its Christian connotations, Palestine came to be regarded as the homeland of the Jews, whose return to Palestine, according to Old Testament prophecies, was the inevitable prelude to the Second Coming of Christ.

It was not long before Puritan England saw an organized movement calling for the return of the Jews to Palestine. When the early millenarianists like Finch, Kett or Brightman had written their Jewish Restoration literature at the turn of the century, the Jews were still a despised minority. Now, with Puritanism and its underlying millenarianism in the position of power, the Jewish Restoration idea came to find general and widespread acceptance.

In 1649 the following petition was sent to the English Government:

> That this Nation of England, with the inhabitants of the Netherlands, shall be the first and the readiest to transport Israel's sons and daughters on their ships to the land promised to their forefathers, Abraham, Isaac and Jacob for an everlasting inheritance.[54]

The authors of the petition were Joanna and Ebenezer Cartwright, two English Puritans residing in Amsterdam.[55] This was the first time in the history of the idea of Jewish Restoration that human action was put forward as the only way to achieve a goal which had previously been regarded, by Jews and non-Jews alike, as a spiritual event to be brought about only by divine intervention.

The seriousness of the Cartwright petition was underscored by the fact that it also included a request to the English Government to repeal Edward's act of banishment and readmit the Jews to England. In Puritan England the idea of Jewish Re-admission and Jewish Restoration to Palestine went hand in hand. This apparent contradiction was sustained through the reading of certain Old Testament passages which implied that the initial dispersion of the Jews (before their Restoration) was an essential precondition for Israel's final redemption and the Second Coming of Christ.[56] Thus England, apparently the only country left without a Jewish presence, had to come to the aid of God the Almighty in helping to speed up the awaited event. But, as Barbara Tuchmann rightly observes, both movements, for Jewish Restoration and for Re-admission, were not for the sake of the Jews themselves, 'but for the sake of the promise made to them . . . The return was viewed, of course, only in terms of a Jewish nation converted to Christianity, for this was to be the signal for the working out of the promise.'[57] Many Puritans also believed that due to their own Hebraism, Jews would find it easy to convert, an attitude we have already detected in Luther's early philo-Semitism.

English Puritan appeals for Jewish Re-admission to England were seconded by some Jewish exponents of Jewish messianism, most notably Menasseh ben Israel, the Chief Rabbi of Amsterdam. His book *Spes Israeli* (The Hope of Israel) very skilfully linked 'the Messianism of the English Puritans with genuine Jewish Messianism and theological speculation with practical politics.'[58] Menasseh was well aware of the new Puritan eschatological teachings. Among his own friends and associates in Amsterdam were many English Puritans who had fled England during the persecution of the reign of Queen Mary. Menasseh's work viewed Jewish Re-admission to England not as an end in itself but as the stepping-stone towards their final resettlement in the land of Palestine.

Sokolow describes Menasseh as 'nothing if not a Zionist, if we look upon Zionism in the light of his time.'[59] By the same token, the general public of Puritan England can be regarded as Zionist in its enthusiastic response to the call for Jewish Re-admission to England and Restoration to Palestine. The English translation of *Spes Israeli* was immensely popular and three editions were rapidly sold out before its author even set foot in England in 1655. In effect, Zionism was the basis of the re-settlement issue. Puritan and Jewish Restorationists knew that the political circumstances in the country were most assuredly in favour. What counted most of all, were Oliver Cromwell's own personal Zionist predispositions in this regard.

Oliver Cromwell and the Jews

Oliver Cromwell, for almost ten years Lord Protector of the newly established Puritan Commonwealth (1649–58), was both a religious fanatic and a political pragmatist. In order to settle the question of Re-admission of the Jews to England, he called the Whitehall Conference in December 1655 to discuss the legality of the Re-admission and the conditions under which this could take place.[60] England's foremost legal and religious authorities were represented at the conference. Cromwell and Menasseh ben Israel were personally present and delivered eloquent pleas in favour of Re-admission, and the opinion of the conference indeed reflected general public opinion. The lawyers confirmed that there could not be any legal objection, but they were unable to agree on conditions and terms. While recognizing in principle the legal right of the Jews to reside in a Christian country, the conference failed to arrive at a practical solution.

This was the point at which Oliver Cromwell personally intervened to sanction the re-entry of the Jews by 'way of connivancy'.[61] Political expediency added its decisive weight to the law and religion. The Whitehall conference had clearly stated that 'the admission of the Jews into a Protestant state should be not only "lawful" but also "expedient".'[62]

For Cromwell, the motive was commercial profit. The Civil War preceding the Puritan era had badly affected England's position as a trade and maritime power. The almost exclusively Puritan commercial class was particularly jealous of the Dutch who had seized the opportunity to gain control over the Near and Far Eastern trading routes. It was well known at the time that the Dutch Jews had been especially active in the expansion of Dutch trade at the beginning of the 17th Century. When Cromwell agreed to the Re-admission of the Jews, he was engaged in a series of trade wars with Portugal, the Netherlands and Spain. Each of these countries had a considerable and important Jewish community known for its wealth, commercial skills and business contacts abroad. Thus, Jewish merchants in England 'could be useful to him as intelligencers whose connections, threading across Europe, could bring him information on trade policies of rival countries and on royalist conspiracies abroad.'[63] An added incentive was the large amount of capital that Jews would bring with them to invest in English industry.

On the religious level, Cromwell showed more interest in the ingathering of the Jews into England than into Zion. But his England was not yet a British Empire and his interests were not imperial but merely commercial and mercantile. The Puritan tradition of Zionism, as it prevailed during the 17th Century, was content with a future Jewish Restoration to Palestine. It saw no political role for England in its immediate actualization, except insofar as Re-admission was a step leading in this direction. Still, the idea of the Jewish Restoration to Palestine as the prelude to the Second Coming of Christ had a secure place in Protestant religious dogma. Later on, the idea of Jewish Restoration would be used to cover up imperial interests in Palestine as they had become linked to requirements of Empire.

Hebraism in English life declined in importance after Cromwell's death in 1658, yet it did not lose its attraction for many Christian sympathizers. Puritanism itself went down to defeat with the return of the Stuarts in 1660 and finally with the Glorious Revolution of 1688. Even so, the established millennial tradition favouring Zionism survived and even flourished in the hostile atmosphere of the Age of Reason in the 18th Century.

Puritanism, like Christian Hebraism at its climax, was not confined to England alone, but occurred in all parts of Europe where Protestantism had gained a foothold. In the Calvinist Netherlands, Zionist ideas were especially entrenched in popular feeling. Spanish Jews fleeing from the Inquisition had found a secure haven in the Netherlands and were welcomed as allies against the common enemy of the Spanish King and the Catholic Church.[64]

Millenarian Zionism in Europe

To a large extent the Revolt of the Netherlands was also an episode in the religious strife stirred up by the Reformation. Long after the Protestant Reformation had started in Germany, the countries today known as the Netherlands and Belgium were still being governed as dominions of the Spanish crown. When Protestantism had gained a major foothold in the cities and in the northern provinces, Spanish Catholic Government interference in freedom of religion led to open revolt in 1565. Protestant forces finally gained victory in 1609 and an independent Dutch Republic was established comprising the territories now included in the Netherlands. Protestant millenarianism was characteristic of the Dutch Calvinist ideology and Judaizing sects flourished during all the the 17th Century, often culminating in support for pseudo-Messiahs.

France at the time also had its share of millenarian Zionists, most notably among the Huguenots in the southern regions. Their distinguished representative was Isaac de La Peyrere (1594–1676) who wrote *Rappel des Juifs*. De la Peyrere called for the Restoration of Israel as the Jewish nation in the Holy Land, despite its unconverted state.[65] He sent his appeal to the French monarch, but his treatise was only allowed to appear in print nearly two centuries later after Napoleon had called for the assembling of a Jewish Sanhedrim in May 1806.[66] The author, nevertheless, remained an influential scholar. He was even appointed French ambassador to Denmark in 1644. Another Frenchman, Philippe Gentil de Langallerie (1656–1717), did not fare so well. When he presented his plan for Jewish settlement in Palestine, offering Rome to the Ottoman emperor in exchange for a Jewish Palestine, he was arrested and tried for conspiracy and high treason.[67] Another French Protestant clergyman, Pierre Jurieu, in his *L'Accomplissement de Prophéties* even predicted the re-establishment of a Jewish kingdom in Palestine no later than by the end of the 17th Century.[68]

Lutheran Germany and Scandinavia knew their share of millenarian Zionism as well. In Germany, the northern city of Hamburg was famous during the 17th Century as the El Dorado of the Jews on the Continent. After London and Amsterdam, this Hanseatic port was the third most important refuge for Spanish and Portuguese Jews fleeing the Inquisition. Hamburg was also a centre of German Pietism, a mystic spiritualist movement which, in the contemporary fashion, centred its futuristic eschatological teachings on the Jewish nation's physical restoration to Palestine. The movement's founder, Philipp Jakob Spener (1635–1703) employed Luther's early writings on the Jewish question in order to promote philo-Semitism as an inducement to Jewish conversion prior to their Restoration.[69] But he also urged understanding and respect for those Jews who chose to remain committed to their religion.

In 1655, Paul Felgenhauer (1593–1677) published his *Good News for Israel* in which he maintained that the Second Coming of Christ and the arrival of the Jewish Messiah were one and the same event.[70] The sign that was to announce the advent of this Judaeo-Christian Messiah would be, in typical millenarian fashion, 'the permanent return of the Jews to their own country eternally bestowed upon them by God through his unqualified promise to Abraham, Isaac and Jacob.'[71]

From Northern Germany these early Zionist ideas of a Jewish Restoration to Palestine easily spread to Scandinavia. In Denmark, Holger Paulli called upon Europe's monarchs to undertake a new crusade, this time to liberate Palestine and Jerusalem from the infidel in order to settle the original and rightful heirs, the Jews.[72] In 1696 he submitted a most detailed plan to William III of England, appealing to the English king to re-conquer Palestine for the Jews so that they might re-establish a state of their own. At the time, his plan represented a bold attempt to associate theological Restorationist aspriations with current political events. In his messianic style and language he even addressed the English king as 'Cyrus the Great and the Almighty's instrument thanks to whom the true Phoenix, the last Temple, shall be born from the ashes of Herod's Temple.'[73] (It was Cyrus who had permitted the Biblical Hebrews to return to Palestine from Babylon.)

In Sweden, Anders Pederson Kempe (1622–89), an ex-army officer turned theologian, was forced to leave Stockholm because of his role in spreading German messianism. He settled near Hamburg where in 1688 he published his own *Israel's Good News*, a violent attack on traditional Christendom:

> You heathen Christians, you let yourselves be persuaded by false teachers, especially the Grandmother of all fornication, Rome, to believe that the Jews were forever disinherited and rejected by God and that you were now the rightful Christian Israel, to possess the Land of Canaan forever.[74]

He called upon the Jews to assert themselves as the Chosen People and to ready themselves for their final Restoration to the Holy Land.

One could easily continue this anthology of noteworthy writers and activists who, through their eschatological teachings, prepared the soil and actually sowed the seeds of Zionism during the century following the Protestant Reformation. The first phase of this kind of non-Jewish Zionism was rather tempestuous. Religious wars and social unrest created a strained atmosphere charged with mystical ideas and expectations. Millenarian waves swept over Europe especially during the Thirty Years War (1618–48) and afterwards. Expectations concerning the End of Time prevailed among all social classes and countries.

Manifestations of early non-Jewish Zionism were thus neither isolated incidents nor espoused only by religious eccentrics and outsiders. They occurred in different corners of Europe and were not confined to England under the Puritans, as some Zionist historians maintain.[75] A voluminous religious literature on the role and the destiny of the Jews spread rapidly during the 17th Century and, by its millenarian nature, never fell out of vogue. Many millenarians were rebuked, persecuted and sometimes even executed for their heretical beliefs. Nevertheless, their writings helped to entrench the notion of a Jewish Restoration to Palestine. It was not long until the more practical questions, as to when and how Restoration was to take place, began to gain importance.

Notes

1. It is a well established fact that Jewish Zionism began as a minority Jewish movement. 19th Century Jewish thought in general was hostile to Zionism, centring instead around assimilation and religious reform. Unlike reform Judaism, by disassociating religion and nationalism Zionism opposed the old Talmudic dictum 'the laws of the land in which Jews live are the laws that must be obeyed.' Orthodox Judaism, on the other hand, objected to the secularism inherent in political Zionism. See Arthur Herzberg (ed.), *The Zionist Idea: A Historical Analysis and Reader* (New York, 1969), pp. 20–1.
2. Talcott Parsons, *The Social System* (Glencoe, New York, 1957).
3. It has been pointed out that contemporary Israeli society relies upon a much greater variety of Zionist myths, but all essentially revolve around the three already mentioned. For a detailed discussion of the basic myths incorporated in Israeli society today see Ferdinand Zweig, *The Sword and the Harp* (London, 1969), especially Chapter 7. Nahum Sokolow, in his *History of Zionism* (London, 1919), calls these myths the Promised Land, Jewish national distinctiveness, and the future of the Jewish People.
4. Louis I. Newman, *Jewish Influence on Christian Reform Movements* (New York, 1966), p. 19.
5. Edwyn R. Bevan and Charles Singer (eds), *The Legacy of Israel* (Oxford, 1944), p. 69.
6. Barbara Tuchmann, *Bible and Sword: England and Palestine from the Bronze Age to Balfour* (London, 1956), p. 37.

7. Friedrich Heer, *The Medieval World: Europe 1100–1350* (New York, 1961), p. 310.
8. Hilaire Belloc, *The Jews* (Boston, 1922), p. 210.
9. Matthew Arnold speaks of the 'Hebraizing Revival' in *Culture and Anarchy* (Ann Arbor, 1965), p. 172. Guedemann observes the Jewish *Kolorit* or tinge in early Protestantism; see Guedemann, *Juedisches im Christentum des Reformationszeitalter* (Vienna, 1870), p. 2.
10. Mayir Verete, 'The Restoration of the Jews in English Protestant Thought, 1790–1840', *Middle Eastern Studies*, Vol. 8, No. 1, p. 14.
11. The term 'Judaizing' denotes the imitation of Jewish ideas, practices and customs.
12. *The Cambridge Modern History*, Vol. 11 (New York, 1907), p. 696.
13. David Ben-Gurion, *The Rebirth and Destiny of Israel* (New York, 1954), p. 100.
14. Robert W. Stookey, 'The Holy Land', *Middle East Journal*, Vol. 30, No. 3, 1976, p. 353.
15. Sokolow, op, cit. p. 60.
16. Barbara Tuchmann, op. cit., p. 18.
17. Newman, op. cit., p. 82.
18. Ibid., p. 24.
19. J. G. Dow, 'Hebrew and Puritan', *Jewish Quarterly Review*, Vol. 3, 1891, pp. 60–1.
20. Bevan and Singer, op. cit., p. 331.
21. Heinrich Graetz, *Geschichte der Juden*, Vol. X (Leipzig, 1888), p. 2.
22. The Jewish historian Cecil Roth has written: 'The personal relations between Jews and non-Jews – not excluding the aristocracy and even members of the ruling families, were more intimate in the Renaissance period than was ever again to be the case in any land in Europe until the 19th century.' See Cecil Roth, *The Jews in the Renaissance* (New York, 1959), p. 21.
23. The Book of Daniel, a representative sample of Jewish messianism, was the only apocalyptical work admitted to the Old Testament Canon. Much of other Jewish messianic literature thus remained outside the Christian Bible. The Book of Revelation, included in the Christian Bible as part of the New Testament, is representative of Christian apocalypticism. While Daniel was written during the 2nd Century BC, the Book of Revelation can be dated to the 1st Century AD when the early Christians suffered severe persecution during the reign of the Roman emperor Nero (AD 37–68).
24. Roland H. Bainton, *The Reformation and the 16th Century* (Boston, 1952), p. 19.
25. Pre-Reformation movements with strong millenarian tendencies included the Waldensians in the 12th Century in southern France, the Passagii sect appearing at the same time in northern Italy and the Hussites of 15th Century Bohemia.
26. Salo W. Baron, *A Social and Religious History of the Jews*, Vol. 2 (New York, 1937), p. 198.
27. As quoted in Verete, op. cit., p. 16.
28. Ibid.
29. Ibid.
30. Franz Kobler, *The Vision was There* (London, 1956), p. 18.
31. Ibid., p. 20.

32. Albert Hyamson, *A History of the Jews in England* (London, 1918), p. 132.
33. As quoted in Christopher Sykes, *Two Studies in Virtue* (London, 1953), pp. 149–50.
34. Baron, op. cit., p. 198.
35. R. Lewin, 'Luther's Stellung zu den Juden', *Neue Studien zur Geschichte der Kirche*, Vol. 10, 1911, p. 17. In Jewish circles Martin Luther was welcomed and often celebrated as a sign that the advent of the Messianic age was near.
36. Ibid., p. 60.
37. Martin Luther, *Saemtliche Werke*, Vol. 29, pp. 46–7.
38. Ibid., Vol. 30, p. 74.
39. Ibid., Vol. 32, pp. 99–358.
40. Ibid.
41. Leon Poliakov, *The History of Anti-Semitism* (New York, 1965), especially p. 220.
42. See Richard Gottheil, *Zionism* (Philadelphia, 1914), p. 96.
43. W. B. Selbie, 'The Influence of the Old Testament on Puritanism', in Bevan and Singer, op. cit., pp. 408–9.
44. This view of Puritanism, Zionism and the 'unique' British tradition is found, for instance, in Nahum Sokolow, op. cit., Vol. I, pp. xxvi–xxvii: 'History shows that the Zionist idea and the continual renewal of efforts in this direction have been a tradition with the English people for centuries. English Christians taught the underlying principles of Jewish nationality. Zionism was thus permanently connected with England. The Jewish national idea has always particularly appealed to English feeling, has touched the heart of the English nation.' A similar perspective is found in Tuchmann's *Bible and Sword*, op. cit. And F. C. Burkitt, in his essay 'The Debt of Christianity to Judaism' wrote: 'English-speaking Christianity is in some respect more Judaic than European Christianity generally. The general biblical tone of English religion ever since the Reformation has given it a Judaic, not to say Semitic, cast and this to some extent obscures the non-Judaic system out of which historically it was derived.' See Bevan and Singer, op. cit., p. 69.
45. Baron, op. cit., Vol. 2, p. 200.
46. Dow, op. cit., p. 69.
47. For example, belief in witchcraft was based on Biblical authority even by such high-ranking Puritans as Milton and Cromwell. And in Protestant countries its legal prosecution, unknown to medieval Jewry, was taken up. See Dow, op. cit.
48. William Cunningham, *Growth of English Industry and Commerce*, 3 vols (Cambridge, 1892), as quoted in Tuchmann, op. cit., p. 82.
49. Ibid.
50. The book of Jewish law.
51. T. B. Macaulay, *History of England*, 5 vols (Philadelphia, 1861), Vol. 1, p. 71.
52. Conversion was especially popular during the reign of James I.
53. Cecil Roth, *England in Jewish History* (London, 1949), p. 7.
54. As quoted by Don Patinkin, 'Mercantilism and the Readmission of the Jews to England', *Jewish Social Studies*, Vol. 8, July 1946, pp. 161–78.
55. At about the same time, Edward Nicholas issued a similar plea under the heading: 'The Apology for the honourable nation of the Jews, and all the sons of Israel'. He connected England's setback with its past maltreatment of the 'most honourable nation of the world, a people chosen by God.' See Roth,

England in Jewish History, op. cit., p. 5.

56. The Old Testament passages referred to were Daniel XII, Verse 7, 'And when he shall have accomplished to scatter the power of the holy people all these things shall be finished', and Deuteronomy XXVIII, Verse 64 talking about the Jewish scattering 'from one end of the earth even to the other'.
57. Tuchmann, op. cit., p. 79.
58. Kobler, op. cit., p. 26.
59. Sokolow, op. cit., Vol. I, p. 16.
60. Mordecai L. Wilensky, 'Thomas Barlow's and John Dury's Attitude towards the readmission of the Jews to England', *The Jewish Quarterly Review*, Vol. 50, No. 2, October 1959, and No. 3, January 1960, pp. 167–75 and 256–68.
61. Ibid.
62. Ibid., p. 260. Menasseh ben Israel in his Humble Address to the Lord Protector based his argument on both religious and profit motives. He referred to the great economic benefits which would accrue to England through the settlement of Jewish merchants in England and he dwelt on the messianic argument linking the Re-admission of the Jews to their ultimate departure for Palestine.
63. Tuchmann, op. cit., p. 89.
64. K. H. Rengstorf and S. Kortzfleisch (eds), *Kirche und Synagoge* (Stuttgart, 1967), pp. 98ff.
65. Sokolow, op. cit., Vol. 1, pp. 41–2.
66. Ibid., p. 41.
67. *Revue des Etudes Juives*, Vol. 89, 1930, pp. 224–236.
68. Verete, op. cit., pp. 5–6.
69. Rengstorf and Kortzfleisch, op. cit., Chapter 2.
70. H. J. Schoeps, *Philosemitismus im Barock* (Tuebingen, 1952), p. 21.
71. Rengstorf and Kortzfleisch, op. cit., pp. 59–60.
72. Schoeps, op. cit., p. 54.
73. As quoted in Kobler, op. cit., p. 37.
74. Rengstorf and Kortzfleisch, op. cit., p. 63.
75. Franz Kobler's and Mayir Verete's studies (both op. cit.) of the Restoration movement are restricted to England, giving the general reader the idea that it was a uniquely English phenomenon.

3. The Zionist Theme in European Culture

In the conclusion of her penetrating analysis of Puritanism and Cromwell's philo-Semitism, Barbara Tuchmann sums up her study of the early English–Zionist connection:

> These first stirrings in Puritan England of interest in the restoration of Israel were unquestionably religious in origin, born out of the Old Testament reign over the mind and faith of the party in power during the middle years of the 17th century. But religion was not enough. No practical results would have come out of the Puritans' sense of ghostly brotherhood with the children of Israel or out of their ideals of toleration or out of their mystical hopes of hastening the millennium, had not political expediency intervened. Cromwell's interest in Menasseh's proposal was dictated by the same factor that dictated Lloyd George's interest in Chaim Weizmann's proposal ten generations later: namely, the aid that each believed the Jews could render in a wartime situation. And from Cromwell's time on, every future episode of British concern with Palestine depended on the twin presence of the profit motive, whether commercial, military, or imperial, and the religious motive inherited from the Bible. In the absence of either, as during the 18th century when the religious climate was distinctly cool, nothing happened.[1]

Without at all disputing the importance of political expediency or the profit motive, we find her analysis underplays Zionism's more integral relation with European culture in the 17th and 18th Centuries, and, in particular underestimates the continued importance of religious ideas in the Enlightenment.

Two 18th Century Inventions: History and Geography

When the Puritan Commonwealth gave way to the Stuarts in 1660, there was no 'eclipse of the Bible', as Tuchmann asserts. Nor was the 18th Century a 'classic age, orderly, mannerly, rational, and as un-Hebraic as possible.'[2] This is far too superficial a view of the era following the Stuart

Restoration. Franz Kobler, on the other hand, shows a much deeper understanding when he writes:

> Far from causing a setback to the Movement, Enlightenment and Deism in their ascendancy actually enriched the [Jewish] Restoration Doctrine by a salutary admixture of realism. Thus the central idea of Restoration was passed on steadily, though with considerable modification, from generation to generation until the French Revolution brought about a sudden and radical metamorphosis.[3]

Zionist ideas, originating from non-Jews during the 16th Century, and most openly displayed in 17th Century Puritan England, were in fact further consolidated during the so-called Age of Reason, despite official opposition.

The Literalization of the Hebrew World

Literature took up where religious doctrine left off. On the stage, 'the sensuous, riotous tone of the earlier plays became more quiet and severe . . . The dominance of the religious element made itself apparent in the atmosphere of the theater.'[4] Old Testament themes became the most common source of inspiration for the artists and poets of the new era, not only in England but also on the Continent. Now modern Jews were themselves portrayed as unique characters, treated with more seriousness and a much deeper understanding. Again the Jewish-Palestine equation was presented with all its Zionist implications.

John Milton's famous *Paradise Regained* had spoken of Israel's Restoration:

> Yet He at length, time to himself best known
> Remembering Abraham, by some wondrous call
> May bring them back repentent and sincere,
> And at their passing cleave the Assyrian flood,
> While to their native land with joy they haste,
> As the Red Sea and Jordan once He cleft,
> When to the Promised Land their fathers pass'd;
> To his due time and providence I leave them.[5]

Milton stated it clearly: Israel would be restored to Palestine, not by conquest but rather by some supernatural event. His *De Doctrina Christiana* (not published until 1825) testifies to Milton's own millenarian convictions and belief in Israel's revival.

Samson Agonistes, directly taken from the Old Testament Book of Judges, marks a new phenomenon: a subjective portrait of a Jew. (This was to recur in the 19th Century with Lord Byron and Coleridge and in the 20th Century with James Joyce.) As a Puritan poet in the Puritan environment, Milton could do little else than choose this subject and treat it as he did. There was no strain to create his characters, they were very much alive in the popular imagination. Old Testament characters, such as Moses, Joshua, David, Ruth, Job or Esther were by now familiar references. The preference for the Hebrew prophets over the Greek classical heroes is easily noticeable when reading an anthology of 17th and 18th Century European literature.

Only a generation later, Alexander Pope renewed this vision of a restored Jewish kingdom in Palestine in his 'Messiah'. His interpretation of scriptural text was along Christological lines, but he included vivid descriptions of Israel's revival as a nation and as a very real event. His new Jerusalam is unmistakably pictured as inhabited by the returning Jews.

Lofty Zionist images of the new Jewish Jerusalem were further employed in 18th Century hymnal poems – most notably those by Charles Wesley. Finally around the turn of the 18th Century William Blake addressed himself to the Jews in the lines:

> England awake! Awake! Awake!
> Jerusalem thy sister calls
> Why wild those sleep the sleep of death
> And close her from thy ancient walls.

On the Continent, Biblical Hebraic subjects made their appearance in French literature. For the French classicist, Jean Baptiste Racine, the Old Testament provided subject matter as well as poetic inspiration. His biblical tragedy *Ester* (1689) is still today regarded as a masterpiece of French drama. His contemporary, Jacques Benigne Bossuet, in his *Discours sur l'Histoire Universelle* (1681), presents Israel as the nation above all nations, the cornerstone of world history.

German language literature, although still in its formative stages during the 17th Century, had a Hebraic Zionist timbre as well. Already in the century before, Hans Sachs had touched upon themes of Jewish history in his *Der Winterich Herodes* (1552) and *Tragedia Koenig Sauls* (1557). Christian Weise picked up the same themes in his *Der Verfolgte David* (1683); *Nebukadneza* (1683) and *Kain und Abel* (1703). In Switzerland, Johann Jakob Bodmer chose as characters Abraham, Noah, Joseph and Solomon for his poetry.

The German poet, Gotthold Ephraim Lessing ranked above all in the period of the Enlightenment. His drama *Nathan der Weise* (1779) leads the reader directly back to Jerusalem, the hometown of the drama's hero, a Jew named Nathan. Lessing's treatment of Nathan as the hero of the drama is unique and innovative. Set during the time of the Third Crusade in the 12th Century, the drama presents Saladin as the ruthless, inconsiderable Muslim ruler and captor of Jerusalem. Even the Christian Templar Knight in his fanaticism appears inferior to Nathan, the wise Jew, to whom both Christian and Muslim turn for advice and counsel. Although

Lessing wrote *Nathan der Weise* to evoke a spirit of tolerance and toleration, his choice of Jerusalem as the locale for the drama and his most favourable treatment of Nathan reflect the Hebraic Zionist influence prevalent in Germany since the Reformation.

Poetic Zionist tones permeated German liturgy during the 18th Century. The Jewish Restoration to Palestine figured as the *leitmotif* in most of the hymns of the new Protestant movement of Pietism. Many of these hymns depict Jewish history at its most glorious stage and often made use of Hebrew words in the midst of the German text.[7]

Zionism and the Philosophers

European espousal of the Jewish Restoration to Palestine can be found in the writings of such outstanding 17th and 18th Century philosophers as John Locke, Isaac Newton, Johann Gottfried Herder, Kant, Fichte, Pascal and Rousseau. John Locke, for example, the father of liberal political theory, in his *Commentaries on St. Paul's Epistles* wrote, 'God is able to collect the Jews into one body . . . and set them in flourishing condition in their own Land'.

The image of the 18th Century as the classical Age of Reason, totally governed by the scientific discoveries of natural laws and their 'challenge' to the authority of the Bible is contradicted by many of the scientist/philosophers' interest in eschatological teachings. Far from un-Hebraic in their interests, they tried to come up with their own 'scientific' interpretations of the Jews' return to Palestine.

Isaac Newton in his *Observations upon the Prophecies of Daniel and the Apocalypse of St. John*, first published five years after his death, concluded that the Jews will indeed return to their homeland: 'The manner I know not. Let time be the interpreter.' He even attempted to set up a timetable for the events leading to the Restoration and expected the intervention of an earthly power on behalf of the dispersed Jews to effect their return.

A generation later, the renowned physician and philosopher, David Hartley, subjected the question of Jewish Restoration to systematic scrutiny in his general scientific work, *Observations on Man, His Fame, His Duty and his Expectations* (1749). He included the Jews among 'the bodies politic' who, despite their present dispersal, constituted a united political entity with a common national destiny. To the prophetic arguments he added his own historical, sociological and psychological accounts of the Jewish people as a living organism held together by their common language, Rabbinical Hebrew, and their historical bonds.[8]

Another scientist who was a strong believer in the messianic mission of the Jewish people was the chemist and discoverer of oxygen, Joseph Priestley. As a unitarian minister, Priestley remained convinced that Judaism and Christianity were complementary and hence conversion to Christianity would be simple. His plea to the Jews to acknowledge Jesus as the Messiah was therefore coupled with his prayer that

the God of Heaven, the God of Abraham, Isaac and Jacob whom we
Christians as well as you worship, may be graciously pleased to put an end to
your suffering, gathering you from all nations, resettle you in your own
country, the land of Canaan and make you the most illustrious . . . of all
nations on the earth.[9]

Palestine and the Jews again went hand in hand in the typical Zionist
fashion. Priestley visualized Palestine as uninhabited, neglected by its
Turkish occupiers, but eager and ready to receive the returning Jews.[10]

A future Jewish state also figures in the writings of both Jean-Jacques
Rousseau, a native of Geneva from a French Protestant family, and
Blaise Pascal, the philosopher of 17th Century French Catholic mysti-
cism. In his greatest book on education, *Emile* (1762), Rousseau wrote,
'We shall never know the inner motives of the Jews until the day they
have their own free state, schools and universities.'[11]

Blaise Pascal wrote his *Penseés sur la Religion* in order to convince the
unbeliever of the existence of God, and found the 4,000-year survival of
the Jewish people good grounds to suppose God must exist. Well versed
in Jewish religious and philosophical literature – the Talmud, Midrash
and the writings of Maimonides – Pascal pondered the role of the Jewish
people, looking upon Israel finally as the symbolic forerunner of the
Messiah. He expressed great respect for the Jews' achievements as the
'foremost nation' and for their faithful adherence to their religion.[12] His
idealization of Jewish history, and of the Jewish people as the oldest
people known to man, met with Voltaire's fierce criticism during the 18th
Century.

German philosophy is often held responsible for inventing the theoretical framework which founded 20th Century anti-Semitism yet it also
had its Zionist tendencies, although the idea of the Restoration was not
incorporated into the structure of the philosophical system *per se*.
Hebraism had exerted its influence upon Johann Gottfried Herder,
philosopher and Protestant theologian, whose admiration for the Old
Testament led him to proclaim the superiority of the 'Hebrew genius'. In
his *Vom Geiste der Hebraeischen Poesie* (1783), he classified the old
Hebrews as a unique nation, set apart from all other nations, with its very
own and special soul.[13] His overall contribution to the emerging force of
modern nationalism is well known. Like the German or any other people,
the Jews constituted a *Volk* whose roots reached deep into the soil of the
remote past and grew in the long unconscious development of the
people.[14] But at the same time Herder harboured a certain contempt for
those contemporary Jews who failed to assert their own nationality and
national consciousness and 'who in spite of all the oppression they suffer
did not long for their own fatherland.[15]

This understanding of Jewry and Judaism as an organic nation rather
than as a religion was also characteristic of Immanuel Kant who once
described the Jews as 'the Palestinians that live amongst us',[16] and of

Johann Gottlieb Fichte whose basic enmity towards the Jews was never-theless coloured by Zionist themes. According to Fichte, there was no place for the Jews in Europe. The Jewish nation had to go back to where its roots had grown – to Palestine. To solve the Jewish question for Europe, he saw 'no other means but to reconquer for them their holy land and to send them all there.'[17]

The Age of Rationalism also saw the emergence of a new type of literature interested in Palestine, not as the Bible's land but as a geograph-ical unit to be explored scientifically. Scientific travellers made pilgrimages to the East now looking for knowledge and information rather than for religious experience, and their accounts of Palestine were not limited to scientific journals but also featured in the increasingly popular travel literature. The geographic features and local customs of the inhabitants interested these new type of travellers far more than the local religious traditions which had attracted the notice of the earlier pilgrims.

But, even so, much of the literature did not rise above the prejudices of the time. Some of the stereotypes developed and portrayed in this new literature were to remain fixed in the Western mind for a long time to come: the image of the 'terrible Turk' or 'cruel infidel'. Further, it was the 'barbarous infidels . . . who by their continuous wars and ravages have made Palestine almost desolate and like a desert . . . a place forsaken by God.'[18] Islam was held responsible for the decay and ruin of the Palestin-ian country, once the garden of mankind.[19] In one of the most famous and widely read 18th Century travel books, the indigenous Bedouin popula-tion was described as 'a very bad people' not to be trusted and totally destructive, parasites to the country.

Even the Christian inhabitants were commonly ridiculed for their superstitious religious practices, such as hallowing certain sacred places or relics. Some of the earlier religious sceptics even refused to enter the Church of the Holy Sepulchre and cunningly described the friars' worship-ping and kissing the relics as a 'singular dotage of the Romish Folly'.[21]

The Jewish inhabitants of Palestine and indeed other nations were, on the other hand, treated in a most favourable light and often idealized even by these rationalist travellers who had no particular interest in Restoration. Looked at closely, this new type of literature inadvertently continued the trend of many Protestant theologians in furthering the Jewish-Palestine connection.

The Apocalypse and the Age of Revolution

Millenarian religious literature and theological abstracts concerning Jewish Restoration had had their heyday during the 17th Century. But although fewer in number during the first half of the 18th Century they were still as influential.

Towards the end of the 18th Century, a new wave of polemical religious literature came off the press, especially in connection with the lively debate between the Christian Zionist, Joseph Priestley and his Jewish opponent David Levi, who rejected the Christian millenarian doctrines. In his book, *Letters to Dr. Priestley, in answer to those he addressed to the Jews*, Rabbi Levi had given the Jewish answer to all the commotion among non-Jews associating contemporary Jewry with an earthly and territorial Restoration to Palestine. He refused to even consider conversion and more important yet, spoke out against the national Restoration of his people, maintaining that the Jewish people were to fulfil their mission of redemption while dispersed rather than by returning to a Homeland.

Yet, heedless of the unpopularity of their ideas among the Jews themselves, these new millenarians went on to find widespread support with their (Christian) public.

> . . . the premises they had set down and the succession of political and military events which they seemed to make intelligible gave their eschatological views a semblance of actuality, thus engendering in the public the belief that what was happening before their eyes was the very apocalyptical sequence of events that had been predicted in the Prophecies on the Latter Days.[22]

The political and military events referred to here all centred on the French Revolution and its implications for the European *status quo*. A further urgency was added by Napoleon's Oriental Expedition and his invasion of Palestine in the spring of 1799 (see Chapter Four).

> History seemed to have assumed apocalyptic proportions, with one kingdom after another being broken up and institutions believed immutable exposed to shattering blows. It had indeed become difficult for students of the prophecies not to find references to these happenings in Daniel or the Revelation.[23]

No longer was Jewish Restoration a topic reserved for mere academic discussion.

Now it was becoming real and actual, bound up with Europe's prevailing political crisis. For the new generation of millenarians the Jewish Restoration required no special proving, it was already foreshadowed by events. Gradually, political themes crept into the heretofore purely religious credo of the unrolling of a divine plan. Rather, earthly powers now had their role to play. Secondly, the repentance and conversion of the Jews to Christianity, which up until that time had been a matter of supreme significance, was no longer seen as the prerequisite for the Jewish return to Palestine.

In 1790, Richard Beere, the rector of Sandbroke, repeated the 1649 Cartwright petition, when he appealed to the English Prime Minister,

William Pitt, to assist in bringing about the impending 'final restoration of the Jews to the Holy Land'.[24] England and its merchant navy could only gain, he claimed, politically as well as economically:

> . . . This island shall be among the first of the nations to convey you [the Jews] to your country . . . it is highly proper for our Government to extend their help for effecting this desirable purpose from motives of sound policy. For whenever our Hebrew brethren shall come to be collected together . . . and again settled in their own land . . . they will stand in need of many manufactured articles, of the necessities of life . . . especially woollens and linens. These things they must purchase from other nations for many years.[25]

Beere's fellow millenarian, James Bicheno, in 1800 published *The Restoration of the Jews — The Crisis of all Nations*. As his title indicated, Bicheno regarded Jewish Restoration as an international issue. According to his own calculations, the Restoration was due 'in these days', and was not at all conditional upon the Jews' conversion.[26] Bicheno was particularly alarmed by Napoleon's Eastern Expedition (see Chapter Four) and by the possibility that 'atheistic France' might gain a foothold in Palestine. The rumours that Napoleon himself was about to restore a Jewish state in Palestine prompted Bicheno to a severe attack on the British Government's alliance with Turkey against France; after all, albeit unconsciously, France seemed to be acting as the instrument of God. By its alliance with Turkey, Britain had joined hands with the infidels who were hindering the Jews from returning to their land, and thus the British Government was directly responsible for holding up the redemption of all mankind. Eventually resigning himself to the British-Turkish alliance, Bicheno still offered the following proposal:

> That the rulers of this country use their influence with the Porte to give up that part of their territory from which the Jews have been expelled, to its rightful owners, and thus whilst they perform the most generous of deeds do all they can at least to prevent those possible consequences, which, were they to take place, would prove most fatal to our government and commerce.[27]

His appeal made the Restoration intelligible in the secular terms of economic issues and current events. He warned of a possible French control over the whole Mediterranean Sea and its implications for British trade with the Far East. The economic and political significance of Palestine for Britain was thus for the first time most clearly and comprehensively stated and was found sufficient to warrant British action on behalf of the Jews' Restoration to Palestine.

Human Intervention: 19th Century Evangelism and Zionism

At the beginning of the 19th Century, England experienced an evangelical revival whose dogmas and beliefs were very similar to those of 17th Century Puritanism. Christopher Sykes calls this revival 'the second spring of the Puritan genius' and Barbara Tuchmann describes this new 'Hebraic interlude' in English history in the following way:

> Now the pendulum had swung back again, after the Hellenic interlude of the 18th century, to the moral earnestness of another Hebraic period. 18th century skepticism had given way to Victorian piety; 18th century rationalism was again surrendering to Revelation.[28]

The English establishment was deeply shocked by the French Revolution which they regarded as the logical outcome of rationalism. The movement back to the Bible and its revelations brought millenarian Restorationalism into vogue once more, and with it non-Jewish Zionism. No longer the old-fashioned creed advocated by 17th Century clergymen and dissenters, non-Jewish Zionism over the past three centuries had matured and developed into 'a new type which had a dual interest in the subject, religious and political which was for the most part the concern of the laymen'.[29]

This new era of Evangelism lasted roughly until the end of Queen Victoria's reign (1837–1901). Typical of the long list of Victorian Christians advocating Jewish Restoration for messianic or more practical considerations, were Edward Bickersteth and Lewis Way, both members of the London Society for Promoting Christianity among the Jews, founded in 1807. But by far the most well known and influential evangelical was Lord Antony Ashley Cooper, seventh Earl of Shaftesbury (1801–85), the 'Evangelical of all the Evangelicals' and a central figure in the tradition of non-Jewish Zionism.

Lord Shaftesbury

Like many before him, Shaftesbury envisaged a Jewish state in Palestine, basing his Zionism on Biblical prophecies, as he had learned them from his friend Edward Bickersteth. But he justified the prophecies by references to the political realities of Victorian England. Like Oliver Cromwell, he was interested in the Jews as a nation, but he concentrated on bringing this nation back to Palestine. Unlike Cromwell, Shaftesbury did not advocate the civil or political emancipation of Jews in England, arguing that religious principles would be violated if Jews were permitted to enter Parliament without taking the traditional oath 'on the true faith of a Christian'. When the Emancipation Bill finally was passed by Parliament in 1861, it was not the Evangelicals with their love for 'God's ancient people' who favoured admitting the English Jews to full citizenship on equal terms, but the much less pious Liberals.

In 1839 the distinguished magazine *Quarterly Review* published Shaftesbury's 30-page article on 'State and Prospects of the Jews' in which the author outlined his concept of Jewish Restoration.[30] The very fact that one of the most influential magazines of the time published an article favourable to Jewish Restoration indicated that support was no longer limited only to certain religious groups, but that it had now gained general and public recognition. In the article, Shaftesbury expressed his concern over the 'Hebrew race'. He vehemently opposed the idea of assimilation and emancipation on the ground that the Jews would always remain aliens in all countries save one, Palestine.

Shaftesbury's constant preoccupation with the Jews' return to Palestine as a nation made him the chief advocate of such a plan long before it gained currency with the British political and imperial establishment. He was convinced, much more than the Puritans had ever been, that human instrumentality could bring about divine purposes – a principle still unacceptable to the majority of Jews at that time. Lord Shaftesbury made it his task to convince his fellow Englishmen that the Jews 'though admittedly a stiff-necked, dark hearted people, and sunk in moral degradation, obduracy, and ignorance of the Gospel were not only worthy of salvation but also vital to Christianity's hope of salvation'.[30]

In Shaftesbury's imagination, Palestine was an empty country. It was he who formulated the early slogan: 'A country without a nation for a nation without a country' which later Jewish Zionists were to transform into their own: 'A land without a people for a people without a land'.[32] When his friend Young was appointed Her Majesty's Vice-Counsul in Jerusalem, Shaftesbury victoriously entered in his diary:

> What a wonderful event it is. The ancient city of the people of God is about to resume a place among the nations, and England is the first of the Gentile Kingdoms that ceases to tread her down.[33]

Although Lord Shaftesbury was by far the most outstanding of all the 19th Century Evangelicals drawn to the cause of the Jewish Restoration, there were many others of stature and influence who laboured to achieve this goal. There were members of the British nobility, led by the Duke of Kent and many members of the House of Lords, such as the Earl of Crawford and Lindsay, the Earl of Grosvenor, Lord Gray, and Lord Bexley. Other members of Parliament included Bishop Manning and Gladstone.[34] The Evangelicals of the 19th Century were not a marginal group and their position was an influential strand of debate in the first half of the Victorian period, when even the opponents of religion were religious:

> . . . as the inevitable accompaniment of the return to Hebraism we find Lord Shaftesbury espousing the restoration of Israel in almost the same terms as the Cartwrights and the Puritan extremists. This was not because

Hebraism in Matthew Arnold's sense had anything to do with modern Jews, but because it was an ethos inherited from the Old Testament. And whenever Christians returned to the authority of the Old Testament they found it prophesying the return of its people to Jerusalem and felt themselves dutybound to assist the prophecy.[35]

For Lord Shaftesbury and his co-religionists this was politically a most opportune time for the promotion of Jewish settlement in Palestine. Three major British interests converged on the area of Palestine during the 19th Century: the European balance of power, the security of India as threatened by France and Russia, and the unimpaired transit route to India via Syria. From now on began what David Polk has described as 'the curious union of empire policy with a sort of paternalistic Christian Zionism which is evident in British policy in succeeding generations.'[36]

Romantic Racism

At the same time that Evangelism swept England at the beginning of the 19th Century, Europe was in the grips of Romanticism. This glorification of the instincts and emotions had come to supersede the Englightenment worship of intellect and reason. Many of those disturbed by the attacks of deists and sceptics now delighted in a philosophy that recognized the merits of faith and exalted the world of the spirit. Romantic idealism cast its influence in many directions, encompassing a deep veneration of nature, tradition, religion and above all the romantic notion of the *Volk* and its *Volksgeist*, a vague concept which in English requires three different words to express its meaning – 'people', 'nation' and 'race'. The 18th Century legal and rationalist concept of 'citizenship' was now replaced by the infinitely more flexible concept of *Volk*,[37] and its associated Romantic doctrines.

As inflected by the rising tide of nationalism, such concepts naturally affected the Jewish Question as well. The Romantic emphasis on faith and tradition generated a new appreciation of the Hebrew nation and race, now based on secular rather than religious precepts. Race was now cast as the very essence and source of human values and existence, and there grew up an almost fanatical conviction among many non-Jews that the Jews constituted a superior nation now living among other nations. The Jews were to be restored to their ancient Homeland in Palestine where they had originally developed their roots and traditions, as well as their peculiarities. Divine agency was now decisively abandoned as the means to effect the return to Palestine, in favour of human activism and achievement, preferably the comined efforts of Jews and non-Jews.

Romantic Zionism found its expression in 19th Century literature as well as political writings. Jewish characters not only make frequent appearances, but they are usually treated most favourably. These characters would be presented not so much as individuals but as members of a nation, sometimes pitied for their national misfortunes, but more often admired for their superior qualities of endurance and survival. The Jews were almost always encouraged to return to their original national existence in Palestine.

Lord Byron

Lord Byron, the illustrious English romantic activist and poet who died while fighting in Greece for Greek national independence, expressed a typical admiration for the greatness inherent in the fate of the Jewish people. Many of the poems in his poetic cycle *Hebrew Melodies* (1815) deal with Biblical and Palestinian themes. The most famous in the collection 'Oh Weep for Those' closes with the following stanza:

> Tribe of the wandering foot and weary breast,
> How shall ye flee away and be at rest?
> The wild dove hath her nest, the fox his cave,
> Mankind his country – Israel but the grave.

The verse exhibits the poet's pity as well as admiration for Israel's fate as a people without a country and regards this as a historical anomaly. In other poems Byron fixes on the 'eternal' linkage between Palestine and the Jews. Byron himself had travelled through Palestine in 1811 and expressed his shock over the apparently miserable and derelict condition of the Holy Land. His poems 'The Wild Gazelle' and 'On the Day of the Destruction of the Temple by Titus' call upon the Jews to return and redeem the land.

Walter Scott

Sir Walter Scott, the first great novelist of the 19th Century, created in his *Ivanhoe* a Jewish character with Zionist leanings – Rebecca.

> She is an ideal figure of true Jewish womanhood, faithful in the defense of her people, her religion, and her honor. In many things she clearly voices the sentiments of her people and gives evidence that Scott had a sympathetic understanding of the position and feelings of the Jews.[38]

Through Rebecca, Scott not only deplores the Jewish people's misfortune but also calls upon the Jews to act since 'the sound of the trumpet wakes Judah no longer'.

William Wordsworth

Like Byron, William Wordsworth struck a similar cord in his poems 'Song for the Wandering Jew' and 'A Jewish Family'. The latter includes the following stanza:

Two lovely sisters still and sweet
As flowers, stand side by side;
Their soul-subduing looks might cheat
The Christian of his pride;
Such beauty hath the Eternal poured
Upon them not forlorn,
Though of a lineage once abhorred,
Nor yet redeemed from scorn.
Mysterious safeguard, that, in spite
Of poverty and wrong,
Doth here preserve a living light,
From Hebrew fountains sprung;
That gives this ragged group to cast
Around the dell a gleam
Of Palestine, of glory past,
And proud Jerusalem.

Robert Browning

During the second half of the 19th Century, Robert Browning and George Eliot stood out among the many English writers who took up the cause of Jewish Restoration to Palestine. In Browning's works, Jewish themes occur more often than in any earlier English poetry. The poet was well versed in Jewish literature and his knowledge of Hebrew served him well in reading the Old Testament. For Browning, the Jewish people were the ideal symbol of continuity whose national future was yet to unfold itself in Palestine. In his poem 'The Holy Cross Day' (1855) he wrote:

The Lord will have mercy on Jacob yet,
And again in his border see Israel yet,
When Judah beholds Jerusalem,
The strangers shall be joined to them;
To Jacob's House shall the Gentiles cleave,
So the Prophet saith and the sons believe.

These lines clearly made Browning the balladeer of Jewish Restoration in Victorian England.

George Eliot

In 1874 George Eliot began to write *Daniel Deronda*, the first truly Zionist novel in the history of non-Jewish fiction. Eliot dispenses with the theories of amalgamation or affinity between Christianity and Judaism. The hero of *Daniel Deronda* is not a Christianized or 'gentilized' Jewish national hero who discovers his Jewish heritage under the influence of non-Jews. Nor are there appeals to Anglican England to follow the example of Cyrus and help to bring about a Jewish return to Palestine.

Eliot's debt to Shaftesbury and Evangelism, though unacknowledged, must be considered. The Gentile author created in *Daniel Deronda* a true Zionist hero who discovers for himself his Jewish nationality and heritage.

The novel represents the apex of non-Jewish Zionism in the literary field, the culmination of a long tradition that began with the Protestant idea of Restoration, but had initially demanded the conversion of the Jews as a first step towards the Palestine goal. Then it was allowed that conversion might happen after Restoration and, by the 19th Century, conversion had been completely dropped as a necessary requirement. Restoration had instead become identified with a return to the Hebrew heritage. The Romantic Revolution, with its emphasis on race, religion and tradition, had finally produced the notion that the great sin was the Jews' secession from Judaism. It followed that acceptance of Jewish values was the only way to redemption.

George Eliot had all the necessary background to write a Zionist novel. She was a deeply religious Christian and in her early life led an almost puritan life, then to be caught up in the full tide of the Evangelical movement. As a devout Evangelical it was only natural that she became familiar with Biblical and post-Biblical Judaism. She regularly visited Jewish synagogue meetings and gradually developed a strong affection for the Jewish religion itself. She had also met Moses Hess, the Jewish Zionist who in 1862 had written (in German) his famous *Rome and Jerusalem*.

Yet even without her knowledge of Hess's Zionist exposition of the Jewish National Question, it seems likely that her interpretation of the Restoration idea would have been the same. Already in two earlier works *Romola* (1863) and *The Spanish Gipsy* (1868), she makes it man's most sacred obligation to accept his origin. Her romantic vision of nature, blended with her own conservative evangelical leanings, made her think of the past as an ideal of human life. *Daniel Deronda* displays the possibility of having contemporary Jewish prophets and leaders as in ancient times. The heritage of the Jews is presented as most worthy of rediscovery and accepted as a way of national revival and final redemption. She strongly believed that 19th Century Jews in Europe were renouncing their own unique national heritage by striving for assimilation and amalgamation with other nations.[39]

Daniel Deronda was the 'literary introduction' to the Balfour Declaration, which made the presence of a Jewish polity in Palestine a historic necessity. The vision, expressed by the character Mordecai, the Jewish mystic, is precisely the Zionist return of the Jews to Palestine and the Restoration of the land as the home of a Jewish nation:

> Looking towards a land and a polity, our dispersed people in all the ends of the earth may share the dignity of a national life which has a voice among the peoples of the East and the West – which will plant the wisdom and skill of our race so that it may be, as of old, a medium of transmission and

understanding . . . There is store of wisdom among us to found a new Jewish polity, grand, simple, just, like the old – a republic where there is equality of protection, an equality which shone like a star on the forehead of our ancient community, and gave it more than the brightness of Western freedom amid despotisms of the East. Then our race shall have an organic centre, a heart and a brain to watch and guide and execute; the outraged Jew shall have a defence in the court of nations, as the outraged Englishman or American. And the world will gain as Israel gains.[40]

In 'The Modern Hep, Hep, Hep' (1879) George Eliot writes:

If we are to consider the future of the Jews at all, it seems reasonable to take a preliminary question: are they destined to complete fusion with the peoples among whom they are dispersed, losing every remnant of a distinctive consciousness as Jews; or, are there, in the political relations of the world, the conditions, present or approaching, for the restoration of a Jewish state, planted in the old centre of national feeling, a souce of dignifying protection, a special channel for special energies, which may contribute some added form of national genius and an added voice in the councils of the world? . . . The hinge of possibility is simply the existence of an adequate community of feeling as well as widespread need in the Jewish race, and hope that among its finest specimens there may arise some men of instruction and ardent public spirit, some new Ezras, some modern Maccabees, who will know how to use all favouring outward conditions, how to triumph by heroic example over the indifference of their fellows and foes, and will steadfastly set their faces toward making their people once more one among the nations.

Notes

1. Barbara Tuchmann, *Bible and Sword* (London, 1956), pp. 93–4.
2. Ibid., p. 95.
3. Franz Kobler, *The Vision was There* (London, 1956), p. 35.
4. Edward N. Calisch, *The Jew in English Literature as Author and as Subject* (Port Washington, 1969), p. 93.
5. John Milton, *Paradise Regained* (London, 1936).
6. William Blake, *Jerusalem* (verse cycle).
7. Siegfried Riemer, *Philosemitismus im deutschen evangelischen Kirchenlied des Barock* (Stuttgart, 1963), p. 72.
8. Kobler, op. cit., pp. 39–40.
9. As quoted in Kobler, op. cit., pp. 41–2.
10. Joseph Priestley, *A Comparison of the Institutions of Moses with those of the Hindus and other Ancient Nations*, 1799.
11. Jean Jacques Rousseau, *Emile* (London, 1957), Book IV, p. 268.

12. K. H. Rengstorf and S. Kortzfleisch (eds.), *Kirche und Synagoge* (Stuttgart, 1967), p. 134.
13. J. G. Herder, *Saemtliche Werke* (Berlin, 1852), Vol. 1, pp. 211ff.
14. G. Kaiser, *Pietismus und Patriotismus im literarischen Deutschland* (Wiesbaden, 1961), pp. 147–8.
15. As quoted in Rengstorf and Kortzfleisch, op. cit., p. 152.
16. Immanuel Kant, *Werke in 6 Baenden* (Darmstadt, 1956), Vol. VI, p. 517.
17. J. G. Fichte, *Saemtliche Werke* (Berlin, 1846), Vol. VI, pp. 149–50; see also A. Lewkowitz, *Das Judentum und die geistigen Stroemungen des 19 Jahrhunderts* (Breslau, 1935), p. 56.
18. Robert Burton, 'Memorable Remarks Upon the Ancient and Modern State of the Jewish Nation' in Nathaniel Crouch (ed.), *Two Journeys to Jerusalem* (London, 1704).
19. Francis Bacon, at the beginning of the 17th Century, depicted the Turks as '. . . a nation without a morality, without letters, arts or sciences . . . a very reproach of human society . . . They made the garden of the world a wilderness.' See Bacon's 'Holy War', *Works* (London, 1874), Vol. II, p. 477.
20. Richard Pococke, *Descriptions of the East*, 2 vols, (London, 1743/45) as quoted in Tuchmann, op. cit., p. 101.
21. Ibid., p. 75.
22. Mayir Verete, 'The Restoration of the Jews in English Protestant Thought, 1790–1840', *Middle Eastern Studies*, Vol. 8, No. 1, p. 5.
23. Kobler, op. cit., p. 43.
24. Ibid., p. 43.
25. Richard Beere, *A Dissertation . . . containing strong and cogent reasons to prove that the commencement of the final Restoration of the Jews to the Holy Land is to take place in the ensuing year, A.D. 1791*, as quoted in Verete, op. cit., p. 11.
26. James Bicheno, *The Restoration of the Jews — The Crisis of all Nations*, cited in Verete, op. cit.
27. Ibid.
28. Tuchmann, op. cit., p. 115.
29. Christopher Sykes, *Two Studies in Virtue* (London, 1953), p. 151.
30. Earl of Shaftesbury, 'State and Prospects of the Jews', *Quarterly Review*, London, January/March 1839.
31. W. T. Gidney, *The History of the London Society for the Propagation of Christianity among the Jews* (London, Centennial Issue, 1908). Lord Shaftesbury served as President of this organization in 1848.
32. Albert H. Hyamson, *Palestine under the Mandate* (London, 1950), p. 10.
33. Edwin Hodder, *The Life and Work of the Seventh Earl of Shaftesbury* (London, 1886), Vol. I.
34. Mel Scult, 'English Missions to the Jews – Conversion in the Age of Emancipation', *Jewish Social Studies*, Vol. 35, No. 1, January 1973, pp. 5–7.
35. Tuchmann, op. cit., pp. 115–16.
36. David Polk, *Backdrop to Tragedy* (Boston, 1957), p. 40.
37. Hans Kohn, *Nationalism* (New York, 1960), p. 30.
38. Calisch, op. cit., p. 125.
39. Here one must remember that the 19th Century is generally regarded as the Golden Age of Jewish emancipation on all levels, intellectual as well as spiritual. At the time the great majority of Jews all over Europe were intensely

involved in a struggle for civil and political emancipation. Jewish hopes were pinned on their complete equality as the prime solution to every aspect of the so-called Jewish Question. As a result, most Jews viewed with great disfavour the Christian Zionists who seemed to deny them their rightful position. See Norman Bentwich and John Shaftesley, 'Forerunners of Zionism in the Victorian Era', op. cit., p. 10.

40. All quotations taken from George Eliot, *Daniel Deronda* (London, 1899), Works of George Eliot, Vol. 8.

4. The Jewish Question Meets the Eastern Question

Napoleon Calls the Jews to Arms

Bonaparte, Commander-in-Chief of the Armies of the French Republic in Africa and Asia, to the Rightful Heirs of Palestine.

Israelites, unique nation, whom, in thousands of years, lust of conquest and tyranny were able to deprive of the ancestral lands only, but not of name and national existence!

Attentive and impartial observers of the destinies of nations, even though not endowed with the gifts of seers like Isaiah and Joel, have also felt long since what these, with beautiful and uplifting faith, foretold when they saw the approaching destruction of their kingdom and fatherland: that the ransomed of the Lord shall return, and come with singing unto Zion, and the enjoyment of henceforth undisturbed possession of their heritage will send an everlasting joy upon their heads (Isaiah 35:10).

Arise then, with gladness, ye exiled! A war unexampled in the annals of history, waged in self-defence by a nation whose hereditary lands were regarded by her enemies as plunder to be divided, arbitrarily and at their convenience, by a stroke of the pen of Cabinets, avenges her own shame and the shame of the remotest nations, long forgotten under the yoke of slavery, and, too, the almost two-thousand-year-old ignominy put upon you; and while time and circumstances would seem to be least favourable to a restatement of your claims or even to their expression, and indeed to be compelling their complete abandonment, she [France] offers to you at this very time, and contrary to all expectations, Israel's patrimony!

The undefiled army with which Providence has sent me hither, led by justice and accompanied by victory, has made Jerusalem my headquarters, and will, within a few days, transfer them to Damascus, a proximity which is no longer terrifying to David's city.

Rightful Heirs of Palestine!

The great nation which does not trade in men and countries as did those who sold your ancestors unto all peoples (Joel 4:6) hereby calls on you not indeed to conquer your patrimony, nay, only to take over that which has been conquered and, with that nation's warranty and support, to maintain it against all comers.

Arise! Show that the once overwhelming might of your oppressors has not repressed the courage of the descendants of those heroes whose brotherly alliance did honour to Sparta and Rome (Macc. 12:15), but that all the two thousand years of slavish treatment have not succeeded in stifling it.

Hasten! Now is the moment which may not return for thousands of years, to claim the restoration of your rights among the population of the universe which had been shamefully withheld from you for thousands of years, your political existence as a nation among the nations, and the unlimited natural right to worship Yehovah in accordance with your faith, publicly and in likelihood for ever (Joel 4:20).[1]

Today it is still a little known fact that Napoleon Bonaparte was the first statesman to propose a Jewish state in Palestine, 118 years before the Balfour Declaration. Weizmann even called Napoleon 'the first of the modern non-Jewish Zionists'.[2]

Napoleon's chosen moment to acknowledge Jewish rights to Palestine occurred during the Syrian campaign of his great Oriental Expedition. In the spring of 1799, he issued a proclamation appealing to the Jews of Africa and Asia to fight under his flags to re-establish the Ancient Kingdom of Jerusalem. The spectacular proclamation's claim to have been issued from Napoleon's 'headquarters in Jerusalem' turns out to have been an even more spectacular piece of military optimism: in fact Napoleon and his troops never even approached the city, retreating from Palestine by sea to Egypt after their defeat at Acre in May 1799.[3] The promises of the proclamation had never had any hopes of being fulfilled.

Yet this does not make the proclamation a 'meaningless gesture'.[4] It is not insignificant that the ground for it had already been prepared by unofficial rumours of Napoleon's Zionist intentions, already flourishing on the eve of the Oriental Expedition. An anonymous letter had circulated among Italian Jews (who considered Napoleon their great liberator) discussing elaborate plans for the Restoration of the Jewish people as a nation. This letter appeared in print in France as well as in England[5] where the English Restorationists jealously watched over Napoleon's Eastern mission, berating English politicians for missing the chance. In April 1798, the French journal *La Decade Philosophique, Litteraire et Politique* published the letter, which expressed the conviction that the Jews would support France in Palestine with men and money: 'They will come in crowds not only to make industry flourish, but also to defray the cost of the revolution in Syria and Egypt.'[6]

Nor is it unimportant that the preamble to the proclamation addresses its Jewish audience directly as 'the rightful heirs of Palestine' and recalls the Biblical prophecies of Isaiah and Joel on the Jewish return to Zion. More pragmatically, the anonymous letter had spoken of the boundaries of the proposed state of Israel in terms less Biblical than commercial:

The country we propose to occupy shall include (subject to such arrangements as shall be agreeable to France) lower Egypt, with the addition of a district which shall have for its limits a line running from Acre to the Dead Sea . . . This position which is the most advantageous in the world, will render us, by the navigation of the Red Sea, masters of the commerce of India, Arabia, the south and east of Africa, Abyssinia and Ethiopa . . .[7]

Yet, as the well known Jewish historian Salo Baron indicates, the acknowledged coexistence of these commercial and Biblical modes is representative; he judges the proclamation to have considerable symbolic importance despite its absence of immediate consequences:

. . . the famous proclamation of Napoleon to the Jewish people during the Egyptian campaign in 1799, although of little immediate consequence, symbolized Europe's acknowledgement of Jewish rights to Palestine. Napoleon was no idealist, seeking to solve the Jewish question on an altruistic basis; his shrewd recognition of the intense interest of the Jews, whom he attempted to enlist in his expeditionary army, and of the support the Jewish hope had received from French and English writers, is a barometer of the extent to which the European atmosphere was charged with these messianic expectations.[8]

The Zionist idea appealed to Napoleon's romantic concept of nationality, as well as to his personal political interest in using the Jews for his imperial designs. In his *Memoires* written while on St. Helena, Napoleon says at one point:

One of my grandest ideas was 'l'agglomeration': the concentration of people geographically united, but separated by revolutions and political action. There are, scattered over Europe, 30 million Frenchmen, 15 million Spaniards, 15 million Italians, and 30 million Germans. My intention was to make each of these peoples into a separate national state.[9]

His proclamation was thus tantamount to an international recognition of a Jewish national existence and a belief in the regeneration of a Jewish nation in Palestine. The millions of Jews scattered all over Europe were finally to be gathered in a Jewish state in Palestine – and it would also happily serve French imperialist interests.

Zionism and French Overseas Ambitions

Napoleon's brief show of Zionism was by no means an isolated incident in the history of French imperialism, although French Zionism lacked the continuity and uninterrupted flow of the British non-Jewish Zionist tradition.

By the end of the 18th Century the Zionist tradition had been well entrenched in France. The Restoration idea had gained a foothold in the 17th and 18th Centuries through the religious teachings, accompanied by the austere Old Testament morality, preached by the Protestant Huguenots and Catholic Jansenites. Jewish Restoration never achieved quite the same measure of popularity it did in England during the same period. Yet Oliver Cromwell had a French counterpart in Jean Baptiste Colbert, Louis XIV's chief minister and the advocate of mercantilism. Like Cromwell, Colbert spoke of the economic benefits which the Jews could offer France with their experience in trade and commerce. He was thus sympathetically inclined towards a Jewish presence in France.[10]

After Napoleon Bonaparte's day, non-Jewish Zionism experienced a revival during Napoleon III's Second Empire (1852–70) when French imperialist activities were renewed on a more vigorous scale. Through his aggressive foreign policy, Napoleon III annexed Algeria in northern Africa and established a French protectorate over Indochina. He also had his own pretensions in the Middle East. In 1854 Napoleon III plunged France into the Crimean War with Russia under the pretext of protecting the Catholic monks in the Ottoman Empire.

The major representative of French non-Jewish Zionism in this era was Ernest Laharanne, private secretary to Napoleon III. As an unequivocal advocate of Napoleon's oriental plans he wrote in 1860 *La Nouvelle Question D'Orient: Reconstruction de la Nationalité Juive*, following English non-Jewish Zionist arguments in favour of Jewish settlement in Palestine. He emphasized the economic gains to Europe if the Jews were to settle in their ancient Homeland and spoke with the highest esteem of the Jewish people, who were 'to open new highways and byways to European civilization'. The Middle East's decadent civilization could be saved only by an injection of European civilization, and hence all of Europe must support the Jewish acquisition of Palestine from the Ottoman Empire. Laharanne clearly demonstrated his Zionist perception of the Jews as a race: 'What an example, what a race! . . . We bow our heads before you strong men. Because you were strong throughout your ancient history, you were strong even after the drama of Jerusalem . . .but the remnant could rise again and rebuild the gates of Jerusalem.'[11]

Strongly reminiscent of Napoleon Bonaparte's 1799 Proclamation, this call equally remained without immediate political effect. Laharanne's views were nevertheless taken over by the new generation of Jewish Zionists who were only now appearing on the stage of Jewish history. Moses Hess, one of the early founding fathers of Jewish Zionists, published his *Rome and Jerusalem* in 1862, quoting extensively from Laharanne's work. He was confident that France would aid Zionist endeavours in Palestine:

> Do you still doubt that France will help the Jews to found colonies which may extend from Suez to Jerusalem and from the banks of the Jordan to the

Mediterranean? . . . France will extend the work of redemption also to the Jewish nation . . . Frenchmen and Jews! It seems that in all things they were created for one another.[12]

European Expansion and a Jewish Palestine

The idea of a Jewish national Restoration to Palestine had resurfaced in Western European culture at a politicaly most opportune time. During the course of the 19th Century, a Jewish presence in Palestine, apart from its previous religious-prophetical, benevolent or philo-Semitic connotations, now came to be a political issue for the secular European powers that aspired to overseas expansion and empires. Religious and philanthropic ideas were now skilfully combined with the hard-headed *Realpolitik* of acquiring or strengthening spheres of influence in the Near East. Secular authorities, as well as the religious ones, were now toying with Zionist ideas for their potential usefulness in the prevailing political situation.

Under the heading of the 'Eastern Question', Palestine suddenly found itself within the orbit of European power politics and under the contending influences of all the major powers: France, Britain and Russia. The crux of the so-called Eastern Question was the precarious condition of the Ottoman Empire of which Palestine was an integral part. Napoleon Bonaparte's ambitious Oriental Expedition, and attempts to break British communications with its Eastern colonies, had set in motion a serious decline of the Ottoman Empire. The dissolution of such a strategically located empire, extending from the Adriatic Sea to the Arabian Gulf, was recognized as posing a dangerous problem to the existing balance of power in Europe.

By the middle of the 19th Century Western Europe's major concern was the Russian ambition to advance southward. Russia, under Nicholas I, was greedily awaiting the breakup of the Ottoman Empire in the hope that it would pave the way for an easy expansion into the Balkans. Already at the beginning of the 19th Century Russia's power in the area had been seen as alarming: not only did it have a fleet in the Black Sea, but also it had taken over some Ottoman territory after a series of Russo-Turkish wars. Furthermore, Russia had gained the right to protect the welfare of the members of all the orthodox churches who were subjects of the Sultan.

Britain's interest in the Near East, and of course Palestine, had been stirred by the Napoleonic expedition of 1799. The area's strategic importance to the British Empire had already been fully recognized. The vital necessity of preventing French control over the area had not only resulted in the battles of the Nile and Acre, but also spawned a British military expedition eastwards. Soon Britain's main concern was to hold back Russia by maintaining Turkish sovereignty at all costs.

Yet British support for the Ottoman Empire's territorial integrity was rather ambivalent at times; witness Foreign Secretary Stratford Canning's support for Greek independence from the Sultan. The 1828 Russo-Turkish war led to the Treaty of Adrianople which, by granting independence to Greece and establishing a Russian protectorate over the various Balkan provinces, contributed to the dismemberment of the Ottoman Empire. Yet Canning did not seem to think the independence of the Greeks incompatible with re-establishing the Ottoman Empire's stability.

When Lord Palmerston first became Foreign Secretary in 1830 the inherent weakness of the Ottoman Empire was generally known, and British policy towards it was in disarray. It was only after the Treaty of Unkiar Skelessi (1833), creating an alliance between the Tsar and the Sultan, that Britain showed itself again resolved to revive its traditional policy of actively bolstering the position of the Sultan through modernizing his administration and military apparatus.[13]

Palmerston and British Imperial Policy in the Near East

Lord Palmerston (1784–1865) was a most valuable political advocate of Lord Shaftesbury's project of Jewish Restoration to Palestine. It was he who first discovered the viable political idea at the core of the evangelical religious dream. Hardly an evangelical himself, Palmerston's Biblical proficiency and versatility in Hebrew history would not have guaranteed that he knew Abraham from Moses. Nor was he a man to be moved by mystical ideas. But he was enough of a politican to recognize the deep impact which evangelical Zionist ideas had left on British public opinion of the time. Lady Palmerston herself once told Princess Lieven:

> We have on our side the fanatical and religious elements, and you know what a following they have in this country. They are absolutely determined that Jerusalem and the whole of Palestine shall be reserved for the Jews to return to; this is their only longing to restore the Jews.[14]

Webster, in his history of the Palmerston era suggests that Palmerston's motivation was less 'for reasons of humanity but mainly to satisfy an important section of public opinion'.[15] But pandering to public opinion was a far less important objective than bringing about a settlement of the Eastern Question through the colonization of Palestine.

Keeping the 'Sick Man' Alive
The political situation which had developed in the Middle East after Mohamet Ali's defiance of his overlord, the Sultan, required that Britain do everything in its power to keep the Ottoman Empire intact. Britain wanted a protégé in the Near East to guard its future interests there. 'In contrast to the French who enjoyed a *locus standi* as the champion of the

Catholics, and to the Russians who supported the Greek-Orthodox, Britain had no comparable group to whom, by merit of common religion, she could extent her protection.'[16] And Britain's fear for its position in the Near East centred on France as well as Russia, both of whom were eagerly awaiting the death of 'the sick man of Europe' in hopes of receiving their share of the Empire.

In the eyes of Palmerston, as British Foreign Secretary, the Jews represented a key element to bolster the Sultan against 'any future evil designs of Mohamet Ali or his successor.'[17] Lord Shaftesbury had skilfully introduced his step-father-in-law, i.e. Lord Palmerston, to the *political* merits of a Jewish Palestine. His diary entry of 1 August 1838, reads:

> Dined with Palmerston. After dinner left alone with him. Propounded my schemes [for Jewish settlement in Palestine] which seems to strike his fancy. He asked questions and readily promised to consider it. How singular is the order of Providence. Singular, if estimated by man's ways. Palmerston had already been chosen by God to be an instrument of good to His ancient people, to do homage to their inheritance, and to recognize their rights without believing their destiny. It seems he will yet do more. Though the motive be kind, it is not sound. I am forced to argue politically, financially, commercially. He weeps not, like his Master, over Jerusalem, nor prays that now, at last, she may put on her beautiful garments.[18]

It was on Shaftesbury's insistence that Lord Palmerston in 1838 finally put into effect an earlier decision to open a British consulate in Jerusalem and appoint a Vice-Consul there.

There are various explanations as to why Palmerston made this decision. Some historians maintain that the opening of the British consulate ensued from Palmerston's interest in the idea of the Restoration of the Jews and his intention of using the Jewish presence within the Ottoman Empire to strengthen British influence in the Near East. Others, like Mayir Verete, view Palmerston's decision merely as part of his general policy 'to set up a network of consulates in the Sultan's dominions for the purpose of introducing new, or defending existing British interests, and resisting those of other Powers, more especially those of Russia'.[19] He dismisses the Jewish factor as completely irrelevant.

There was certainly no official discussion of the Jewish issue in relation to the decision to open the British consulate in Jerusalem. But certainly interest in the Jewish factor was bound to crop up as soon as the consulate was set up in 1834. Palmerston's correspondence with his Ambassador to the Porte, Viscount John Ponsonby, and his choice in 1838 of William Young, a devout evangelical and friend of Lord Shaftesbury, as the first British Vice-Consul to Jerusalem, testify to the fact that the Jewish factor indeed played a role in Palmerston's final decision to open the consulate.

William Young, Protector of the Jews in Palestine

When Palmerston appointed Young as Vice-Consul to Jerusalem his instructions specifically stated that one of the Vice-Consul's tasks was protecting all the Jews residing in Palestine. Palmerston also instructed Young to report back to the Foreign Office on the state of the Jewish population within the territory of his consular jurisdiction.[20] His specific instruction to 'afford protection to the Jews generally' clearly implied recognition of the Jews as a nation with an inseparable attachment to Palestine long before the Jewish Zionist programme was itself formulated. Adhering to Palmerston's instructions, Vice-Consul Young in May 1839 reported back to the Foreign Office that 9,690 Jews currently resided in Palestine and he added that their condition was deplorable and that they were completely dependent upon outside help.[21]

Young's own zeal in affording protection 'to the Jews generally' often brought him into conflict with the British Consul-General stationed in Egypt, Colonel Patrick Campbell. Campbell felt that Young's exaggerated zeal had led him to overstep his authority. According to established treaty rights, British consular protection applied only to foreign national Jews (the *hamaya* Jews) residing in Palestine. Native Jews of the Ottoman Empire (*rayah* Jews), on the other hand, were still under the sole jurisdiction of the Sultan as subjects of the Ottoman Empire. Campbell wrote, 'You have no more right to protect [them], than Austria or France would have to protect Rayah Catholics, or Russia or Greece to protect Rayahs of the Greek religion.'[22] Young defended his practice as being in accordance with Lord Palmerston's personal instructions of 31 January 1839: 'Palmerston's distinct wish . . . was to make the Hebrews in Palestine appreciate how kindly the British government was disposed toward them, and to show that it was willing to shield them from oppression of their neighbours, as well as the local authorities.'[23]

The national unity of the Jewish people was made one of the principal affirmations of Jewish Zionism at the end of the 19th Century. Yet Palmerston, half a century earlier, had implicitly held this position when he failed to make a distinction between *rayah* and *hamaya* Jews. He supported Young in his dispute with Campbell. From the accepted legal point of view, however, British intervention on behalf of *rayah* Jews was tantamount to interference in the internal affairs of a foreign country.

Palmerston's active promotion of Jewish settlement in Palestine was complementary to his Zionist predispositions. In this international context, his support of Lord Shaftesbury's plan to return the Jews collectively to Palestine shows his political sensibilities.

Jewish Settlement/British Interests

General public opinion had long been favourably disposed towards Jewish settlement in Palestine but, on the political level, it was still a relatively new and unexplored issue. Palmerston, as a pragmatist, was mainly concerned with the political benefits that such a Jewish settlement scheme would yield for Britain. He was also aware that English political circles were still to be convinced. In January 1839, Palmerston received a memorandum supposedly drawn up by the British Secretary of the Admiralty, Henry Innes, sent 'on behalf of many who wait for the redemption of Israel'. It was addressed to 'all Protestant Powers of North of Europe and America'. This document called upon European rulers to follow in the footsteps of Cyrus and to fulfil God's will by allowing the Jews to return to Palestine. Although composed along evangelical lines and filled with Biblical quotations, the document still marked the transition of non-Jewish Zionism from pious evangelical anticipation to active – and political – intervention. Palmerston brought it to the attention of Queen Victoria who was known for her piety.[24]

The memorandum was widely covered in the press. Prestigious papers, like *The Times* and *The Globe*, the semi-official organ of the Foreign Office, regarded the Jewish settlement of Palestine as an established topic. *The Times* reprinted the 'Memorandum to the Protestant Sovereigns' over a year after it had been first issued.[25] Five months later an article appeared under the heading 'Syria – The Restoration of the Jews', indicating that 'the proposition to plant the Jewish people in the land of their fathers, under the protection of the five powers, is no longer a mere matter of speculation, but of serious political consideration'.[26] This article publicly raised for the first time the issue of Jewish willingness and preparedness to collaborate with the non-Jewish Zionists in such a scheme.

Non-Zionist Judaism

Although public discussion was increasing, Jewish participation remained conspicuously low key. Only a very small part of the Anglo-Jewish community wanted anything to do with a Restoration scheme. When Lord Palmerston himself approached the London-based Jewish Board of Deputies to inquire about possible Jewish co-operation in the Jewish settlement projects, he got a very meagre response. He then sent an astonishing letter to Ponsonby, his Ambassador to Constantinople, on 11 August 1840 stating that:

> There exists at present among the Jews dispersed over Europe, a strong notion that the time is approaching when their nation is to return to Palestine . . . Consequently their wish to go thither has become more keen, and their thoughts have been bent more intently than before upon the means of realizing that wish. It is well known that the Jews of Europe possess great wealth; and it is manifest that any country in which a considerable number of them might choose to settle, would derive great benefit from the riches which they would bring into it . . . it would be of manifest importance to the Sultan to encourage the Jews to return to, and settle in

Palestine, because the wealth which they would bring with them would increase the resources of the Sultan's dominions; and the Jewish people, if returning under the sanction and protection and at the invitation of the Sultan, would be a check upon any future evil designs of Mohamet Ali or his successor . . .[27]

The opening paragraph of this letter represents at most wishful thinking. In fact, Palmerston's appraisal of Jewish keenness to settle in Palestine was based solely on a memorandum by E. S. Calman, a Jewish subject of the Sultan, who had earlier written to Palmerston:

> The Jews are aware that there is no remedy for them as a People than that of returning to the Holy Land . . . A Proclamation like that of Cyrus would be echoed by hundreds of thousands of Jews in Poland, Russia, and elsewhere, and by the rich as well as by the poor who would gladly exchange their present harassed and uncertain mode of life for the more quiet and more certain one that would result from the cultivation of the soil.[28]

Calman's memorandum was just as unfounded and misleading as Palmerston's dispatch to Ponsonby. Even Zionist historians testify to the fact that European Jewry at the time of Palmerston's agitation were far from willing to engage in any plan to settle in the Ottoman province of Palestine.[29] They were far more concerned with their struggle for full civil and political emancipation in Britain.

Lord Shaftesbury was closer to reality when he wrote to Palmerston cautioning him against his undue optimism:

> The rich will be suspicious and take counsel with their fears; the poor will be delayed by the collection of funds – a few will prefer a seat in the House of Commons in England to a seat under their vines and figtrees in Palestine; and some perhaps of the French–Israelites . . . may entertain like sentiments. The reformed, or infidel Jews of Germany would probably reject the proposal.[30]

Yet, in spite of this lack of enthusiasm among the Jews, the Sultan's opposition and Shaftesbury's warning alike, Palmerston continued to press his idea on the diplomatic level. On 4 September 1840 he again reminded his Ambassador to Constantinople, another opponent of the scheme:

> . . . don't lose sight of my recommendation to the Porte to invite the Jews to return to Palestine. You can have no idea how much such a measure would tend to interest in the Sultan's cause all of the religious party in this country, and their influence is great and their connexion extensive. The measure moreover in itself would be highly advantageous to the Sultan, by bringing into his dominion a great number of wealthy capitalists who would employ the people and enrich the Empire.[31]

The 'Rejuvenation' of Turkey

Palmerston was determined to settle the Eastern Question through Jewish colonization of Palestine, although his only source of public encouragement was the Tory press. For the British Foreign Minister, a Jewish presence in Palestine offered two advantages to British interests. The direct advantage was the presence of a pro-British partisan group in an area where previously Britain had none, an area which was becoming increasingly vital for British imperial interests abroad. An indirect advantage was the envisaged influx of Jewish capital and labour urgently needed by the Sultan in order to prop up his almost bankrupt economic system.

Palmerston's plan for the rejuvenation of Turkey was dependent not only on thoughts of Jewish finance but also on a high and idealist assessment of Jewish culture and know-how and the effect this would have on 'mediocre and backward Turkey'. Thus the racist element of Zionism was already clearly discernible, in fact, all the non-Jewish Zionists of the time tended to belittle Oriental civilization and Islam. A detailed study of public opinion would most likely have shown a positive correlation between holders of pro-Zionist views and anti-Ottoman bias. As early as the Greek Revolution (1820–21), public opinion in Europe, especially in Britain, had rallied around the Greek cause, as it opposed the 'backward and barbarous' Ottoman Empire. It became commonplace to associate the Empire's 'backwardness and barbarism' with its religion. Islam came to denote inefficiency and despotism and was even thought to be responsible for the Ottoman Empire's decay.[32] Stratford Canning, arriving as Ambassador in Constantinople in January 1832, remarked in an official despatch to the Foreign Office in London, 'I know no conceivable substitute for it [Ottoman civilization] but civilization in the sense of Christendom.'[33]

The Jews were commonly assigned a character different from the rest of the population in Palestine, and regarded as the symbol of Europeanism within the Islamic Empire. Palmerston and his associates in the Foreign Office concluded that the Empire could only survive if it was modernized – rejuvenated – along Western lines, and associated this with the Jewish settlement plan.[34] This is the background to Palmerston's overture to the Sultan to invite the Jews to return to Palestine. Writing again to Ponsonby, Palmerston emphasized that the Jewish presence, including its wealth and industry, would promote 'the progress of civilisation'.[35]

Pre-Herzlian English Zionists

Palmerston did have some allies within the British foreign policy establishment. Two typical representatives in the Colonial Office in London were Edward L. Mitford and Colonel George Gawler.

Edward Mitford: Mitford eventually came to advocate a far more radical form of Zionism, and argued for the establishment of a full-blown Jewish state. In 1845, his 'An Appeal on behalf of the Jewish Nation in Connection with British Policy in the Levant' put forward his plan:

> The plan I would propose is, first, the establishment of the Jewish nation in Palestine, as a protected state, under the guardianship of Great Britain . . . secondly, their final establishment, as an independent state, whensoever the parent institutions shall have acquired sufficient force and vigour to allow of this tutelage being withdrawn . . .[36]

Among the 'incalculable advantages' economic and strategic ones were primary. A Jewish state would place the 'management of our steam communication entirely in our hands and would place us in a commanding position in the Levant from whence to check the process of encroachment, to overawe our enemies and, if necessary repel their advance.'[37] The advent of steam navigation during the 1840s also made the Near East important for British control over the route to India. Steamships required frequent re-coaling and therefore British ships used the Mediterranean-Red Sea route with trans-shipment at Suez, rather than the long Cape route.

Mitford also shared the other Zionists' positive biases towards the Jews. He described them as a far superior people, incorporating the peculiar qualities of fortitude and perseverance which made them deserving of an independent state of their own in Palestine. But he also had the foresight to raise the problem of Palestine's own Arab population:

> The country, compared with its extent, is at present thinly populated, yet the pressure caused by the introduction of so large a body of strangers upon the actual inhabitants might be attended with injurious results. Before, however, attempting to make a settlement, it would be desirable that the country should be prepared for their reception. This might be done by inducing the Turkish government to make the Mohammedan inhabitants fall back upon the extensive and partially cultivated countries of Asia Minor . . .[38]

George Gawler: The first Governor of the Colony of South Australia, Gawler was equally convinced that only the Jews were capable of propping up the Ottoman Empire through colonization, but his position was a more orthodox Palmerstonian one. In his pamphlet *Tranquillisation of Syria and the East* (1845), he recommended the gradual establishment of Jewish colonies under British protection by agreement with the Ottoman Government. The Jews were eventually to be granted self-government but under the protection of Great Britain. He, too, regarded a Jewish Palestine as the only guarantee for Britain's continued influence in the Orient. On 1 October 1847 he wrote to Jacob A. Franklin, an English Jewish rabbi:

> For this I never cease to yearn, and if I desire justification for the share I took in the foundation of South Australia, it is in the first place, that I may have a greater plea for publicity urging the colonisation of Palestine. I really believe the Enemy of Israel has a large share in the singularly persevering attacks which are made upon my proceedings in South Australia – they are from high quarters so unprincipled . . . Conservative in politics as I am, I am truly rejoiced to see the progress of civil emancipation for your brethren in England and throughout Europe for the reason because I think they highly deserve it at the hands of the civilized world, and for another, that I believe every step towards emancipation is a movement towards *Palestine*. . . . privileges in Gentile states menace your nationality – you must have a point of centralization to preserve it.[39]

His angle on Jewish emancipation is not untypical of many other non-Jewish Zionists at the time when Jewish emancipation was the first priority for European Jewry.

Charles Henry Churchill: Another of these first-generation political non-Jewish Zionists, Churchill was a staff officer in the British expedition to Syria, which had aided the Sultan in the overthrow of Mohamet Ali. He became critical of Palmerston's Eastern policy of trying to keep the Ottoman Empire alive as long as possible. Instead, Churchill called for the early liberation of Syria and Palestine from Turkey in order to place them under British protection. For the Jews he envisaged the role of colonizers and guardians of British interests.

Compared to Palmerston, however, Churchill displayed a much more realistic understanding of the Jewish condition in Europe at the time. He knew very well that there was no 'strong notion among Europe's Jews to return to Palestine' and so set about selling the idea to them. He wrote on 14 June 1841 to Moses Montefiore, President of the Jewish Board of Deputies in London:

> I cannot conceal from you my most anxious desire to see your countrymen endeavour once more to resume their existence as a people. I consider the object to be perfectly obtainable. But two things are indispensably necessary: Firstly that the Jews themselves will take up the matter, universally and unanimously. Secondly that the European powers will aid them in their views.[40]

Again in 1842 Churchill sent a letter to Montefiore asking him to transmit to the German Jews a 'German Address' which he enclosed in the letter. In the address he proposed that 'the Jews of England conjointly with their brethren on the continent of Europe should make an application to the British Government through the Earl of Aberdeen, the Foreign Secretary, to accredit and send out a fit and proper person to reside in Syria for the sole and express purpose of superintending and watching over the interests of the Jews in that country'.[41] But the Jewish response was once more a refusal. In a resolution passed on 7 November 1842, the Jewish Board of Deputies resolved that it 'is precluded from originating any measures for carrying out the benevolent views of Colonel Churchill respecting the Jews of Syria'.[42]

Zionism Pre-Formed, Not Pre-Figured

Thus by the middle of the 19th Century Zionism had remained a completely non-Jewish prerogative. Those who chose to champion the Jewish people and their right to return to Palestine were self-appointed and acting of their own accord, rather than in conjunction with the Jewish people. Modern Zionist historians generally refer to non-Jews such as Palmerston, Mitford, Gawler or Churchill as having foreshadowed the real Zionist movement. But they were more than mere forerunners of a future movement. They were already true Zionists in the same sense as Weizmann or Herzl or Nordau. The principal Zionist propositions were already present and distinctly marked: the concept of the unity of the Jewish people and the concept of their inseparable attachment to Palestine with a view to return. Palmerston and his Zionist colleagues grasped and utilized both concepts many decades before the Jews took them up as their own.

Notes

1. As cited in Franz Kobler, *Napoleon and the Jews* (New York, 1975), pp. 55–7.
2. See Weizmann's letter to Winston Churchill, as quoted in Richard Crossman, *A Nation Reborn* (London, 1956), p. 130.
3. In fact the full text of duplicity involved in the proclamation has come to light only relatively recently, when in 1940 Franz Kobler discovered a German transcript of the actual text of the proclamation in the possession of a Viennese German immigrant in London (the original had long since vanished, presumably with the defeat at Acre). Before this discovery, historians had relied on the official French gazette, *Moniteur Universelle* which on 22 May 1799 had summarized: 'Bonaparte a fait publier une proclamation, dans laquelle il invite tous les juifs de l'Asie et de l'Afrique à venir se ranger sous ses drapeaux pour rétablir l'ancienne Jerusalem' (as quoted by Philip Guedella, *Napoleon and Palestine* (London, 1925), p. 24).
4. As Barbara Tuchmann claims in *Bible and Sword* (London, 1956), p. 105.
5. Republished in *St. James Chronicle*, 14 July 1798 and *The Monthly Visitor and Pocket Companion*, Vol. 4, pp. 383–6, under the title 'Letters recently written from a Jew to his Brethren'.
6. *La Decade philosophique, litteraire et politique*, Vol. 6, Nos. 20–21, 9 and 19, April 1798.
7. See also Albert M. Hyamson, *Palestine: The Rebirth of an Ancient People* (London, 1917), pp. 162–3.

8. Salo W. Baron, *A Social and Religious History of the Jews* (New York, 1937), Vol. 2, p. 327.

9. Las Casas (ed.), *Memoires* [of Napoleon] (Paris, 1823), Vol. 1, p. 247.

10. W. Sombart, *Jews and Modern Capitalism* (New York, 1939), p. 39.

11. As quoted in Ferdinand Zweig, *Israel: The Sword and the Harp* (London, 1969), p. 243.

12. Moses Hess, *Rome and Jerusalem. A Study in Jewish Nationalism*, translated by Meyer Waxman (New York, 1918), pp. 149, 167, 168.

13. For a more detailed study and astute analysis of Palmerston's Near Eastern policy during these early years of his Foreign Ministry see Frederick S. Rodkey, 'Lord Palmerston and the Rejuvenation of Turkey, 1830–1841', *Journal of Modern History*, Vol. 1, No. 4, December 1929, pp. 570–93; and Part II in ibid., Vol. 2, No. 2, June 1930, pp. 193–225. See also Harold W. Temperley, *England and the Near East: The Crimea* (London, 1936).

14. As quoted in Sir Charles Webster, *The Foreign Policy of Palmerston 1830–1841* (London, 1951), Vol. 2, p. 761.

15. Ibid., p. 762.

16. Isaiah Friedman, 'Lord Palmerston and the Protection of the Jews in Palestine, 1839–1851', *Jewish Social Studies*, op. cit.

17. Palmerston to Ponsonby, Public Record Office MSS, F.O. 78/390 (No. 134) 11 August 1840.

18. As quoted by Norman Bentwich and John M. Shaftesley, 'Forerunners of Zionism in the Victorian Era', p. 210. See also Edwin Hodder, *The Life and Work of the Seventh Earl of Shaftesbury* (London, 1886), Vol. 1, pp. 310–11.

19. Mayir Verete, 'Why was a British Consulate established in Jerusalem?' *Zion*, Vol. 26, Nos. 3–4, 1961, pp. 215–37.

20. Bidwell (Foreign Office) to Young, Public Record Office MSS, F.O. 78/368, (No. 2) 31 January 1839. The draft of this memo was initialled by Palmerston.

21. Young to Palmerston, Public Record Office MSS, F.O. 78/368, (No. 13) 25 May 1839.

22. Campbell to Young, Public Record Office MSS, F.O. 78/368, (No. 6) 28 May 1839.

23. Friedman, op. cit., p. 26.

24. Palmerston to Queen Victoria, 22 January 1839, reprinted in N. Sokolow, *History of Zionism* (London, 1919), Vol. 2, Appendix 65, pp. 231–4.

25. *The Times* (London), 9 March 1840.

26. Ibid., 17 August 1840. A similar article in the *Globe* on 14 August 1840 entitled 'A Regard for the Jews' referred to England's special role and responsibility to aid the Jews in their return to Palestine.

27. Palmerston to Ponsonby, Public Record Office MSS, F.O. 78/390, (No. 134) 11 August 1840.

28. Enclosure No. 1 in Palmerston to Ponsonby, Public Record Office MSS. F.O. 195/165, (No. 261) 25 November 1840.

29. Non-Jewish Zionist endeavours to have the Jews settle in Palestine received very little support from British Jewry. The London Jewish Board of Deputies refused to get involved, although Moses Montefiore, an advocate of Jewish agricultural settlements in Palestine was its President at the time. See Franz Kobler, *The Vision was There* (London, 1956), pp. 65–6 and 68–71; see also Bentwich and Shaftesley, op. cit., pp. 207–9. As for Continental Jewry, it suffices here to point to the 1845 Frankfurt Rabbinical Conference which

renounced the Restoration idea completely, voting that 'all petitions for the return to the land of our fathers, and for the restoration of a Jewish state, should be eliminated from the prayers.' *Protokolle und Aktenstuecke der Zweiten Rabbiner Versammlung* (Frankfurt, 1845), p. 106. Even as late as 1872 international Jewry still refused to accept the Zionization of its future. During the first international Jewish conference meeting during this year, Jewish respresentatives from England, France, Germany, Austria and the United States met to consider the condition of the Jews in Romania. It did not once touch on a solution through Jewish immigration into Palestine.

30. Included as Enclosure No. 2 in ibid.
31. As quoted in Webster, op. cit., Vol. 2, p. 762.
32. See, for example, Webster, op. cit., Vol. 1, pp. 84–7. Also Aberdeen to Gordon, Public Record Office MSS, F.O. 78/179, 21 November 1829, wherein Aberdeen called the Ottoman Empire 'a clumsy fabrick of barbarious power' soon 'to crumble into pieces from its own inherent causes of decay'.
33. As quoted in Webster, op. cit., Vol. 1, p. 264.
34. Finn to Palmerston, Public Record Office MSS, F.O. 78/874, (No. 20) 7 November 1851.
35. Palmerston to Ponsonby, Public Record Office MSS, F.O. 78/427, (No. 33) 17 February 1841. This dispatch was approved by Queen Victoria.
36. See Kobler, op. cit., 1956, p. 76.
37. Israel Cohen, *The Zionist Movement* (New York, 1946), p. 52.
38. As quoted in Kobler, op. cit., 1956, p. 77.
39. As quoted in Bentwich and Shaftesley, op. cit., p. 218.
40. Cohen, op. cit., p. 51. Charles Henry Churchill was a grandson of the Duke of Marlborough and therefore also an ancestor of Winston Churchill.
41. Kobler, op. cit., 1956, pp. 65–6.
42. Ibid., p. 66.

5. The Road to the Balfour Declaration

Scientific Zionism

During the second half of the 19th Century the new scientific revolution provoked controversy between faith and science. In 1859 Charles Darwin published his *The Origin of Species*, and in 1871 his *The Descent of Men* while in 1863 Thomas Huxley published his *Man's Place in Nature*. One of the by-products was the transformation of Zionism, which developed its own unique theories of evolution. In 1865 the 'Palestine Exploration Fund' was founded by English Zionists in order to prove their religious principles through modern science.

Charles Warren and Claude Reignier Conder were sent to Palestine to investigate the future economic potential of the country. In his book *The Land of Promise* (1875) Charles Warren predicted Palestine's future productivity, but only through Jewish colonization. His collaborator, Conder, was equally convinced: 'The energy, industry and tact which are so remarkable in the Jewish character, are qualities invaluable in a country whose inhabitants have sunk into fatalistic indolence.'[1]

At the time many other explorers, geographic surveyors, archaeologists and plain adventurers made their voyages to Palestine and reported back their 'scientific' findings. In most cases, their results were nothing more than foregone conclusions. They saw what they wanted to see – the neglect and devastation of a once flourishing land. This deplorable state of the land of Palestine was naturally blamed on the 'indigenous Arab tribes' whose only attributes were 'indolence and outright stupidity' and who were thus totally incapable of managing their own affairs, let alone those of a country with such a promising future prosperity as Palestine.

In sharp contrast stood the 'rightful but absent' owners of the land – the Jews – whose return to the land was regarded as the only viable solution to the problems confronting Palestine. In keeping with such a deep-rooted Zionist belief, the famous geologist, John William Dawson wrote in 1888, after an extended field trip to Palestine:

. . . No nation has been able to establish itself, as a nation in Palestine up to this day, no national union and no national spirit have prevailed there. The motley, impoverished tribes . . . have held it as mere tenants at will, temporary landowners, evidently waiting for those entitled to the permanent possession of the soil.[2]

Thus when it came to Palestine and the Jews, even the most agnostic scientists harboured Puritan feelings in their Zionist outlook.

Any truly scientific investigation into the state of affairs in Palestine would have revealed a quite different set of facts. First and foremost, the condition of the few Jews living at the time in Palestine was no better and no more promising than that of the Arab majority there. Both groups were exploited by the Turkish overlords and thus lived in the same kind of desolation. Nor was there any indication that a so-called Jewish national spirit was in the making there. Jewish and even Zionist historical studies on the subject reveal quite the contrary.[3] The first colonization initiatives had to come from non-Jewish Zionist enthusiasts and facts had to be created if they were not already there – a real foreshadowing of Jewish Zionist exhortations in the 20th Century!

From early on the destinies of Zionism and imperialism were interlocked. Initial attempts to settle the Jews as agricultural colonists were all connected to Palestine's place in political and strategic spheres:

> Two arguments particularly were brought forward by Christian and Jewish proponents of the Return. The first was the advantage of having a friendly, industrious population such as the Jews in a vital, 'neutralised' spot, Palestine, on the overland route to India, which, taken from the enfeebled hand of the 'Sick Man of Europe' at the Porte, might become a British protectorate. Secondly, a further inspired idea was put forward by some English officers, the cutting of a canal from the Mediterranean down to the Gulf of Akaba. The 'neutralisation' of Palestine was to be bound up with the development of the Middle East by an 'Eastern International Society', on the analogy of the East India Company, the Jews returning to Palestine as colonists under a Charter.[4]

The Palestine Exploration Fund represented only one of the many organizations and foundations that cropped up during the last decades of the 19th Century in England and offered their advice, personnel and financial assistance to those Jews willing to settle in agricultural colonies in Palestine. Non-Jewish advocates preferred to publish their schemes in the Jewish press in order to gain access to the largest possible Jewish audience. Most notably the *Jewish Chronicle*, the *Hebrew Observer* and the *Voice of Jacob* published a series of articles written by non-Jewish Zionists. In one of the articles, quoted above, Isaac Ashe in 1871 suggested the formation of a chartered company similar to the existing East India Company or Hudson Bay Company. He anticipated by 30 years the Jewish National Fund. The following are some more of his suggestions:

three or four steps only are necessary at once to restore a Jewish nationality in Palestine; viz., first to buy the soil from its present proprietors; secondly to make it of value to tenants, cultivators, by an outlay of capital; letting it, when thus improved, to such tenants of the Jewish race in perpetual tenure at fixed valuations. Thirdly, that this outlay of capital be so directed as not only to result in the improvement of the soil, but in the production of works of national character and importance. Fourthly, that such works, and others with them, be so directed as to place the country in such an attitude and position of military defence as shall enable the nation successfully to maintain its independence against all comers when the time shall have arrived for asserting it . . .[5]

Laurence Oliphant Draws Up the Blueprints

The most representative and influential non-Jewish Zionist of this era was Laurence Oliphant (1829–88), a Member of Parliament, foreign service officer, journalist and above all religious eccentric. An advocate of the 'revitalization' theory for the preservation of the Ottoman Empire against the Russian rival, he proposed a detailed settlement scheme for Jews. Following personal visits to Palestine to survey the land and study the conditions for settlement and agricultural colonization, in 1880 he published his book *The Land of Gilead* proposing Jewish settlement east of the Jordan river under Ottoman sovereignty and British protection.

It remains for England to decide whether she will undertake the task of exploring its ruined cities, of developing its vast agricultural resources, by means of the repatriation of that race which first entered into its possession, 3000 years ago and of securing the great political advantages which must accrue from such a policy.[6]

His proposal of a million-and-a-half-acre colony east of the Jordan was the most detailed and carefully worked out settlement scheme at the time. The Jewish settlers were to be drawn from Romania, the Russian Pale of Settlement and other parts of the Ottoman Empire.

He also included recommendations about the existing Arab population of Palestine. The Bedouins, whom he described as 'warlike', were to be driven out while the peasant Arabs were to be conciliated and placed on 'reserves' like the Indians in North America. Some of the Arab peasants might also serve as a source of cheap labour under Jewish direction. In his eyes, the Arabs had 'very little claim to our sympathy [having] laid waste to the country, ruined its villages and plundered its inhabitants until it has been reduced to its present condition.'[7]

But Laurence Oliphant is important above all for initiating the first contacts between non-Jewish and Jewish Zionists. Like Colonel Churchill four decades earlier, Oliphant realized the importance of getting the Jews themselves involved in the settlement and colonization projects. In 'The Jews and the Eastern Question', in the September 1883 issue of *The*

Nineteenth Century, he called upon the Jews to co-operate. His initial contact with like-minded Jews were the Chibbath Zion (Love of Zion) movement, mainly Eastern European Jews whose main objective was to escape from the new wave of pogroms after Tsar Alexander II's assassination in 1881. Jewish Zionism slowly gained ground from 1880 onwards, although its support was still mainly confined to Russian and other East European Jews. (At this point the most significant shift in Jewish polemics was simply the proposal that their persecution would have to be dealt with in a secular way, by finding *some* nation to call their own. But if Leo Pinsker's 1882 pamphlet, *Auto-Emancipation*, can be taken as typical, there was no reason why this territory should be Palestine. Indeed Pinsker poured as much scorn on the sentimental attachment to Palestine as he did upon hopes of a messianic solution.)[8]

Oliphant attended various conferences of the Chibbath Zion movement in Russia and Romania and met with their leaders. He also approached non-Jewish religious leaders and statesmen, including the Prince of Wales, the future King Edward VII. Indeed, the prospects seemed very bright. The British Prime Minister Lord Beaconsfield (Disraeli)[9] and his Foreign Secretary, Lord Salisbury, had similar ambitions and granted Oliphant permission to negotiate with the Ottoman Government over a possible territory for Jewish settlement. He even secured the consent of the French Foreign Minister.

The Reversal of Britain's Ottoman Policy

Domestic political developments within England brought a premature end to Disraeli's diplomatic efforts. The Liberal Party won the 1880 general elections and the Conservative Lord Beaconsfield was replaced by the Liberal Gladstone. A Gladstone government automatically meant a change in the British Eastern policy. Suddenly Britain ceased to be the Sultan's friend and protector. 'Mr. Gladstone was disgusted with the Turks, hated the whole business of imperialism, and appeared to believe that, by ignoring the responsibilities that Britain had acquired for herself through imperial expansion, he could make them vanish.'[10]

Finally, the great moment for non-Jewish Zionism in Britain had arrived. All along the Zionists had felt that they were forced to make their arguments in the name of a policy already doomed to failure. Nonetheless, as long as the British Government had remained committed to its pro-Ottoman policy, the non-Jewish Zionists skilfully managed to adjust their own schemes and projections to the overall British Eastern policy. Every defeat of Turkey on the battlefield, even if it was inflicted by the anti-Semitic Russian Tsar, raised the hopes of the non-Jewish Zionists only to have them subdued again by the ensuing peace conferences, which generally maintained the existing *status quo* in the Sultan's Asian provinces. For instance, in 1878, after Russia defeated Turkey, the peace of San Stefano did not resolve the crisis. Then a European Congress had met once again, in June 1878, in Berlin to settle another Eastern crisis: in accordance with British traditional policy, Turkey's Asian possessions remained untouched and the existing order in Palestine unchanged.

But the Zionists had never been disillusioned over these apparent setbacks. Instead, they had adopted a step-by-step approach towards the creation of a Jewish state in Palestine through indirect means, such as Jewish colonization under Turkish sovereignty and British protection; or even the strengthening of British influence in the Near East which was to bring Palestine within the orbit of British imperial interests. The growth of British influence – Disraeli's contribution towards the building of a Jewish Palestine – compensated Oliphant and his colleagues for the disappointments of the Berlin Congress.

And even when in 1885 the Conservatives under Lord Salisbury came back into office, the changed geo-political realities called for a major revision in Britain's Eastern policy, Lord Salisbury no longer thought it necessary to restore Britain's influence at Constantinople. For him, the Ottoman Empire was now a lost cause. In his reminiscences of British policy during the Crimean War he once sadly remarked; 'We put our money on the wrong horse.' He confessed that perhaps it would even have been better for England to have agreed to the Tsar's suggestion to partition the Ottoman Empire before its inevitable downfall.

During the last decade of the 19th Century, non-Jewish Zionists in England were finally able to engage in a direct approach. The changed geo-political situation, partly caused by British penetration into the region north and west of Palestine (Egypt and Cyprus), and the Sultan's turn to the Kaiser, called for a revision in Britain's Eastern policy. With British concern centred on Egypt, there was now ample reason for the government to deviate from its traditional policy of maintaining the territorial integrity of the Ottoman Empire in order to annex part of it.

The new significance of Palestine in the British imperial plan came to rest primarily in its proximity to Egypt. Lord Kitchener, as one major proponent of the new Eastern policy, called upon his Government to 'secure Palestine as a bulwark to the British position in Egypt as well as an overland link with the East.'[11]

At last Zionism was not merely in tune with British imperialism, but had developed into a unique branch of it. The staunchest advocates of Zionism were now men of the inner government circles in England. Gone were the days when Zionism was still neatly wrapped in Lord Shaftesbury's style of religious ideas. During the last decade of the 19th Century, the demands of empire also demanded political Zionism. The Zionist programme's actual realization was now more possible than at any time before. Non-Jewish Zionism was reinforced by the growth of Zionism among European Jewry. At last some Jews had come to head the Zionist calling and expressed interest in political action to bring about the re-settlement of the Jews in Palestine.

William Hechler, a Modern Zionist

Another connecting link between non-Jewish Zionism and the nascent modern Zionist movement was William H. Hechler (1845–1931), the Anglican minister and British Embassy chaplain in Vienna. Born in South Africa to German Protestant parents, Hechler was reared in the popular evangelical tradition of religious Zionism. Very much like Shaftesbury, he expressed his great love for 'God's ancient people' by his ever-increasing promotion of Jewish settlement in Palestine. The very embodiment of British evangelism entering the realm of politics, he was, by background and by training, ideally suited to act as mediator between Jewish and non-Jewish Zionism, combining religious, humanitarian and political Zionism. Imbued with evangelical millenarianism, he even formulated his own exact date for the re-establishment of a Jewish state. Equally, he was moved by his concern over the vast stream of East European Jewish refugees now fleeing towards the West.

In May 1882, he assembled a conference of prominent Christians to consider a solution to the 'Jewish Problem' confronting England as a result of increasing Jewish immigration. During the same year, he himself visited Palestine to investigate conditions for eventual Jewish settlement there. His booklet, *The Restoration of the Jews to Palestine* (1894), predating Herzl's *Der Judenstaat* by two years, spoke of the need for 'restoring the Jews to Palestine according to Old Testament prophecies'.

In his quest for Jewish settlement, he had learned how to add political and practical arguments to his religious and humanitarian pleas. Early in 1896, when he had become chaplain to the British Embassy in Vienna, he was introduced by a friend of Herzl to the latter's *Der Judenstaat*. Upon reading this Zionist *chef-d'oeuvre*, Hechler immediately requested a meeting with the author. The fateful meeting took place on 10 March 1896 and both men took a liking to each other. Herzl recorded this visit in his diary:

> The Reverend William Hechler, Chaplain of the English Embassy here, came to see me. A sympathetic, gentle fellow, with the long grey beard of a prophet. He is enthusiastic about my solution of the Jewish Question. He also considers my movement a 'prophetic turning-point' – which he had foretold two years before. From a prophecy in the time of Omar (637 CE) he had reckoned that at the end of forty-two prophetic months (total 1260 years) the Jews would get Palestine back. This figure he arrived at was 1897–98.[12]

For Herzl this crucial meeting opened the doors of European state chancellories to the modern Zionist movement. Hechler not only was a born diplomat but also had excellent personal contacts with high-ranking personalities in England and Germany. Shortly after their first encounter, Hechler arranged a meeting between his new Zionist friend and the Grand Duke of Baden, an uncle of Kaiser Wilhelm II. Both Herzl and

Hechler hoped that the German Kaiser might be persuaded by his esteemed uncle to adopt the role of Cyrus within the framework of a German-protected Zionism in Palestine.[13] Herzl's audience with the Grand Duke of Baden in Karlsruhe was his first diplomatic success. It resulted in Herzl's two audiences with the Kaiser himself in Constantinople and Jerusalem in October and in November 1898, when he hoped, a hope ultimately unrealized, to make use of Germany's growing influence with the Sultan.

The Basle Programme of 1897

Hechler's as well as Laurence Oliphant's active co-operation with the Jewish Zionist movement were the first links in a long chain of contacts between non-Jewish and Jewish Zionists at the turn of the century. With the birth of the Zionist Organization in August 1897 at the 1st Zionist Congress in Basle, Jews themselves for the first time framed the political platform that was to serve as a basic reference point for the 20th Century Zionist movement.

> Zionism strives to create for the Jewish people a home in Palestine secured by public law. The Congress contemplates the following means to the attainment of this end: 1) The promotion on suitable lines of the colonization of Palestine by Jewish agricultural and industrial workers; 2) The organization and binding together of the whole of Jewry by means of appropriate institutions, local and international, in accordance with the laws of each country; 3) The strengthening and fostering of Jewish national sentiment and consciousness; 4) Preparatory steps towards obtaining Government consent where necessary to the attainment of the aims of Zionism.[14]

Yet the main features of this Zionist programme were not new. A tradition of four centuries of non-Jewish Zionism endorsed the historical connection between a separate Jewish nationality and the land of Palestine and saw that connection as the grounds for reconstituting the Jewish National Home in that country. Both non-Jewish and Jewish Zionism stood, as they still do today, for the transformation of an Arab Palestine into a Jewish National Home or state. The essential fact was that the Jews were envisaged as a nation, a nation without a territory, but in due time to be restored to their rightful inheritance.

Joseph Chamberlain Colonizes Zionism

Joseph Chamberlain (1836–1914) in many ways personified the new type of non-Jewish Zionist which became so numerous at the turn of the century. His first concern was the British Empire, whose 'national mission' was to become 'predominant as a force of world history and universal civilization'.[15] Biblical prophecy was of no concern to him; neither was he moved by humanitarian considerations or a sense of moral debt to 'God's ancient people'.

But, like Palmerston and others before him, he recognized that Zionist prognostications presented legitimate opportunities for extending the British Empire. 'He saw the Jews as a ready-made group of European colonizers available to settle, develop and hold all but empty land under the British aegis.'[16] In his efforts to extend the borders of the Empire, Chamberlain constantly sought colonizers and settlers who would bring civilization to the 'lesser breeds without the law'. His Zionism was not philosophical, but very practical. In 1903, he offered Herzl El Arish in the Sinai for Jewish settlement. He did not mind compromising a major axiom of Zionism, namely that Palestine was the only possible territory for the Jewish homeland.[17]

There is some disagreement among scholars as to why Chamberlain accepted Zionism. His biographer, Julian Amery, suggests that Chamberlain initially acted through humanitarian motives, and only later recognized that a 'Jewish colony in Sinai might prove a useful instrument for extending British influence in Palestine proper when the time came for the inevitable dismemberment of the Ottoman empire.'[18] Christopher Sykes, on the other hand, offers quite another picture of Chamberlain's Zionism:

> In Chamberlain's enthusiasm for Zionism, and it was a passionate thing with him, we must not suppose that we see another manifestation of the Millennial tradition. Here was no successor of Lord Shaftesbury, no spiritual brother of Hechler and Sibthrop. Chamberlain's interest in Jewish fortunes was financial.[19]

However genuine, Chamberlain's humanitarian concern was soon subordinated to the concept of the Jews as a *problem*. When Chamberlain was colonial Secretary, during Salisbury's third permiership between 1895 and 1903, England's chief domestic problem was unwanted immigration – chiefly Jewish immigration from Eastern Europe. In the 1880s the great stream of Jewish immigrants had begun to flow from Russia and Romania, most of them to England and the United States. In common with English Jewish Zionists,[20] Chamberlain favoured a policy restricting the influx of Jewish refugees. His major fear was for the competition of cheap labour and 'the evils' which 'unrestricted immigration would inflict upon English working class people'.[21] Once again we find a Zionist position part and parcel of an anti-Semitic immigration and civil rights policy.

Herzl Finds His Audience
Herzl himself was most eager to meet the British Colonial Secretary in order to 'gain Mr. Chamberlain's support for a Jewish settlement on a considerable scale within the British dominions'.[22] Rebuffed by German

indifference, the founder of Jewish political Zionism now concluded that England was to be 'the Archimedean point where the lever can be applied'.[23] During the 4th Zionist Congress, held in London in 1900 he confidently proclaimed in his opening address: 'From this place the Zionist movement will take a higher and higher flight . . . England the great, England the free, England with her eyes fixed on the seven seas, will understand us.'[24]

Herzl made his debut in British official government circles in 1902 when he was summoned to London to testify as one of 175 witnesses before the 'Royal Commission of Alien Immigration', appointed 'to inquire into and to report upon the character and extent of the evils which are attributed to the unrestricted immigration of aliens, especially in the Metropolis, and the measures which have been adopted for the restriction and control of Alien Immigration in Foreign countries, and in British colonies.'[25] Herzl was the only witness who offered the Commission a practical solution to the problem along Zionist lines:

> Nothing will meet the problem the Commission is called upon to investigate and advise upon, except a diverting of the stream of migration that is bound to go on with increasing force from Eastern Europe. The Jews of Eastern Europe cannot stay where they are – where are they to go? If you find they are not wanted here, then some place must be found to which they can migrate without that migration raising the problems that confront them here. Those problems will not arise if a home is found for them which will be legally recognized as Jewish.[26]

Herzl made a great impression upon the members of the Commission, particularly its Jewish representative, Lord Rothschild. Long been antagonistic to Herzl, he was won over by his testimony and saw how he could make use of both Herzl and political Zionism. The realization of the Basle Platform would solve the question of the East European refugees without having to absorb them in England.

Herzl's argument was thus taken up by British politicians attempting to decrease Jewish immigration into England, most notably Joseph Chamberlain and Arthur Balfour, the newly installed Prime Minister. A few months after his appearance before the Alien Commission, Herzl was received by Chamberlain. For the first time since Menasseh ben Israel's negotiations with Cromwell, the Restoration of the Jews to Palestine was the topic of discussion between a British statesman and a Jewish leader. In their meeting, Jewish political Zionism and non-Jewish Zionism converged, revealing the direction of Zionist strategy and the philosophy of British imperialism.

Chamberlain's Territorial Shopping-List

For Chamberlain, the prophet of domestic social reform turned promoter of imperial schemes, Zionism offered 'legitimate opportunities' for extending the British Empire. His personal anti-Semitism, for which he was well known in Anglo-Jewish circles,[27] was no obstacle, consistent as it was with his Zionist conception of a 'separate Jewish race'. Further, their racial inferiority compared to the Anglo-Saxon race, did not disqualify the Jews as convenient European colonizers readily available for settlement within the expanding British Empire. Chamberlain's offer of El Arish in the Sinai seemed Zionist enough, if taken as an 'assemblage centre' for the Jewish people in the neighbourhood of Palestine.[28] Equally, a Jewish colony in Sinai 'might prove a useful instrument for extending British influence into Palestine proper, when the time came for the inevitable dismemberment of the Ottoman empire'.[29] According to Herzl's own calculations, once the Jews were 'under the Union Jack at El Arish' Palestine too would fall into the British sphere of influence.[30]

The scheme ultimately failed, despite Chamberlain's enthusiasm for it. A Zionist commission of experts dispatched to El Arish to explore the existing conditions for settlement reported back that the land would require massive irrigation by diverting the Nile river. Jewish interest in the project was further dimmed by the Foreign Office's reluctance to risk troubles in Egypt over El Arish. Together, these obstacles were enough to shelve the whole idea.

However, Chamberlain had no difficulty in finding another spot on the map of the British Empire in need of European colonization. This time it was Uganda, but this was too far removed from the ultimate goal of Palestine to be of any value. Even as a *Nachtasyl*[31] (a temporary asylum for Jews in immediate danger), the Uganda offer was rejected at the 6th Zionist Congress meeting in 1903. Uganda could never have been reconciled with the original Basle Programme and therefore it was not in the spirit of true Jewish Zionism. Yet, for the record, Uganda represented the first territorial offer officially made by a government to the Jews as a national entity.

The Anti-Semitism of English Non-Jewish Zionism

When the British Government made its first official territorial offer to the Jewish people in 1903 in the form of the Uganda proposal, the head of the Government was no one other than Lord Arthur James Balfour. In July 1902 he had succeeded his uncle, Lord Salisbury, as Prime Minister. Thus Balfour was promoting Zionism long before the controversial Balfour Declaration in 1917. Nor had he in 1903 yet become the friend of Chaim Weizmann, the Zionist leader who had established an executive apparatus in England designed to win the support of the British Government for Zionist plans in Palestine. This earlier relationship to the Herzlian phase of the Zionist movement is often overshadowed by Balfour's later more pronounced philo-Semitic attachment to Zionism, exhibited so deliberately when he was Foreign Secretary under Lloyd

George. Although he continued to express support for Zionism for the rest of his life, in fact his earlier Zionist leanings are far more revealing for their harmonious blend of anti-Semitism on the Jewish Question and racism on the subject of history in general.

Balfour, like Chamberlain, believed in the unique virtues of the Anglo-Saxon race. His unambiguous racial patriotism often slipped into anti-Semitism, as revealed in the debates around the 1905 Aliens Act. Not only had he been the head of the government that introduced the Bill, but he 'had personally taken an active part in piloting it through the House of Commons'.[32] During the Committee stage, Balfour had replied to Sir Charles Dilke:

> The right hon. Baronet had condemned the anti-Semitic spirit which disgraced a great deal of modern politics in other countries of Europe, and declared that the Jews of this country were a valuable element in the community. He was not prepared to deny either of these propositions. But he undoubtedly thought that a state of things could easily be imaged in which it would not be to the advantage of the civilization of the country that there should be an immense body of persons who, however patriotic, able and industrious, however much they threw themselves into the national life, still, by their own action, remained a people apart, and not merely held a religion differing from the vast majority of their fellow-countrymen, but only intermarried among themselves.[33]

This statement also left no doubt that the reason for the Bill was to curb Jewish immigration from Eastern Europe and to save England from 'the undoubted evils that had fallen upon the country from an immigration which was largely Jewish.'[34] The reaction of the 7th Zionist Congress was to accuse Balfour of 'open anti-Semitism against the whole Jewish people'.[35]

Even as late as 1914 Balfour confessed to Weizmann that he shared many of Cosima Wagner's anti-Semitic sentiments. He had met with her in Beyreuth and discussed the Jewish predicament in Germany.[36]

The Balfour Declaration, often regarded as the embodiment of political Zionism, does not absolve Balfour of his anti-Semitism nor did his repeated public denouncements of the Jewish persecution in Eastern Europe where, in his own words, 'the treatement of the race has been a disgrace to Christendom'.[37] On the contrary, Balfour's rather ambiguous and enigmatic attitudes on the Jewish Question demonstrate a case in point for our contention that Zionism, racism and anti-Semitism are all part of one phenomenon: the very nature of Zionism not only accommodated anti-Semitism, but often welcomed it. Balfour's hostility to Jewish immigration therefore was not looked upon as 'anti-Semitism in the ordinary or vulgar sense of that word' but merely as 'a universal social and economic concomitant' of this immigration.[38] Balfour must have thought along the same lines when in 1917 he refused to intercede with the Russian Government for the removal of Jewish civic disabilities. In answer to Lucien Wolf's request, Balfour is reported to have indicated that:

> Wherever one went in Eastern Europe one found that by some way or another the Jew got on, and when to this was added the fact that he belonged to a distinct race and that he professed a religion which to the people about him was an object of inherited hatred, and that moreover, he was . . . numbered by millions, one could perhaps understand the desire to keep him down and deny the right to which he was entitled. He [Balfour] did not say that this justified the persecution, but all these things had to be considered when it was proposed that foreign Governments should intervene in order to obtain emancipation for the Russian Jews.[39]

Balfour's ardent and often passionate Zionism emanated from his perception of the 'racial uniqueness' of the Jew, for whom 'race, religion and country' were interrelated. Furthermore, Zionism also appealed to his own conservative philosophy:

> His view of the expediency of acknowledging the historic right of the Jews to a special position in Palestine was a long range view, stretching further into the past and the future than was perhaps the case with some of his colleagues. He thought of the Zionists as guardians of a community of religious and racial tradition that made the unassimilated Jew a great conservative force in world politics, and he felt strongly about the way in which the Jewish contribution to culture and to religion had for the most part been requited by the Christian world.[40]

Balfour shared with many other non-Jewish Zionists their major dilemma, namely how to reconcile two apparently contradictory notions. On the one hand, they expressed admiration for the Jewish race, much like Balfour who once described the Jews as 'the most gifted race that mankind has seen since the Greeks of the 5th century.'[41] But on the other side, they were unable to reconcile the 'Jewish otherness' or 'separateness' from their non-Jewish environment. The non-Jewish Zionists generally displayed 'a kind of pro-Semitism which put all emphasis on the distinctiveness of the Jews and seemed almost to imply that emancipation had done them a wrong by blurring their identity as a nation'.[42]

Zionism provided an easy answer to this predicament when it accepted the essential unassimilable Jewishness of the Jews as its *a priori* postulate. In Balfour's own evaluation of Zionism, its value to the non-Jewish world lay precisely in its 'endeavour to mitigate the age-long miseries created for Western civilization by the presence in its midst of a Body which it too long regarded as alien and even hostile, but which it was equally unable to expel or to absorb.'[43]

Palestine as the bound variable in the Zionist equation was accepted by Balfour shortly after the failure of the Uganda project. Although well-intentioned, Chamberlain's project of Jewish settlement in East Africa, had had one serious defect – it was not Zionism. In Balfour's Zionism, Palestine was the indispensable element and he entertained no illusions about the future of Palestine's Arab inhabitants. In his Memorandum *Respecting Syria, Palestine and Mesopotamia* he straight-forwardly proclaimed:

> For in Palestine we do not propose even to go through the form of consulting the wishes of the present inhabitants of the country, though the American Commission has been going through the form of asking what they are. The Four Great Powers are committed to Zionism. And Zionism, be it right or wrong, good or bad, is rooted in age-long traditions, in present needs, in future hopes, of far profounder import than the desires and prejudices of the 700,000 Arabs who now inhabit that ancient land.[44]

And with regard to Jewish settlement in Palestine, he recommended towards the end of this same memorandum:

> If Zionism is to influence the Jewish problem throughout the world, Palestine must be made available for the largest number of Jewish immigrants. It is therefore eminently desirable that it should obtain the command of the water-power which naturally belongs to it, whether by extending its borders to the north, or by treaty with mandatory Syria, to whom the southward flowing waters of Hamon could not in any event be of much value. For the same reason Palestine should extend into the lands lying east of the Jordan.[45]

Lloyd George's Zionism

Balfour and Lloyd George were both self-confessed Zionists, ardent and united in their support for the Zionists even though Balfour was a Conservative and Lloyd George a Liberal. Their backgrounds were similar. Balfour, who had once described his mother as 'a woman of profound religious conviction', was reared within the tradition of Scottish Protestantism with all its affection for the Old Testament and the strong belief in the Restoration of the Jews as heralding the Second Coming of Christ. His own personal philosophy, as outlined in his *Theism and Humanism*, reflects Judaic influence. He regarded history as 'an instrument for carrying out a Divine purpose'.

Owing to his father's early death, Lloyd George was raised by his maternal uncle Richard Lloyd, a volunteer preacher belonging to a Welsh Baptist sect called 'Campbellites' or 'The Disciples of Christ'. Thus he was given a rigid Old Testament background. In his own account of his youth, Lloyd George admitted that he had been trained more in Hebrew history than in the history of England:

> I was brought up in a school where I was taught far more about the history of the Jews than about the history of my own land. I could tell you all the kings of Israel. But I doubt whether I could have named half a dozen of the kings of England, and not more of the kings of Wales . . . We were thoroughly imbued with the history of your race in the days of its greatest glory, when it founded that great literature which will echo to the very last days of this old world, influencing, moulding, fashioning human character, inspiring and sustaining human motive, for not only Jews, but Gentiles as well. We absorbed it and made it part of the best in the Gentile character.[46]

In the same speech, Lloyd George attributed his Zionism to Chaim Weizmann's personality and professional genius as a chemist: 'I am his [Weizmann's] proselyte . . . Acetone converted me to Zionism.'[47] The same acknowledgement was made again in his *Truth About the Peace Treaties* and in his *War Memoirs*.[48] These statements are part of the myth that the Balfour Declaration was a reward to Chaim Weizmann for services rendered to the British war effort (he worked under Lloyd George as an industrial chemist in the Ministry of Munitions). Weizmann's skills notwithstanding, Lloyd George was most certainly already predisposed to be receptive to Weizmann's arguments in favour of a Jewish National Home in Palestine.

On 15 October 1905, the *Jewish Chronicle* had described him as a 'doughty Welsh nationalist' and 'an ardent believer in the Zionist Movement'.[49] Chaim Weizmann personally recalled that Lloyd George's 'advocacy of the Jewish national homeland long predated his succession to the Premiership.'[50] Weizmann's own personal acquaintance with Lloyd George began only in January 1915. But already in 1903 Lloyd George had been in active contact with Herzl and the Zionist Movement.

It was Lloyd George, Roberts & Co., Lloyd George's legal firm who, on the recommendation of the Zionist Organization, had drawn up a draft scheme for Chamberlain's East Africa project. Lloyd George later told Herbert Samuel, a member of the Asquith cabinet and a Jewish sympathizer of Zionism, that he was 'very keen to see a Jewish state established in Palestine'.[51] When Samuel circulated his Memorandum *On the Future of Palestine* in January 1915, Lloyd George, then Minister of Munitions under Asquith, together with Edward Grey, the Foreign Secretary, were the only Cabinet members in favour of Samuel's proposal to combine British annexation of Palestine with British support for Zionist aspirations in Palestine.[52]

When Lloyd George became Prime Minister in December 1916, the British Government seriously began to consider a public statement of British policy on Palestine and opened official talks with the Zionists on the question. By then Palestine had become part and parcel of World War

I's most entangled diplomatic manoeuvres. With Lloyd George as Prime Minister, and Arthur James Balfour as Foreign Secretary, non-Jewish Zionism had reached the innermost circles of British policy-making, flanked by a host of lesser luminaries, all of whose Zionism was no less sincere and obliging.

In the controversy of how to conduct the war, Lloyd George, following his Zionist intuitions, chose to support the 'Easterners' who advocated making the Near East the major theatre of British war efforts after the deadlock on the Western front. To him the Palestine campaign was the one really interesting part of the war, for 'the very names of the battle-fields stirred his imagination . . . moved by his memories of the sacred writings, familiar to him from childhood, which foretold the restoration of the Jewish people to the Holy Land.'[53] In his own *Memoirs* he recalled; 'We realized the moral and political advantages to be expected from an advance on this front and particularly from the occupation of Jerusalem.'[54]

But his fears were not centred only on the German-Turkish alliance. Above all he wanted to preclude any future French influence in the area. He once told Lord Bertie, the British Ambassador to France, that France 'will have to accept our protectorate, we shall be there by conquest and shall remain.'[55]

British Imperialism the Match-Maker

At last British and Zionist interests coincided. Jewish Zionists like Chaim Weizmann and Nahum Sokolow did their part in identifying their own interests with those of Britain and Western imperialism. For Britain in 1917 the acquisition of Palestine had become an irreducible strategic requirement. But a claim based on military conquest alone could not be reconciled with Woodrow Wilson's principle of non-acquisition of territory by war and would have alienated world opinion. Thus, open annexation by Britain was out of the question. The only course open for Britain was to link its own war aims with the principle of self-determination. British non-Jewish Zionists thus found it most appropriate to enter Palestine as a trustee for its Old Testament proprietors, 'God's ancient people'. It not only quieted the British conscience, but left the door open for future British interests in the region. With this in mind, Mark Sykes once wrote in a letter to Lord Robert Cecil:

> We should so order our policy that, without in any way showing any desire to annex Palestine or to establish a Protectorate over it, when the time comes to choose a mandatory power for its control, by the consensus of opinion and desire of its inhabitants, we shall be the most likely candidate.[56]

Within the framework of non-Jewish Zionism, the Balfour Declaration provided an effective moral attitude and a good cause. The subsequent British Mandate over Palestine was no more than the inevitable recognition of an already accomplished fact. The Balfour Declaration was incorporated in the British Mandate for Palestine, entrusted by the Allied Powers' Supreme Council at San Remo in 1920. It was granted by the League of Nations in 1922 for the specific purpose of 'the establishment in Palestine of A National Home of the Jewish People'.

Why the Balfour Declaration?

There are differing views among historians as to why the British Government under Lloyd George finally issued the Balfour Declaration, on 2 November 1917. The reasons stretch from humanitarian sentiment for the Jews, to interest of state and wartime strategy. The official explanations vary as widely as those given by the general observer.[57] While all these elements may have been present, they needed a further factor finally to tip the scale in favour of the Declaration. The essential reason in the end must be sought in the Zionist predispositions of the many and diverse individuals involved in the original decision-making process and right through to the formulation of the Declaration itself.

Lloyd George and Arthur Balfour were not the only ones who wholeheartedly and single-mindedly supported the Zionist goals in Palestine. Rather they were heading a whole generation of non-Jewish Zionists, all of them distinguished figures in public life and government. Mark Sykes, Leopold Amery, Lord Milner, Major Ormsby-Gore (later Lord Harlech), Herbert Sidebotham, Robert Cecil, J. C. Smuts, Richard Meinertzhagen, Josiah C. Wedgewood, C. P. Scott and many others all held positions of influence and were determined exponents of Zionist policies.

In fact the only anti-Zionists of high standing seem to have been Edward Montagu and Lord Curzon who, as the most knowledgeable member of the War Cabinet on Middle Eastern Affairs, expressed serious misgivings about Zionism. On 26 October 1917 Lord Curzon circulated a memorandum in which he advised against the proposed Balfour Declaration on the grounds that it involved far-reaching commitments which Great Britain could never fulfil. He already foresaw the future trouble in Palestine whose Arab population would 'not be content either to be expropriated for Jewish immigrants or to act as hewers of wood and drawers of water for the latter.'[58] But his warnings were not heeded.

For all their other differences, Curzon's opponents shared a Zionism now precisely honed to imperial aspirations. The identity of interest between British imperialism and Zionism was now also accepted by the Jewish Zionists. As early as 2 April 1905 the South American Zionist official, Samuel Goldreich, wrote in a letter to Herzl; 'I did my best to convince Lord Milner that what he called Imperialism is identical with Zionism, and that the highest and noblest ideals of Britain and the world demand the restoration of Israel to Zion.'[59] Lord Milner was only one of many whose imperialism had made them Zionists.

The New Generation of Imperial Zionists

Herbert Sidebotham: The new vision of Zionism was promoted by Sidebotham in his various articles in the *Manchester Guardian*, a newspaper edited by Charles Prestwich Scott, another non-Jewish Zionist and the mutual friend of Lloyd George and Chaim Weizmann.

Sidebotham, like the majority of his non-Jewish Zionist contemporaries, was a self-made Zionist. He only met Weizmann in 1916 after Weizmann's attention had been drawn to Sidebotham's military essays in the *Manchester Guardian*, where he had argued, for instance, on 22 November 1915 that Palestine was crucial to the defence of Egypt and the Suez Canal. These early articles had emphasized the great political and strategic value to the British Empire of Zionist settlement in Palestine.

Yet his reputable military essays, widely read in government circles, were filled with typically Zionist imagery. In one of his early essays Sidebotham evoked the 'ancient connection between Egypt, Palestine and Mesopotamia', applying it to the contemporary situation:

> Mesopotamia was the cradle of the Jewish people and the place of its exile in the captivity. From Egypt came Moses, the founder of the Jewish State. The wheel of destiny will have come full circle round if at the end of this war the extinction of the Turkish empire in Mesopotamia and the need of securing a more defensible frontier in Egypt were to lead to the re-establishment of a Jewish state in Palestine.[60]

His description of Palestine is also characteristic and speaks for itself:

> Nor is there any indigenous civilization in Palestine that could take the place of the Turkish except that of the Jews, who, already numbering one-seventh of the population, have given to Palestine everything that it has ever had of value to the world.[61]

He spoke of Palestine with the old Biblical names of Judaea and Samaria:

> Palestine, in fact, had no separate national or geographic existence apart from that which the classic history of the Jews had given it, and this disappeared with Jewish independence. In assigning Palestine therefore as a national home, Mr. Balfour was not giving away anything that belonged to someone else. It was a ghost of the past which two thousand years had not succeeded in laying and which could assume an actual physical existence only through the Jews. To the Christian, Palestine was the Holy Land . . . To others Palestine might indifferently be regarded as an appendage of Egypt or a part of Syria or Arabia. Only to the Jews could Palestine be a country by itself.[62]

The Jews, 'the oldest of living races', were to radiate their civilizing influence throughout the East while the indigenous Arab population of

Palestine was described as 'a more mixed and feebler race than the Arabs of the Yemen or the Hedjaz'.[63] Sidebotham's condescending attitude towards the Arabs in general, and the Palestinian Arabs in particular, was neither astonishing nor exceptional among non-Jewish Zionists. Sidebotham's appraisal of Zionism concluded with the following revealing statement: '. . . so strong is the argument for Zionism to our own security that if there had been no Zionism ready made to our hands . . . we should have had to invent it.'[64]

Sir Mark Sykes: Another influential Englishman converted to Zionism through imperialism, Sykes was one of the Assistant Secretaries to Lloyd George's War Cabinet. His job was mainly to provide the Cabinet with information and advice on Middle Eastern affairs. Although not a decision-maker himself, he was very powerful because of his reputation as an expert on Middle Eastern affairs and because of his access to those in power. His biographer argued that he was the driving force behind the British Palestine policy that led to the Balfour Declaration and then to the Mandate.[65]

Raised as a Catholic, Sykes' Zionism seems to go against the general rule associating non-Jewish Zionism with the evangelical Protestant milieu. Indeed, Sykes did not hold the usual attitudes towards the Jews 'as God's ancient people' to be restored to their ancient Homeland. Prior to his conversion to Zionism, he had negotiated the famous Sykes-Picot agreement, a secret treaty in 1916 carving up the Ottoman Empire between Russia, France and Britain, and placing Palestine under international administration. Although not unaware of the Zionists and the whole Jewish Question, at the time Sykes saw it as irrelevant to these Anglo-French negotiations over a post-war settlement for the Ottoman Empire. Still, in one respect, the Sykes-Picot agreement was in fact what the Zionists wanted: it gave a geographical identity to Palestine for the first time in modern history:

> In a sense the Sykes-Picot Agreement was of Zionist origin, the special provision for Palestine being to a large extent the result of the Samuel Memorandum, of Dr Gaster's interrupted conversion of Sykes, and of Sykes' influence on Picot. Further, it protected the future of Palestine (in an unscrupulous manner as some thought) from the consequences of the British promises to the Sherif of Mecca for Arab independence in the Arab speaking world. In only one respect did it run counter to Zionist wishes, and that was in the insistence on the international zone.[66]

The 'Dr Gaster' mentioned in the quote was Dr Moses Gaster, Mark Sykes' tutor in Zionism, a Romanian Jew and the Chief Rabbi of the Sephardic community in London. Sykes met Gaster at one of the learned Orientalist societies during 1915. According to Sykes' own account, the rabbi had opened his eyes to the meaning of Zionism at the end of 1915, just after Sykes' appointment to his post as one of the Assistant Secretaries to the War Cabinet.[67]

His education in Zionism was further reinforced by Herbert Samuel, who in February 1916 had sent him a copy of his memorandum on Palestine calling for a 'British protectorate' over Palestine whereby 'facilities would be given to Jewish organizations to purchase land, to found colonies, to establish educational and religious institutions'. Sykes was impressed by Samuel's memorandum and from that moment on began to interest himself actively in Zionism. He immediately grasped the principal object of Zionism, namely 'the realization of the ideal of an existing centre of nationality rather than boundaries or extent of territory'.[68] Zionism had a special appeal for Sykes, as a fervent believer in nationalism and all its virtues, even more so when interpreted by Samuel within the larger framework of British imperialism.

Before his own personal encounter with the Jewish Zionists, Gaster and Samuel, Sykes was known for anti-Jewish attitudes that often came close to plain anti-Semitism. For Sykes, the Jew represented 'the archetype of the cosmopolitan financier whose iniquities were among his favourite themes',[69] and he voiced contempt for the many 'Anglicized Jews' who seemed to have blended their Jewish religion with English nationality. Indeed, as Sokolow even had to confess, Mark Sykes 'had no liking for the hybrid type of assimilating Jew'.[70] Through the Zionist looking-glass he suddenly discovered the 'real Hebrew' as opposed to the Anglicized Jew.

Non-Jewish Zionism and the Balfour Declaration

It has been said that the Balfour Declaration came to the Jewish Zionist leaders of the time, Chaim Weizmann, Nahum Sokolow et al, 'like water seeking its source',[71] in other words, that it was mainly non-Jewish Zionists who initiated and were responsible for the issuance of the Declaration. Weizmann once explicitly declared: 'We Jews got the Balfour Declaration quite unexpectedly . . . We never dreamt of the Balfour Declaration, to be quite frank, it came to us overnight.'[72] But, as we have argued, this did not really happen 'overnight'. All the Balfour Declaration did was to combine the basic principles of Zionism in an official government document for the first time.

The diplomatic background to this momentous declaration has been discussed at length elsewhere. We have concentrated our analysis rather on the motivations of some of the political decision-makers.

A textual analysis of this 67-word declaration gives a good insight into the central tenets of Zionism. First and foremost, it recognized the existence of 'the Jewish people' as a nation. Following the Declaration's incorporation into the Mandate and approval by the League of Nations, the 'Jewish people' became a national entity recognized by international law. The contention of the majority of the Jews at the time that Judaism was merely a religion was dismissed as 'palpably false'.[74] Moreover, while granting recognition to the Jews as a nation, non-Jewish Zionism, as expressed in the Balfour Declaration, denied the existence of the Palestinian Arab people. Ninety per cent of Palestine's total population at the time were referred to in the Declaration merely as 'the existing non-Jewish communities in Palestine'. This preposterous nomenclature, avoiding even the very word 'Arab', served the sole purpose of concealing the fact that Palestine was an Arab country. The whole non-Jewish Zionist tradition, as it emerged from the early Protestant revolution of the 16th Century, built up the image of Palestine as a non-Arab land, i.e. as the Jewish Homeland. Its Arab inhabitants went either unmentioned or were casually dismissed as the left-over remnants of other races that had strayed into the Holy Land. But, it may be said, the Declaration offers to guarantee the 'civil and religious rights' of these 'non-Jews'. However, the term 'civil rights', if indeed it meant anything at all, could only have referred to the rights of aliens in a foreign country.

The legend of Palestine as the ancestral home of all Jews had now become accepted on the highest levels of political decision-making. Palestine was not regarded as part of the Arab homeland. Lord Milner made this explicit:

> If the Arabs go to the length of claiming Palestine as one of their countries in the same sense as Mesopotamia or Arabia proper is an Arab country then I think they are flying in the face of facts, of all history, of all tradition, and of associations of the most important character – I had almost said, the most sacred character. Palestine can never be regarded as a country on the same footing as the other Arab countries . . . The future of Palestine cannot possibly be left to be determined by the termporary impressions and feelings of the Arab majority of the present day.[75]

The same tone was struck by Robert Cecil when he called the Balfour Declaration 'the rebirth of a Jewish nation' and called for 'Arabia for the Arabs, Armenia for the Armenians, and Judaea for the Jews, and real Turkey for the Turks'.[76]

The language of the Balfour Declaration is notoriously vague, especially as to the precise territory involved in the Jewish Homeland in Palestine. But non-Jewish Zionists were again the first to concern themselves with Jewish Palestine's boundaries. Palestine was of course 'Biblical Palestine', a geographic area including parts of what are today Lebanon, Syria and Jordan. Hechler, Lloyd George and Smuts were all too familiar with Biblical geography and they were under no illusions as to the future result of the British National Home policy.

Lord Balfour himself had gone on record as saying that by the Declaration they had always meant an eventual Jewish state.[77] Lloyd George, too, confirmed this interpretation in the evidence he provided before the Peel Commission.[78] They had settled as early as 1917 in their minds, if not on paper, the future status of Palestine, as a Jewish state.

Non-Jewish Zionism thus reached its peak during the first two decade of this century. Ushering in the official stage of Zionist-British co operation, the Balfour Declaration came to set the terms of Wester policy towards Palestine.

Notes

1. C. R. Conder writing in *The Jewish Chronicle* in 1878, as cited in Fran Kobler, *The Vision was There* (London, 1956), p. 87.
2. J. W. Dawson, *Modern Science in the Bible*, cited in Kobler, op. cit., pp 105–6.
3. See, for example, Leonard Stein, *Zionism* (London, 1925), pp 47–72; o Bentwich and Shaftesley, 'Forerunners of Zionism in the Victorian Era', op cit., pp. 209–13. According to Stein 34,000 Jews resided in Palestine in 1878 the great majority of which were *halukah* Jews, i.e. living on foreign dona tions. Only a very few Jews were engaged in agricultural colonization t rehabilitate themselves and the land. The few attempts to found agricultura colonies, and many of them indeed failed, would all have ended in total failur had it not been for the influx of foreign capital as requested by non-Jewis Zionists.
4. Bentwich and Shaftesley, op. cit., p. 213.
5. As quoted in Bentwich and Shaftesley, op. cit., p. 215.
6. Cited in Barbara Tuchmann, *Bible and Sword* (London, 1956), p. 173.
7. Ibid.
8. Pinsker, a true secularist, summed up his argument for Jewish self emancipation and territorial statehood in the following points: 1) The Jew are not a living nation, they are everywhere aliens, therefore they ar despised; 2) The civil and political emancipation of the Jews is not sufficient t change this estimation; the proper, the only remedy, would be the creation o a Jewish nationality, of a people living upon its own soil, the auto-emancipatio of the Jews; 3) The international Jewish question must receive a nationa solution; 4) A way must be opened for the national regeneration of the Jew by a congress of Jewish notables; 5) The undertaking would, in the presen state of affairs, present no insuperable difficulties. See Leo Pinsker, *Auto Emancipation*, edited by A. S. Eban (London, 1932).
9. Benjamin Disraeli (later Lord Beaconsfield), himself of Jewish origin, wa already well known before assuming the premiership in 1874, for his two Zionist novels, *The Wondrous Tale of Alroy* (1833) and *Tancred* (1847). Some historians also think he is the author of an anonymous memorandum writter for the 1878 Berlin Congress and offering a Zionist programme for the solution of the Palestine problem. But Disraeli's major contribution to Zion ism rests in his efforts to expand and solidify British interests in the Near East It was Disraeli who, in 1875 negotiated the British purchase of Egypt's share in the Suez Canal Company. And it was under his premiership that Britair occupied first Cyprus and then Egypt in 1882.
10. Tuchmann, op. cit., p. 174.
11. George Antonius, *The Arab Awakening* (London, 1938), pp. 261–2; see also Leonard Stein, *The Balfour Declaration* (London, 1961), p. 52.

12. *The Diaries of Theodor Herzl* (New York, 1956).
13. Bessi and Hermann Ellern, *Herzl, Hechler, and the Grand Duke of Baden and the German Emperor, 1896–1904* (Tel Aviv, 1961), p.52.
14. For the Basle Programme, see Stein, *Zionism*, op. cit., p. 88.
15. Julian Amery, *The Life of Joseph Chamberlain* (London, 1951), Vol. 4.
16. Tuchmann, op. cit., p. 189.
17. An offer which did not prove workable, as explained later in this chapter.
18. Amery, op. cit., p. 260.
19. Christopher Sykes, *Two Studies in Virtue* (London, 1953), p. 162.
20. *Protokoll des 7. Zionisten Kongress*, Wien, Verlag Erez Israel, 1905.
21. See *Jewish Chronicle*, 23 December 1904, especially p. 13. This includes his speech at Limehouse in December 1904 speaking vehemently against alien immigration into England.
22. Diaries of Herzl, op. cit., p. 373.
23. Paul Goodman, *Zionism in England* (London, 1949), pp. 18–19.
24. *Protocols of the Fourth Zionist Congress* (London, 1900), p. 5.
25. The final report of the Commission was published on 14 August 1903. See Cmd. 1741; Minutes of Evidence, Cmd. 1742, 'Report of the Royal Commission on Alien Immigration, 1902–1903'.
26. As quoted in Oskar K. Rabinowicz, *Winston Churchill on Jewish Problems* (New York, 1960).
27. During the luncheon with the Italian Jewish Finance Minister Baron Sonnino, Chamberlain was quoted as having said to the former: 'Yes Sir, I have been called the apostle of the Anglo-Saxon race, and I am proud of the title. I think the Anglo-Saxon race is as fine as any on earth . . . There is in fact only one race that I despise – the Jews. Sir, they are physical cowards.' As quoted in Amery, op. cit., p. 236.
28. See *Diaries of Herzl*, op. cit., p. 376.
29. Amery, op. cit., Vol. 4.
30. *Diaries of Herzl*, op. cit., p. 384.
31. It was the Zionist leader Max Nordau who called Uganda a *Nachtasyl*, a temporary shelter for the Jews fleeing from the pogroms in Eastern Europe.
32. Stein, *Balfour*, op. cit., p. 149. The Bill was twice introduced by the Balfour Government. The first draft had been submitted to the House of Commons on 29 March 1904, but had finally been withdrawn on 7 July 1904, due to the heavy opposition from the Liberals. A modified form of the original draft was reintroduced on 4 April 1905. This bill ultimately passed on 11 August 1905 and came into force beginning 1 January 1906.
33. Hansard, H.C., 10 July 1905, Vol. 149, col. 154/155. See also *Jewish Chronicle*, 14 July 1905, p. 7 for a Jewish critique of Balfour's speech.
34. Hansard, ibid., col. 155.
35. *Protokoll des 7. Zionisten Kongress*, op. cit., p. 85.
36. For Weizmann's account of this meeting with Balfour on 12 December 1914 see Stein, *Balfour*, op. cit., p. 154. Cosima Wagner was Richard Wagner's widow and the prototype of pre-Nazi anti-Semitism.
37. Hansard, H.C., 2 May 1905, col. 795. See also Blanche E. C. Dugdale, *Arthur James Balfour* (London, 1936), Vol. 2, pp. 216–17.
38. Chaim Weizmann, as quoted in Richard Crossman, *A Nation Reborn* (London, 1960), p. 27.
39. Wolf's note of his conversation with Balfour is found in Stein, *Balfour*, op. cit., 1961, p. 164.

40. Dugdale, op. cit., Vol. 2, p. 216.
41. Balfour in an interview with Harold Nicolson in 1917; see *Jerusalem Post*, 2 November 1952.
42. Stein, *Balfour*, op. cit., p. 163.
43. Nahum Sokolow, *History of Zionism* (London, 1919), Vol. 1, pp. xxixff.
44. For the complete text of the memorandum see E. L. Woodward and J. Butler (eds.), *Documents on British Foreign Policy, 1919–39* (London, 1952), 1st Series, Vol. 4, pp. 340–7.
45. Ibid., p. 347.
46. Lloyd George to the Jewish Historical Society of England on 25 May 1925, reprinted in Philip Guedalla, *Napoleon and Palestine* (London, 1925), pp. 45–55, esp. pp. 48–9.
47. Ibid., p. 48.
48. Lloyd George, *The Truth About the Peace Treaties* (London, 1938), Vol. 2, p. 117; see also his *War Memoirs* (London, 1933–36), Vol. 2, p. 584.
49. *Jewish Chronicle*, 15 December 1905.
50. Chaim Weizmann, *Trial and Error* (New York, 1965), p. 192.
51. Viscount Samuel, *Memoirs* (London, 1945), pp. 139ff.
52. Ibid., p. 142.
53. Stein, *Balfour*, op. cit., 1961, p. 146.
54. Lloyd George, *War Memoirs*, op. cit., Vol. 4, p. 189.
55. *The Diary of Lord Bertie of Thame* (London, 1924), Vol. 2, p. 122. The entry was recorded on 20 April 1917.
56. Shane Leslie, *Mark Sykes: His Life and Letters* (London, 1923).
57. Balfour at various times propounded his humanitarian concern 'to give the Jews their rightful place in the world', see *Parliamentary Debates*, House of Lords, Vol. 50, No. 47, cols 1018–1019, 21 June 1922; also Dugdale, op. cit., pp. 216–17. In his autobiography, Lloyd George referred to the propaganda value among the American and Russian Jews, while Winston Churchill counted on the 'moral and financial support' of world Jewry; see *Parliamentary Debates*, H.C., Vol. 156, col. 3289, 4 July 1922. Lord Curzon, on the other hand, proclaimed the strategic factor as chief reason; see *Parliamentary Debates*, House of Lords, Vol. 40, col. 1028, 29 June 1920.
58. For the complete text of the Memorandum, see Lloyd George, *Treaties*, op. cit., Vol. 2, pp. 1123ff.
59. Goldreich to Herzl, 2 April 1905. A copy of the letter can be found in the Zionist Archives in Jerusalem.
60. Herbert Sidebotham, *England and Palestine. Essays Towards the Restoration of the Jewish State* (London, 1918).
61. Ibid.
62. Herbert Sidebotham, *British Policy and the Palestine Mandate: Our Proud Privilege*, as quoted in Joseph M. Jeffries, *Palestine The Reality* (London, 1929).
63. Herbert Sidebotham, British Interests in Palestine (London, 1934), p. 8.
64. Ibid., p. 11.
65. Leslie, op. cit., pp. 288–9, also p. 85. See also Leopold S. Amery, *My Political Life* (London, 1953), Vol. 2, pp. 114–15.
66. Sykes, op. cit., pp. 195–6.
67. Mark Sykes' address to the London Opera House meeting reported in *The Times*, 3 December 1917.

68. As quoted in Stein, *Balfour*, op. cit., pp. 233–4.
69. Ibid., p. 272.
70. Sokolow, op. cit., Vol. 2, p. xxi; see also Leslie, op. cit., p. 269.
71. Joseph M. N. Jeffries, *Palestine: The Reality* (London, 1939) Longmans Green & Co., p. 172.
72. As quoted in Paul Goodman (ed.), *Chaim Weizmann* (London, 1945), Chapter 14.
73. For a most detailed study of the Declaration's political background see Stein, *Balfour*, op. cit.
74. F.O. 371/3388/1495, 27 October 1918.
75. Lord Milner in the House of Lords, on 27 June 1923, as quoted in Jeffries, op. cit., pp. 695–6.
76. Speech at London Opera House, 2 December 1917, printed in full in Sokolow, op. cit., Vol. 2, pp. 101–2.
77. Balfour in a conversation with Weizmann, Churchill, Mark Sykes and Meinertzhagen on 22 July 1921. As quoted in Richard Meinertzhagen, *Middle East Diary, 1917–1956* (London, 1960), pp. 103–5.
78. Lloyd George, *Treaties*, op. cit., Vol. 2, p. 1139. The Peel Commission published in July 1937 concluded that an 'irrepressible conflict' had arisen over the question of who was to rule Palestine. The report recommended the division of Palestine. A White Paper was simultaneously issued to support the Report as official British policy – the notorious 1937 White Paper.

6. Zionism in America

The New World as the New Jerusalem

Up until World War I, the American Government had no interest in Zionism as a political movement. But Zionism as a spiritual movement had constituted an important element in American thought and political life since the earliest days of European settlement in the New World during the second half of the 17th Century. English Puritanism, with its celebration of Hebraism, furnished the background for American Puritanism. The Judaic elements were in fact even more pronounced in the New World and the Pilgrims carried with them the tradition of Hebrew scholarship as well. In the words of Lecky, 'the Hebraic mortar cemented the foundations of American democracy.'[1]

As in England, Puritan theology relied upon the literal inspiration and acceptance of the Bible. Their American experiences brought the Puritans to identify with the Biblical Hebrew exiles and settlers. America became the 'New Canaan', and like the ancient Hebrews, they had escaped the servitude of a 'Pharoah' (King James I of England) and fled the 'land of Egypt' (England), seeking refuge from religious persecution in the new promised land. Declaring war on the native Indians, they invoked the Old Testament:

> It clearly appears that God calls the colonies to war. The Narrohaigansetts and their confederates rest on their numbers, weapons and opportunities to do mischief, as probably the old Asher, Amalek and the Philistines with others did confederate against Israel.[2]

The Hebrew Bible, i.e. the Old Testament, was turned into the standard sourcebook for names, as well as the guide for their legislation. Children were named after the old Hebrew patriarchs while their towns and settlements were called Bethlehem, Eden, Hebron, Judaea, Salem, Zion or even Jerusalem. The place names of Biblical Palestine were thus reproduced again and again in the newly conquered colonies. Puritan identification with Hebraic Biblical characters permeated the newly created national life in colonial America and this heritage became inseparable from the so-called American tradition.[3]

When the *saeculum theologicum* of the 17th Century came to an end, Palestine as the Jewish Homeland had already begun to occupy a special place in American secular culture. The return of the Jews to this 'traditional home' remained a favourite theme and generally accepted principle in both religious and popular literature. Early American thought on Palestine was mainly derived from these traditional and literary sources.[4]

Towards the end of the 18th Century the belief in the Jewish Restoration came to constitute an important aspect of the American Protestant theology, where messianic and millenarian doctrines occupied an important place. In the United States, Evangelism took on a much more dominant form than in England and finally culminated in a distinct popular culture incorporating many of its spiritual and religious Zionist precepts. Thus from the very beginning of American history,

> there was a strong Christian tendency to believe that the Second Advent must await the restoration of the Jewish state. This was not a unanimous opinion among Christian theologians, but it formed part of the matrix of American intellectual history, comprising a persistent millennial strain in American Christian thought.[5]

This particular conservative stream in American Protestantism attracted mainly Calvinists to its pessimistic *Weltanschauung*. The most important denominations in this fundamentalist tendency included the Baptists, Lutherans and certain Presbyterians. Subscribing to the literal interpretation of Biblical prophecies and a belief in the national revival of the Jewish people, fundamentalists represented a large portion of American Protestantism towards the end of the 19th Century. Their Zionism led them to regard the Jews as the key to the future.[6]

All prophecies concerning the Jews were taken to refer to 'natural Israel', i.e. the secular and spiritual Jewish nation as against the 'spiritual Israel', i.e. the Christian Church.[7] They believed that 'throughout the ages God is pursuing two distinct purposes, one related to the earth with earthly people and earthly objectives involved, which is Judaism, while the other is related to heaven with heavenly people and heavenly objectives involved, which is Christianity.'[8] Accordingly 'the boundaries of the land given in the promise to Abraham will literally be restored during the millennium, Christ will return to a literal, theocratic political kingdom on earth with a government patterned after the existing national government'.[9]

This distinct form of millenarian thinking not only made fundamentalist congregations effectively Zionist, but it produced leaders demanding public action to restore the Jews to Palestine.

William Blackstone
One of the most outstanding of the American fundamentalist non-Jewish Zionists was William E. Blackstone (1841–1935), a 'financier, world

traveller, author, missionary, evangelist, dispenser of millions for missions, and outstanding champion of Zion.'[10] Stimulated by his religious conviction, he campaigned actively on behalf of the Jews and their Restoration decades before the advent of modern political Zionism. His book *Jesus is Coming* (1878) had a tremendous influence on evangelical American Protestantism. With over one million copies sold, and translated into 48 languages, including Hebrew, it became a best-seller propagating the Zionist ideal within the spirit of millenarianism. 'Probably the most wide-read book in this century on our Lord's return was the famous volume, *Jesus is Coming*, by William E. Blackstone. More Christian leaders had their interest in the second advent awakened by this book than any other volume that had been published for decades.'[11]

During 1888 Blackstone had visited Palestine and was struck by the 'astonishing anomaly – a land without a people and a people without a land.'[12] In the typical non-Jewish Zionist fashion of the time, he was convinced that the Holy Land could be developed agriculturally and commercially by the returning Jewish 'heirs'. The Arab indigenous population was non-existent for him since they did not figure in his Zionist equation of Palestine and the Jews. Blackstone's efforts on behalf of Jewish Restoration culminated in his petition of 5 March 1891, submitted to the American President, Benjamin Harrison, and his Secretary of State, James G. Blaine, urging them 'to consider the situation of the Israelites and their claims to Palestine as their ancient home, and to promote in all other just and proper ways the alleviation of their suffering condition.'[13]

The petition was prompted by the Russian pogroms. Where were these Russian Jews to go? Blackstone thought it 'both unwise and useless to undertake to dictate to Russia concerning her internal affairs.'[14] In America these Jewish refugees were just as unwanted as in England. Thus the Blackstone petition went on to offer the following, most logical and least offensive, solution:

> Why not give Palestine back to them [the Jews] again? According to God's distribution of nations it is their home, an inalienable possession from which they were expelled by force. Under their cultivation it was a remarkably fruitful land, sustaining millions of Israelites, who industriously tilled its hillsides and valleys. They were agriculturists and producers as well as a nation of great commercial importance – the center of civilization and religion. Why shall not the powers which under the treaty of Berlin, in 1878, gave Bulgaria to the Bulgarians and Servia to the Servians now give Palestine back to the Jews?[15]

This Zionist petition was not the eccentric endeavour by a religious fanatic as it might appear at first sight. It was supported by the signatures of 413 very important Americans who could have made up a 19th Century

Who's Who in America. They included the editors of the country's major newspapers, members of Congress, judges – led by Chief Justice Melville W. Fuller himself – Governors, Senators, both Protestant and Catholic churchmen and such representatives of American business and capitalism as J. Pierpont Morgan, John D. Rockefeller, William Rockefeller, Russel Sage and Charles Scribner.[16]

Strongly supporting the petition, the American press spoke not only of moral necessity but also of political advantages to the United States. Six years before the 1st Zionist Congress was convened in Basle, the idea of a Jewish National Homeland in Palestine had already penetrated deep into American culture. The Zionist novel *Daniel Deronda* by George Eliot had found a good reception in America where the general press centred mainly on its political feasibility and usefulness.[17] Laurence Oliphant's ideas had been popularized in the United States by Claude R. Conder who maintained that only the Jews could serve Palestine's needs.[18] The association of the land of Palestine with the Jews became automatic and the growing idea of a Jewish national Restoration was constantly being reinforced by publicity in the general press as well as the religious and secular literature of the time.[19]

President Harrison acknowledged receipt of Blackstone's petition but, although he had promised 'to give it careful consideration', no concrete results materialized at the time. However, a protest note was dispatched to the Russian Government by the American Secretary of State, stating that the huge and uncontrolled outflow of destitute Jews settling in America was due to the 'oppressive measures' of the Russian Government and that the 'hospitality of a nation should not be turned into a burden'.[20] Reading between the lines of this diplomatic correspondence, one cannot help but notice that American verbal intercession on behalf of the persecuted Russian and Romanian Jews did not spring from either general philanthropy or genuine philo-Semitism: the American Government was unwilling to have the expelled Jews come to the United States.

Woodrow Wilson, the 'Non-Interventionist'

On 31 August 1918, President Wilson sent the following letter to the leader of American Zionism, Rabbi Stephen Wise, officially endorsing the British Balfour Declaration:

> I have watched with deep and sincere interest the reconstructive work which the Weizmann Commission has done in Palestine at the instance of the British government, and I welcome an opportunity to express the satisfaction I have felt in the progress of the Zionist Movement in the United States and in the Allied countries since the declaration of Mr Balfour on behalf of the British Government of Great Britain's approval of the establishment in

Palestine of a national home for the Jewish people, and his promise that the British Government would use its best endeavors to facilitate the achievement of that object, with the understanding that nothing would be done to prejudice the civil and religious rights of non-Jewish people in Palestine or the rights and political status enjoyed by the Jews in other countries.[21]

This official endorsement of the Balfour Declaration was a foregone conclusion, although there are different accounts of the personalities involved. The American Jewish historian, Selig Adler,[22] concludes from his investigation of the Wilson Papers and of the General Records of the State Department that Wilson finally succumbed to the pressures of American Zionist Jews, in particular his friend and associate Justice Louis Brandeis. Adler also believes that Colonel House, the Presidential adviser, was anti-Semitic and therefore opposed to Zionism, although this is disputed by the British Jewish historian, Leonard Stein,[23] who sees Colonel House as responsible for Wilson's pro-Zionist attitude and final approval of the Balfour Declaration.

Wilson's interest in Zionism was also greatly stimulated by his Zionist Jewish friend Louis Brandeis, in addition to other influential Zionist Jews such as Felix Frankfurter, Rabbi Stephen Wise and Josephus Daniels. All of them had equal access to the President and all were highly regarded by him. Thus, Wilson's Zionist sympathies could easily be attributed to their influence and solicitation. But then, Wilson also had anti-Zionist Jewish friends and associates: Henry Morgenthau, who once called Zionism 'the most stupendous fallacy in Jewish history', Bernard M. Baruch, Jacob Schiff, or Abram I. Elkins, all were hostile to Zionism and did not hide their anti-Zionist feelings from the President.[24]

The existence of this double pressure, plus the lack of any conclusive documentary evidence with regard to Brandeis' special role, make it rather speculative to see his role as the determining factor. The missing link could only have been the President's own personal Zionist predispositions, part and parcel of his very own cultural and religious heritage.

A descendant of Presbyterian parsons on both sides, Wilson was reared within that tradition of American Protestantism which perpetuated a Zionist mythology, even if conceived only within the spiritual realm. Nevertheless, it provided an indirect fund of feelings and concepts which were to have a bearing on his future attitude towards the Zionist movement and its goals. Wilson could not but enjoy the role of being instrumental in the return of the Jews to 'their land'. His own confession that he, 'the son of the manse, should be able to help restore the Holy Land to Its people'[25] is most telling. He was genuinely attracted to Zionism and all his statements on the subject, in public and in private, were consistent in endorsement of the Zionist idea. It is our contention that Wilson's decision concerning Palestine and Zionism were guided by his subjective personal sentiments rather than by the objective considerations of *Realpolitik*. This is confirmed by the fact that his approving note on the Balfour Declaration was sent via his counsellor, Colonel House, entirely bypassing the State Department and his Foreign Secretary, Robert Lansing.

On 13 October 1917, Wilson sent to Colonel House the following note: 'I find in my pocket the memorandum you gave me about the Zionist Movement. I am afraid I did not say to you that I concurred in the formula suggested by the other side. I do, and would be obliged if you would let them know it.'[26] His unilateral personal agreement with the phraseology and final issue of the Balfour Declaration was regarded by the British Government as essential; Wilson's approval removed the last obstacle still standing in its way.

But, after the official proclamation, no further official American Government endorsement was forthcoming. The Secretary of State, Robert Lansing, objected on political grounds, sending the following note to the President on 13 December 1917:

> My Dear Mr President:
> There is being brought considerable pressure for the issuance of a declaration in regard to this Government's attitude as to the disposition to be made of Palestine. This emanates naturally from the Zionist element of the Jews.
>
> My judgement is that we should go very slowly in announcing a policy for three reasons. First, we are not at war with Turkey and therefore should avoid any appearance of favoring taking territory from that Empire by force. Second, the Jews are by no means a unit in the desire to reestablish their race as an independent people; to favor one over the other faction would seem to be unwise. Third, many Christian sects and individuals would undoubtedly resent turning the Holy Land over to the absolute control of the race credited with the death of Christ. For practical purposes I do not think that we need go further than the first reason given since that is ample ground for declining to announce a policy in regard to the final disposition of Palestine.
> Faithfully yours,
> Robert Lansing[27]

Wilson, however, did not heed his Secretary of State's advice. Instead, he continued to assure the Zionist leaders that they could rely on his personal support.[28] And when at the beginning of 1919, prior to the Paris Peace Conference, the Zionist leaders seemed to have questioned United States co-operation, Wilson himself wrote to Felix Frankfurter:

> I never dreamed that it was necessary to give you any renewed assurance of my adherence to the Balfour Declaration and so far I have found no one who is seriously opposing the purpose which it embodies . . . I see no ground for discouragement and every reason to hope that satisfactory guarantees can be secured.[29]

Wilson thus again reaffirmed his Zionist sentiments, though without explicit and real commitment. He nonetheless remained convinced of Zionism's ultimate realization in Palestine. He was quoted by the *New York Times* as having told Justice Julian W. Mack: 'I am persuaded that the Allied Nations with the fullest concurrence of our own government and people are agreed that in Palestine shall be laid the foundation of a Jewish Commonwealth.'[30]

Recommendations made by the Section of Territorial, Economic and Political Intelligence of Wilson's delegation to the Paris Peace Conference confirmed that the American Government was in favour of a Jewish National Home in Palestine. The recommendations became a part of the President's working paper for the conference, calling for the establishment of a separate state in Palestine to be placed under a British protectorate within the framework of the League of Nations. Additionally it recommended 'that the Jews be invited to return to Palestine and settle there, being assured by the Conference of all proper assistance in so doing . . . being further assured that it will be the policy of the League of Nations to recognize Palestine as a Jewish state as soon as it is a Jewish state in fact.'[31]

All Wilson's statements and decisions on Palestine and Zionism tend to show that he was not a mere convert of Brandeis. He was a Zionist in his own right and of his own persuasion, fully conversant with its main issues and aware of their implications for Palestine. His interest in Zionism even outweighed his personal diplomatic invention at the Paris Peace Conference, his famous 14 Points, in which he rejected the right of territorial acquisition by force, condemned secret agreements and proclaimed the principle of self-determination of peoples. Point 12 even stated specifically that the 'non-Turkish nationalities of the Ottoman Empire should be assured an unmolested opportunity of autonomous development.'

Secretary of State Lansing actually pointed out that the President's Zionist posture was in clear contradiction to his principle of self-determination. But from the Zionist perspective, the principles of Zionism and self-determination were by no means contradictory. To the Zionists, the 'non-Turkish nationalities' of the Ottoman Empire were the Jews and the Armenians and to them only were the principles of self-determination to apply.

In the Zionist vision, the Palestinian province of the Ottoman Empire was 'a land without a people' and above all it was morally 'right that Palestine should become a Jewish state', since it was 'the cradle and home of their vital race'.[32] Contrary to the general consensus among scholars of Zionism, President Wilson's decision to identify American policy with the Zionist programme in Palestine was not simply an acquiescence to the pressures exerted by certain Jewish Zionists. Rather his decisions and pronouncements present a case in point where considerations of sentiment and 'morality' entered the policy-making process and in the end prevailed over all the other 'objective' considerations of *Realpolitik*.

Above Party Politics

After Woodrow Wilson's unqualified endorsement of the Balfour Declaration, all of his presidential successors committed themselves in one way or another to the Zionist position. Since then, every American President has expressed at least his sympathies with the Zionist movement and accepted its goal in Palestine.

Yet, the extent of practical aid granted to the Zionists varied greatly depending mostly on the degree to which a President felt personally committed to Zionism. During the inter-war period, such presidential support was restricted mainly to verbal assurance. The three Republican Presidents following Wilson – Warren G. Harding, Calvin Coolidge and Herbert Hoover – expressed the same Zionist sympathies as their Democratic predecessor. President Harding stated his attitude very clearly on 1 June 1921:

> It is impossible for one who has studied at all the services of the Hebrew people to avoid the faith that they will one day be restored to their historic national home and there enter on a new and yet greater phase of their contribution to the advance of humanity.[33]

And in May 1922 he also expressed his eager support for the Palestine Foundation Fund:

> I am very glad to express my approval and hearty sympathy for the effort of the Palestine Foundation Fund on behalf of the restoration of Palestine as a homeland for the Jewish people. I have always viewed with an interest, which I think, is quite as much practical as sentimental, the proposal for the rehabilitation of Palestine, and I hope the effort now being carried on in this and other countries in this behalf may meet with the fullest measure of success.[34]

Both statements were representative of the non-Jewish Zionist tradition. The analogy between the contemporary Jews and the Old Testament Hebrews is very clear in the first statement, as is the theme of Jewish Restoration to 'their historic national home'. Calvin Coolidge's statement of 13 June 1924 was less specific in this regard, but still he expressed his basic belief in Palestine as 'the Jewish National Homeland' in speaking to an audience of the Zionist Movement of America:

> I have so many times reiterated my interest in this great movement that anything which I might add would be a repetition of former statements, but I am nevertheless glad to have this opportunity to express again my sympathy with the deep and intense longing which finds such fine expression in the Jewish National Homeland in Palestine.[35]

Finally President Herbert Hoover on 21 September 1928 congratulated Zionism on its great achievements in Palestine, echoing the theme of revitalization:

> I have watched with genuine admiration the steady and unmistakable progress made in the rehabilitation of Palestine which, desolate for centuries, is now renewing its youth and vitality through the enthusiasm, hard work, and self-sacrifice of the Jewish pioneers who toil there in a spirit of peace and social justice. It is very gratifying to note that many American Jews, Zionists as well as non-Zionists, have rendered such splendid service to this cause which merits the sympathy and moral encouragement of everyone.[36]

Roosevelt Before and After the 1939 British White Paper

During the 1920s, up until the end of Roosevelt's second administration, Zionism and Palestine were not issues of great public debate in the United States and thus called for no American action. The United States saw no reason to involve itself in the Middle East, an area which she had mandated to Great Britain. Great Britain was pursuing its Mandate in Palestine within the true spirit and letter of the Balfour Declaration, at least as far as the Zionists were concerned. The spirit of isolationism and the economic problems of the Great Depression left no room for American political involvements outside the Western hemisphere. America's 'spiritual' involvement in the nascent Palestine problem existed merely in its continued acceptance of Zionism on the popular as well as political level.

During Roosevelt's second term as President this situation changed. The White Paper containing British so-called 'policy' limiting Jewish immigration to Palestine, was in direct opposition to the Zionist principle of reconstituting a Jewish Palestine through massive Jewish immigration. The operational centre of the World Zionist Movement had already begun to shift its main efforts to the United States.

The Zionists' aim during Roosevelt's era was twofold: the attainment of a Jewish majority in Palestine and then the eventual establishment of an independent Jewish state or commonwealth there. It was therefore deemed an absolute priority to get a reversal of the 1939 British White Paper. Zionist pressures were exerted towards getting the American President to help achieve these aims.

Much to the Zionists' liking, Roosevelt once supported the 'Iraq plan' suggested by former President Hoover, whereby 2–300,000 Arabs were to be removed from Palestine to Iraq, a three billion dollar operation to be financed by the Jews, the British and the French on equal footing. But Roosevelt was as pragmatic and realistic as he was naive. Once convinced of this plan's unworkability, he jumped to another. 'He turned from one plan to another in kaleidoscopic fashion. He often leaned toward an extra-territorial solution, with a token Jewish state in Palestine, but with the majority of homeless Jews in Angola, British Guyana, Madagascar or many other places that flashed through his mind.'[37]

Roosevelt's Personal Zionism

President Roosevelt's personal beliefs in regard to Zionism and a Jewish state in Palestine are difficult to determine. Many Jewish Zionists are still not certain whether he was friend or enemy. All the documentary evidence now available suggests that, although he was sympathetic, Roosevelt never believed that Jewish statehood was a genuine possibility. Rabbi Solomon Goldman, the President of the Zionist Organization of America, wrote to Chaim Weizmann; 'We have every reason to believe that the President has the finest understanding of, and the deepest sympathy with, our movement.'[35] Roosevelt was also happy to use Zionism to further his own political ends in re-election.

His own background as an Episcopalian played a role in his deep-seated scepticism about Zionism and a Jewish state in Palestine. Episcopalian teachings did not see Palestine as belonging to the Jews as a gift of God nor did it recognize Jewish historic claims to Palestine as their rightful Homeland. It is significant that another Episcopalian, Dean Acheson, the son of an Episcopalian bishop of Connecticut, once remarked regarding his personal friends, the Jewish Zionists, Louis Brandeis and Felix Frankfurter; 'They were never able to sell me on this mystical dream of Zionism.'[39] To Roosevelt, the pragmatist and realist, Zionism indeed seemed a mystical dream, although he displayed a more sympathetic concern for the suffering of the Jewish people.

Overall, his Zionism, such as it was, was probably due to pressure from close Jewish friends and collaborators as well as from organized American Zionist groups, which were even more powerful and widespread than at the time of Woodrow Wilson.

Rabbi Stephen Wise had been a close friend of Roosevelt since his term as Governor of New York from 1929 until 1933. He had worked as his campaign adviser during his presidential campaigns. Yet when Wise drafted a statement to be issued by the President in full support of unrestricted immigration and colonization of Palestine, Roosevelt rejected making any such declaration on behalf of Zionism.[40]

Roosevelt's dislike for Rabbi Silver, Rabbi Wise's successor as leader of the Zionist Organization of America, was well known. Nahum Goldmann reported to the Jewish Agency in 1944 that Roosevelt 'who always thought of Palestine as a noble and idealistic venture, is beginning to think of it as a nuisance.'[41] Also Stettinius once informed Nahum Goldmann of the 'disservice' that some of his co-religionists were doing to the Zionist cause because of their 'stubbornness and selfish actions'.[42]

But when, on 12 October 1944, the Republican presidential candidate,

Governor Thomas E. Dewey, announced his endorsement of the Republican Party's Palestine plank , unrestricted immigration and support of the Balfour Declaration,[43] Roosevelt did not hesitate to make public his own support for a similar plank on Palestine in his party's platform:

> We favor the opening of Palestine to unrestricted Jewish immigration and colonization, and such a policy as to result in the establishment there of a free and democratic Jewish commonwealth.[44]

And furthermore he added:

> Efforts will be made to find appropriate ways and means of effecting this policy as soon as practicable. I know how long and ardently the Jewish people have worked and prayed for the establishment of Palestine as a free and democratic Jewish commonwealth. I am convinced that the American people will give their support to this aim and if re-elected I shall help to bring about its realization.[45]

This statement proved to be an empty election promise: after his election to a fourth term nothing was undertaken in this direction. Some observers listed it as yet another example of the kind of duplicity Roosevelt practised with the Zionist leaders, to his own political advantage.[46]

Another reason for Roosevelt's involvement with Zionism was his concern for the Jewish victims of Nazism's racist policies. It was his initiative behind the Evian Conference, which convened on 8 July 1938 to help alleviate the European refugee problem. Initially, Roosevelt wanted the conference to discuss the issue of Jewish immigration to Palestine. But he later agreed to the British demand that the conference should deal with all refugees, and not merely with the Jews fleeing from Germany. The Zionists were furious over the President's decision to drop his original proposal and go along with the British.

Their 'hostile indifference' to the conference was not just because Palestine was dropped from the agenda but because the alternative proposals – freedom of emigration for the Jews and the liberalization of the strict immigration laws of the Western countries – were in no way congenial to the spirit of Zionism.[47] The Zionist idea was predicated on the assumption that Palestine should be the only country where the Jews would be welcomed.

Roosevelt's efforts were focused in another direction. He wanted the existing immigration barriers against the Jews to be lifted by Western democracies, including the United States. 'To Roosevelt it seemed dishonest to demand immigration concessions from the Arabs while the United States retained its tight and selective quota laws.[48]

Yet in spite of Roosevelt's sincerity, the Evian Conference failed. Again under Roosevelt's pressure, a second meeting was convened, in Bermuda in April 1943, to consider the question of the overall refugee situation. Roosevelt proposed a new programme for free immigration, which was matched by Winston Churchill agreeing to admit 100,000 Jewish refugees into England. But again Roosevelt's proposal was defeated, this time by the United States Congress whose interests seemed to coincide with those of the Zionists – both favouring the continuation of restrictive immigration laws for the Western countries while requesting open and free immigration into Palestine. Roosevelt in the end bowed to Congress and retreated from his original intention of raising the issue of general immigration reform and an international open door policy for the Jewish refugees. For the Zionists, this was a major victory for, from now on, they had clear support for their favourite argument that Palestine offered the only refuge for the Jews.

Postponing the Unresolvable

Roosevelt was never able to formulate a clear policy on Palestine or the Middle East in general. He could not resolve the conflict between the military, strategic and economic necessity of placating the Arab states and the apparently 'humanitarian' claims of the Zionists, fortified by their own considerable economic and political pressures. His policy was essentially one of postponement: the Middle East was a region of British responsibility and any final decision on Palestine would have to be left until after the war, and then only with full consultation with Jews and Arabs. All along he hoped that the Arabs and the Jews might still come to terms by themselves. But he had also discovered the fact that any solution to the Palestine dilemma would be far from easy.[49] Roosevelt never fulfilled any of his promises to the Zionists, because he never finally accepted the argument that Zionist and American interests coincided in the Middle East.

Truman and the Formation of Modern US Policy

Harry S. Truman assumed the office of President as a result of Roosevelt's death on 12 April 1945, but he had inherited no coherent Palestine policy. He was free to follow his own leanings. The repercussions of Truman's decisions have affected US Middle East policy to this day.

President Truman was the personification of American non-Jewish Zionism on the political level, as is universally agreed in Zionist histories. But there has always existed a controversy over the reasons for his Zionism, with one historian even portraying him as an indecisive opportunist oscillating under Zionist pressure and allowing the Jewish vote to dictate his Palestine policy.[50] Some of Truman's contemporaries also point to motives of political advantage and expediency.[51] Other historians argue that Truman's Palestine policy was motivated entirely by humanitarian considerations for Jewish suffering and persecution, as urged by Truman's former White House Counsel and Defense Secretary under

Kennedy, Clark Clifford, in an address to the American Historical Association in December 1976. He dwelt on Truman's sympathy for the underdog, recalling that the President envisaged the recognition of Israel 'as the logical culmination of his three years of personal diplomacy and sheer human concern for a people who had endured the torments of the damned and whose instincts for survival and nationhood still refused to be extinguished'.[52]

Without disputing the validity of any of these factors, we seek merely to point out the omission of perhaps the most important of all, namely Truman's own personal participation in the non-Jewish Zionist tradition. Shortly after succeeding President Roosevelt, Truman made the following press statement:

> The American view of Palestine is, we want to let as many of the Jews into Palestine as it is possible to let into that country. Then the matter will have to be worked out diplomatically with the British and the Arabs, so that if a state can be set up there they may be able to set it up on a peaceful basis.[53]

And in his *Memoirs* he described his approach to the Palestine problem in the following way:

> My purpose was then and later to help bring about the redemption of the pledge of the Balfour Declaration and the rescue of at least some of the victims of Nazism. It was not committed to any particular time schedule for its accomplishment. The American policy was designed to bring about, by peaceful means, the establishment of the promised Jewish homeland and easy access to it for the displaced Jews of Europe.[54]

From Refugee Status to Jewish Majority
Truman departed from Roosevelt's established precedent of separating the general Jewish refugee question from the Palestine situation, and instead fused them in the typical Zionist fashion. Jewish immigration into Palestine was to bring about a Jewish state 'in fact' by attempting to create a Jewish majority. By the expression 'on a peaceful basis', he did not mean in co-operation with the Arabs, but simply without having to commit American troops. At the end of his first presidential press conference, Truman stated that he had 'no desire to send 500,000 American soldiers there to make peace in Palestine.'[55] His major concern was a Jewish presence in the land – strong enough to make its own stand.

His official request to Prime Minister Attlee on 31 August 1945 to admit immediately 100,000 Jewish refugees into Palestine must be seen within this Zionist perspective. Truman adopted the same two goals which the Zionists had set for themselves on the eve of World War II: the attainment of a Jewish majority under the British Mandate in Palestine and the eventual establishment of an independent Jewish state.

Truman made no secret of his Zionist inclinations, even in his dealings with the Arabs. In a letter to Ibn Saud on 28 October 1946, he combines the humanitarian issue of Jewish refugees with the Zionist issue of the Jewish National Home. Justifying his request for the immediate admission of large numbers of Jewish refugees, he wrote:

> It was only natural that this government should favor at this time the entry into Palestine of considerable numbers of displaced Jews in Europe, not only that they may find shelter there, but also that they may contribute their talents and energies to the up-building of the Jewish National Home.[56]

In the same letter Truman also maintained that support of the Jewish National Home had been a consistent American policy. He did not consider that the admission of a considerable number of displaced Jews into Palestine represented 'an action hostile to the Arab people'.[57]

His letter to the Saudi King no longer followed the established pattern of trying to cover up the existing pro-Zionist position. On the contrary, an American President forthrightly declared American policy on Palestine to be in line with the Zionist aims. 'The letter became the first diplomatic document to a foreign power in which the United States . . . stated its historic obligations towards the Jewish homeland.'[58]

The occasion for this statement of intent was King Ibn Saud's response to Truman's rejection of the Morrison-Grady proposals, the last in a series of Anglo-American efforts to arrive at a joint solution of the Palestine problem. Ibn Saud accused Truman of altering 'the basic situation in Palestine in contradiction to previous promises'.[59] The Morrison-Grady plan in July 1941, had recommended a federal state for Palestine with separate Jewish and Arab cantons, a district of Jerusalem and a district of the Negev. The question of immediate Jewish immigration was made conditional upon Arab acceptance.

In rejecting the plan, Truman went along with the new Zionist strategy of accepting 'a viable Jewish state in an adequate area' of Palestine, the first move towards partition.

Partition or Trusteeship for Palestine? A Personal Setback for Truman

On 18 February 1947, the British Foreign Secretary, Ernest Bevin, announced his government's decision to submit the Palestine question to the newly organized United Nations and the first regular session of the General Assembly agreed to convene a special session to consider the problem. Truman spotted this move as the best way to advance his Palestine policy under the cover of international consensus.

Not only did he instruct the American UN delegation to vote for partition on 20 November 1947, but he also had American officials exert all their influence on third party governments to vote likewise. 'By direct order of the White House every form of pressure, direct and indirect was brought to bear by American officials upon countries outside the Moslem world that were known to be either uncertain or opposed to partition.'[60]

Truman's Palestine policy was a presidential policy unilaterally carried out despite the opposition of various government advisers and the over-whelmingly negative view of the Department of State. On 19 March 1948, the State Department did succeed in making its position public when the United States United Nations Ambassador, Warren Austin, presented the Security Council with a new American trusteeship proposal, a con-siderable retreat from the partition plan. Suddenly the realization of Jewish sovereignty in Palestine seemed far removed and Zionist pressure was seen to be much less effective than had been thought. The Zionists had failed to convince the American foreign policy élite that the creation of a Jewish state in Palestine was in the national interest of the United States.[61] In fact, the partitioning of Palestine and the setting up of a Jewish State was opposed by practically every member of the Foreign Service and of the State Department engaged with the Near East.

However, President Truman's commitment to partition, and the set-ting up of a Jewish state, on at least a portion of 'historical Palestine', remained irreversible. Only the day before Ambassador Warren's Security Council statement he had received Chaim Weizmann and as-sured him of his continued support for partition. 'They have made me out a liar and a double crosser,' he later told Clark Clifford, his White House Counsel, and asked him to set up an immediate investigation of how Austin had come to make his surprise statement. Truman's private diary records his anger over the incident:

> The State Department pulled the rug from under me today. I didn't expect that would happen. In Key West or enroute there from St. Croix I approved the speech and statement of policy by Senator Austin to the UN meeting. This morning I find that the State Department has reversed my Palestine policy. The first I know about it is what I see in the papers. Isn't that hell? I am now in the position of a liar and a double crosser. I have never felt so in my life. There are people on the third and fourth levels of the State Department who have always wanted to cut my throat. They've succeeded in doing it.[62]

The truth was deemed too humiliating and damaging to the presidency to be exposed to the American public. Truman's hands were therefore tied by the Austin statement especially after he discovered that both his Secretary of State, George Marshall, and his Under Secretary, Robert Lovell, had known in advance of the *de facto* policy reversal. To repudi-ate his own Secretary of State would have created the impression that the President had lost all control of the United States foreign policy.

Truman's way of salvaging the situation was to have Clark Clifford adapt the Austin trusteeship proposal to his own designs. The resulting document reaffirmed American support for partition in the long term and represented trusteeship only as an interim measure to prevent large-scale violence in Palestine when the British Mandate came to an end.[63]

And trusteeship at least had the virtue of minimizing the possible need to commit American troops to enforce partition.[64]

Between 19 March 1948, the day of the Austin statement, and 14 May 1948, the day of Truman's *de facto* recognition of the newly founded Jewish state, even the American Zionist establishment underestimated the depth and genuineness of Truman's own Zionism. All outward appearances led them to believe that the official American position was a retreat from partition. Perhaps the only one who had really grasped Truman's commitment to partition was Chaim Weizmann. Eddie Jacobson, Truman's old personal friend and business associate interceded personally with the President to arrange a meeting for Weizmann, and Weizmann later assured Jacobson of his continued trust in the American President: 'I do not believe that President Truman knew what was going to happen in the United Nations on Friday when he talked to me the day before.'[65]

The general misunderstanding of the circumstances surrounding the Austin statement only served to reinforce Truman's critics. The American Zionist leadership argued that the President's speedy recognition of the state of Israel in May 1948 was the outcome of effective pressure from the Zionist lobby, and was motivated by domestic political considerations to gain the Jewish vote in the elections of that year. To be sure, tremendous pressure was exerted by the Zionist organizations, non-Jewish Zionist organizations, Congress and the press.

Yet, as with Roosevelt, this pressure had resulted in the opposite of what the Zionists wanted, in some instances even undermining Truman's own Zionist enthusiasm. There exist many accounts of the President's very negative response to Zionist pressure. One of the reasons why Truman first refused to receive Chaim Weizmann early in 1948, was precisely his bitterness 'against Zionist leaders for unbecoming conduct and unusual discourtesies.'[66] After personally having pleaded with Truman to meet Weizmann, Eddie Jacobson wrote; 'But the President remained immovable. He replied how disrespectful and how mean certain Jewish leaders had been to him.'[67] Jacobson then continued his observation:

> I suddenly found myself thinking that my dear friend, the President of the United States, was at that moment as close to being an anti-Semite as a man could possibly be, and I was shocked that some of our own Jewish leaders should be responsible for Mr Truman's attitude.[68]

The greatest defeat of Jewish diplomacy since the 1939 White Paper was the American foreign policy establishment's retreat from partition. Zionist pressure, power and influence, though significant, could not decisively align American policy with Zionism in the Middle East in 1949. The same holds true of the common notion of the decisive 'Jewish vote' in the United States.

Truman's Zionism: Vote-Catching or Personal Conviction?

In the case of Truman's 1948 election, insiders refute the notion that the Jewish vote was the decisive factor in the President's Palestine policy. Congressman Sol Bloom argued that this Jewish vote as 'illusory' and that only 20% of this vote would be influenced by a Palestinian policy.[69] Furthermore, Clark Clifford in a memorandum submitted to Truman in November 1947 maintained that the Jewish vote was of no importance to the forthcoming presidential election campaign:

> The strategy recommended was based on the premise that if the Democrats won the South, and the states west of the Mississippi, we could afford to write off the electoral votes of New York, New Jersey, Illinois and Ohio with their large Jewish urban constituencies. I suggested that if we were to win the Jewish vote, it could be won on the Democratic Party's long-standing commitment to political and economic liberalism.[70]

Thus Truman's *de facto* recognition of Israel in 1948 – even before it had been officially requested by the Provisional Government of Israel – was no mere appeal to the Jewish vote nor even a tribute to the success of Zionist pressure. It was totally in accordance with Truman's own personal sentiments, themselves nothing less than Zionist. This was the moment of triumph of non-Jewish Zionism in America, although the decision to recognize the Jewish state was not that crucial in itself, since it was only the logical outcome of Truman's earlier commitment to partition of Palestine as the only solution.

Long before he had become President, Truman had shown a sympathetic understanding of Zionism. His own Southern Baptist background and training stressed the theme of the Jews' Restoration to Zion. The members of the Southern Baptist convention were the most enthusiastic pro-Zionist congregations, championing both the religious and historical claims of the Jews to the land of Palestine. Most Baptists were theologically conservative or even fundamentalist and tended to regard the creation of the Jewish state as the evident fulfilment of Biblical prophecies.[71]

There is no doubt that Truman's religious background played a great part in his later life. By and large a self-taught man, like Abraham Lincoln, he had educated himself in part through the Bible itself. 'As a student of the Bible he believed in the historic justification for a Jewish homeland and it was a conviction with him that the Balfour Declaration of 1917 constituted a solemn promise that fulfilled the age-old hopes and dreams of the Jewish people.'[72] Truman's autobiography, full of Biblical quotations and allusions, also indicates his marked tendency to dwell upon the Judaeo-Christian tradition.

As a Baptist, Truman sensed something profound and meaningful in the idea of Jewish Restoration. It was a known fact that his favourite Biblical passage was the Psalm 137, beginning 'By the rivers of Babylon, there we sat down, yea, we wept, when we remembered Zion'. Truman once confessed that he could never read the account of the giving of the Ten Commandments at Sinai without a tingle going down his spine. 'The fundamental basis of this nation's law,' he declared, 'was given to Moses on Mount Sinai.'[73]

When Eddie Jacobson introduced Truman in 1953 to an audience at a Jewish theological seminary as 'the man who helped create the State of Israel', Truman's response invoked the enduring Zionist theme of exile and Restoration: 'What do you mean "helped create"? I am Cyrus, I am Cyrus.' Who could forget that it was Cyrus who made possible the return of the Jews to Jerusalem from their exile in Babylon?[74]

American Public Opinion on the Zionist Case

American public opinion had been overwhelmingly in favour of the Balfour Declaration in 1906. Charles Israel Goldblatt surveyed a very representative sample of the general American press, including religious periodicals, for his study of the impact of the Balfour Declaration in America. He discovered that general Zionist sentiments were cross-national and to be found at all levels of the social strata. 'The only anti-Zion sentiments that could be detected in the press were those that emanated from statements by anti-Zionist Jewish personalities.'[75]

Congressional Support

Within the ranks of both Houses of Congress, approval of the declaration was astonishingly consistent. A survey conducted by the Zionist Organization in June 1918 regarding Congress's position on the declaration was published in 1919 by Reuben Fink.[76] Sixty-nine Senators and 231 Representatives answered the Zionist Organization's inquiry. All of them approved of the declaration. There was no division between Democrats and Republicans. Nor was there any indication that these members of Congress were influenced by the presence of a Jewish electorate and the so-called Jewish vote.

Their replies were genuinely Zionist in their phraseology as well as in their content. Many evoked the image of the Old Testament Hebrew prophets and cited Biblical prophecies to show that the Jews were to 'become the governing people of Palestine'. Others called for Jewish statehood and wanted to see action by the United States Government in line with the Balfour Declaration. The following quotation is a representative sample of this early Congressional Zionism:

> Just as Moses has led the Israelites out of bondage, so the Allies are now redeeming Judaea from the land of the unspeakable Turk, as a fitting finale to this World War. Judaea should be established as an independent nation, an independent sovereign, with power to govern itself and to forward and

complete its ideals of life. I feel that I am expressing the thoughts of the American people, and certainly of those with whom I have discussed this question, that the Government of the United States should use its proper influences in seeing that this Jewish state be created, wherefrom will emanate the teachings and principles of old Judaea.[77]

The climax of Congressional approval came in June 1922, when the United States Senate resolved 'that the United States of America favor the establishment in Palestine of the National Home for the Jewish people, in accordance with the provisions contained in the Declaration of the British Government of November 2, 1917, known as the Balfour Declaration.'[78] The powerful force behind the Resolution was the well-known chairman of the Foreign Relations Committee, the Republican Senator Henry Cabot Lodge of Massachusetts whose Zionism, deriving from his own religious persuasion, was enhanced by his anti-Turkish prejudices. In June 1922, during a speech in Boston, he made the following remarks:

> It seems to me that it was entirely becoming and commendable that the Jewish people in all portions of the world should desire to have a national home for such members of their race as wished to return to the country which was the cradle of their race and where they lived and labored for several thousand years . . . I never could accept in patience the thought that Jerusalem and Palestine should be under the control of the Moham-medans . . . that Jerusalem and Palestine, sacred to the Jews . . . a land profoundly holy to all the great Christian nations of the West, should remain permanently in the hands of the Turks, has seemed to me for many years one of the great plots on the face of civilization, which ought to be erased.[79]

On 30 June 1922, the House of Representatives followed suit and passed a similar resolution sponsored by Congressman Hamilton Fish. Their version of the resolution differed from that of the Senate by the inclusion of a preamble reading:

> Whereas the Jewish people have for many centuries believed in and yearned for the rebuilding of their ancient homeland;
> and
> Whereas owing to the outcome of the World War and their part therein, the Jewish people are to be enabled to recreate and organize a national home in the land of their fathers, which will give to the House of Israel its long-denied opportunity to re-establish a fruitful Jewish life and culture in the ancient Jewish land.[80]

To cement the consensus between both Houses of Congress on the issue of the 're-creation of Palestine as the National Home of the Jewish Race', both Houses unanimously passed the Lodge-Fish Resolution which, on 21 September, was signed by the new Republican President, Warren G. Harding.

The extent to which the Zionist idea had permeated American culture, decades before the appeareance of the 'Zionist lobby', is reflected in the general public's enthusiastic support for the British Mandate over Palestine and later its outspoken condemnation of Britain's inter-war policy in Palestine whenever it seemed to run counter to the 'spirit' of the Balfour Declaration.

On the Congressional level and the realm of public officialdom, Zionism became identical with Americanism in many minds. One Congressman from Pennsylvania echoed Brandeis when he said; 'Any Jew who is a Zionist must be not alone a better Jew, for that fact, but also a better American.'[81]

Non-Jewish Zionism was not confined to urban centres and States with large Jewish populations. Many Senators and Representatives who pressed the Zionist cause on Capitol Hill came from States where Jews made up only very small fractions of the total population, such as the Southern and Mid-Western States, where Protestant fundamentalism was particularly well entrenched.

The 1922 resolutions calling for a Jewish Homeland in Palestine were only the first link in a whole chain of Zionist resolutions and activities by the American Congress on behalf of Zionism. Another example was the 1944 resolution resolving 'that the United States shall use its good offices and take appropriate measures, to the end that the doors of Palestine shall be opened for free entry of Jews into that country, and that there shall be full opportunity for colonization so that the Jewish people may ultimately reconstitute Palestine as a free and democratic Jewish commonwealth.'[82] The text was *almost* identical to a Zionist resolution adopted by the Biltmore Conference, a conference convened in 1942 by the Emergency Council of the Zionist Organization of America. Discarding either partition or a bi-national state, this conference demanded the creation of a 'Jewish commonwealth' in the post-war era within the 'historic boundaries of Palestine'. But there is an interesting difference in the two texts: the Congressional resolution had substituted the word 'reconstitute' for the Biltmore resolution's 'to be established'. Non-Jewish Zionism thus, in the 20th Century, perpetuated the vision of a modern Jewish state as the fulfilment of Biblical prophecies, and created the impression that a Jewish state had once already existed in Palestine so that its Restoration was only proper.

The immediate occasion for this new congressional Zionist action was Great Britain's 1939 White Paper stipulating that Jewish immigration into Palestine was to be limited to 75,000 for the five-year period ending on 31 March 1944. All Jewish and non-Jewish Zionists denounced the White Paper as a virtual betrayal of the Balfour Declaration and Britain's Mandate trust. The speeches delivered on the floor of both Houses of

Congress in support of the resolutions have been compiled by Reuben Fink; an anlaysis of them clearly reveals the thinking for Congressional Zionism.[83] Most Congress members held a deep-rooted belief in the 'historic rightness of the Zionist goal'. Most Congress members generally thought that the Jews had 'an historic right not only to nationhood but also to the land of Palestine'. This lofty idea of 'historic right' was necessarily based on Biblical grounds. Thus the Representative from Massachusetts, Thomas J. Lane, proclaimed:

> To build the Kingdom of God, the Jews must not be dissipated among other nations. Always as ineffective minorities, as the Prophets preached, they must have their own nation – there to work and develop the ideal social order, as a model and example from which other nations may learn.[84]

Senator James J. Davis of Pennsylvania expounded the same theme when he said: 'there in Palestine . . . they can reassemble the remnants of their scattered nation, and can rebuild them once again into a united democratic state, under which they can master their own problems and create their own destiny as a proud and independent people.'[85]

The Zionist image of Palestine as the 'for centuries barren, desolate and forsaken country' to be 'transformed' by the Jews into the new garden of Eden, was the generally accepted view. The status of the indigenous Arab population is hardly even mentioned except as the cause of Palestine's backwardness and desolation. The Senator from Kentucky, Alben W. Barkley, who visited Palestine in 1937, enthusiastically reported the great improvement made by the Jews in land reclamation and maintained that a 'natural link' bound the Jews to Palestine.[86] Bennett Champ Clark, the Senator from Missouri, presented a similar description of the land:

> Following the proclamation of the mandate, Jews from all parts of Europe began moving into Palestine. Their coming converted a barren land into a literal Biblical land of 'milk and honey' . . . A barren country, desolate and forsaken for centuries, Palestine has been transformed by Jewish idealism and labor into a thriving country, and it stands today as the world's most marvelous example of reclamation.[87]

And Representative Everett M. Dirksen of Illinois maintained that the Jewish dream 'in the shape of a wilderness which has been made to blossom in accordance with the Biblical tradition as a land of milk and honey is now ready to receive additional millions of people.'[88]

Despite the general Congressional consensus on the resolutions in both houses, a joint resolution was not forthcoming in 1944 because the American Secretary of War, Henry L. Stimson, was opposed to it on military grounds. It was 'the considered judgement of the War Department that without reference to the merits of these resolutions, further action on them at this time would be prejudicial to the successful prosecution of the War.'[89]

Still, the United States had once again recorded its Zionist position on Palestine. The attitudes in both Houses of Congress reflected the opinions of the American people at large. During the inter-war period, the idea of political Zionism had penetrated all levels of society and goverment and even brought forth a leadership among non-Jews who were fully committed to the ultimate pursuance of the Zionist goal: a Jewish state in Palestine. The Jewish *halutzim* (pioneers) in Palestine were compared to the early American pioneers who opened up the land for settlement and civilization in the New World.

> The draining of marshes, the laying out of orchards, the gathering of crops, the planning of cities – all done by the Palestine 'halutzim' – evokes in the hearts of Americans the unforgettable picture of their own pioneering days in the not distant past. Even the hostility of certain Arab elements to Jewish colonization efforts recalls to Americans their own struggle to establish civilization in a sparsely settled land.[90]

An opinion poll in the mid-1930s showed that 76% of the Americans questioned were in favour of unlimited immigration and unrestricted settlement of Jews in Palestine; 7% were against; 8% were undecided and 5% had no opinion at all on the matter.[91]

The Palestine Committees
During the 1930s and 1940s various non-Jewish Palestine Committees were set up expressly to mobilize public opinion for the Zionist cause. All of these organizations were sponsored by well-known public personalities – clergymen, educators, as well as politicians. Most of them also coordinated their efforts with the Zionist Organization of America.

One of the first such organizations was the Pro-Palestine Federation of America, formed in 1930 by the Reverend Charles E. Russell and attracting mostly evangelical clergymen and Christian educators. Its publication *The Pro-Palestine Herald* defined the organization's principles as 'dedicated to the task of encouraging closer cooperation between Jew and Gentile, and also to the defense of the Jewish national home cause as defined in the Mandate for Palestine.'[92] In May 1936 this organization had requested the British Prime Minister, Stanley Baldwin, to allow increased Jewish immigration into Palestine maintaining that 'the restoration of the land of Israel to the Children of Israel is the guiding star in this great struggle for a better world and a better humanity.'[93]

During the same year the Pro-Palestinian Federation sponsored an American Christian Conference on the Jewish problem, held on 15 December 1936 in New York City. This conference was attended by over 200 public personalities from government and religious circles who jointly declared that it was the duty of all 'civilized communities' to help the Jewish refugees fleeing from persecution in Germany and Eastern Europe to get to Palestine, 'their natural place of refuge'.[94]

Another, more secular, non-Jewish group was organized in May 1932 under the name of the American Palestine Committee. This organization included among its original founding members 10 senators and 18 members of the House of Representatives as well as several Cabinet officials.

The object of the Committee was 'to organize more effectively our endeavours as non-Jews to cooperate with this great idealistic cause' and 'to foster the development of an informed public opinion in the United States among non-Jews concerning Zionist activities, purposes and achievements in Palestine'. This Committee remained rather dormant, until it was reconstituted in April 1941 by Senators Robert M. Wagner of New York and Charles F. McNary of Oregon. On 28 March 1941, the Office of Senator Wagner issued a statement to the press entitled 'US Cabinet Members, Members of Congress Governors, Noted Educators and Church and Civil Leaders Join in Establishing Body to Encourage Reconstruction of the Jewish Homeland in Palestine'.[95] This document also listed the names of the Committee's members, including over 700 distinguished leaders in all spheres of American public life. In a speech delivered in connection with the 24th anniversary celebration of the Balfour Declaration at Carnegie Hall, New York, on 1 November 1941, Senator Wagner outlined this Committee's principle as follows:

> The American Palestine Committee stands committed to the principles laid down in the Balfour Declaration and reaffirmed by congressional resolutions and presidential statements to the present day. We declare that Palestine is an important bulwark on the world democratic front, and that the Jewish national home in Palestine shall be an important and integral part of the world order that must follow the victory . . .[96]

In 1946, just in time to labour for the creation of a Jewish state in Palestine, the American Palestine Committee and the Christian Council on Palestine merged and formed the American Christian Palestine Committee, combining the 'political' and the 'spiritual' branches of Christian American Zionism. This new organization conducted a vigorous and systematic campaign allowing American public opinion to influence government policy in favour of a Jewish state in Palestine. Through publications, seminars, lecture tours, public advertisement, its members tried to spread information about Palestine and sway the American public toward the Zionist view.

Liberal Theologians
The Christian Council on Palestine had been founded in 1942 by such noted theologians as Dr. Henry A. Atkinson, Professor Reinhold Niebuhr, Paul Tillich, Daniel A. Poling and William F. Albright with the active support of the American Zionist Movement.[97]

Reinhold Niebuhr, Professor of Social Ethics at Union Theological Seminary, and the foremost representative of liberal American theology justified his Zionism in a two-part article in *The Nation* in 1941.[98] Niebuhr saw the basic Jewish dilemma as their open persecution in Germany and Eastern Europe coupled with their inability to find a haven in the West because of the existing restrictive immigration laws. He thus recognized the right of the Jews to constitute a unique and separate people and consequently to have the 'moral right' to a collective national survival in Palestine. 'Under the compulsion of their great need' the Jews were to have a higher claim to Palestine than the Arab population who, nevertheless, were to be justly compensated for their loss of rights in the land of Palestine. Niebuhr admitted that there existed no just solutions to the problem of conflicting rights in Palestine:

> There is in fact no solution to any political problem. The fact however that the Arabs have a vast hinterland in the Middle East, and the fact that the Jews have nowhere to go, establishes the relative justice of their claims and of their cause . . . Arab sovereignty over a portion of the debated territory must undoubtedly be sacrificed for the sake of establishing a world Jewish homeland.[99]

The only solution Niebuhr could envisage in order to solve the 'Jewish problem' was a political existence for the Jews in a Jewish state. A binational Palestinian state was automatically ruled out. Protestant America, as best represented by Niebuhr, had now added the moral and pragmatic argument to its spiritual one in its defence of a Jewish Palestine. The new pragmatic approach had a special appeal to Americans for 'to say that it is internationally unethical to take Palestine away from the Arabs and give it to the Jews has about as much rightness to it as to say Europeans had no right to settle on what has become the great continent of America, because it happened to be peopled by the American Indians.'[100]

The many 'Christian' committees and organizations which sprang up in the years before and during World War II wielded considerable influence. Themselves deeply committed Zionists, they also found American Protestantism a milieu already favourable to Zionist ends, and the liberal theologians like Niebuhr, however influential, represented only one end of the spectrum. The largest religious group in the United States, comprising well over 200 different denominations, Protestantism represented perhaps the most effective socializing agent in American culture. Of course, Zionism was not equally strong in all Protestant churches. The Presbyterian, Episcopalian and Methodist churches, were critical of the basic premises of political Zionism.[101] Support was most commonly found in the theologically conservative and fundamentalist American liberal theology, as was the case with Reinhold Niebuhr. Daniel Poling, the editor of the influential *Christian Herald*, said in his defence of Zionism before the Anglo-American Committee of Inquiry:

Christians believe overwhelmingly . . . that Palestine was divinely selected as the site of the Jewish nation . . . I am trying as the representative of the Christian groups to present what is, we believe, the Christian viewpoint . . . I may say this viewpoint has been and is now being with increasing fervor, expressed by representatives of the Evangelical Christian peoples of this country.[102]

The American Labour Movement

On the level of organized American civic life, the American labour movement had for a long time been favourable to Zionism and since 1917 effectively has added its weight in favour of Zionism. The American Federation of Labor (AFL) was one of the first groups to endorse the Balfour Declaration. During its 37th Annual Convention on 19 November 1917 in Buffalo, the AFL passed a resolution recognizing 'the legitimate claims of the Jewish people for the establishment of a national homeland in Palestine on a basis of self-government.'[103]

In fact the American Federation of Labor had arrived at a Zionist perspective long before. When Russian and East European Jews faced persecution at the turn of the century, the AFL clearly linked the general oppression of the Jews to the absence of a Jewish national existence in a national home. The victims of oppression and persecution were regarded as victimized by their own lack of statehood. This was in line with the labour movement's traditional stand on the nationality question, favouring national autonomy or independence for all oppressed minorities and nationalities. Domestically this policy had served a specific purpose, since it provided a vehicle for placating domestic ethnic groups within the movement itself.

Accordingly, the AFL in 1917 also expressed its 'unqualified' support for the American Government's decision to enter World War I with the plea 'to secure for the small nationalities the right to live their own lives on their own soil, and to develop their own culture under free national auspices.'[104] The doctrine of self-determination was also applied to the Jews.

This concern for Jewish 'national rights' within the ranks of the American labour movement at this early stage is attributable to a predominantly non-Jewish leadership within the movement. Jewish trade unions were generally opposed to Zionism. During the deliberations of the 1917 Buffalo Convention, the two most prominent Jewish trade union leaders, Benjamin Schlesing, President of the International Ladies' Garment Workers' Union, and Max Zaritsky, Assistant General Secretary of the United Clothes, Hat and Cap Makers of North America, vigorously spoke out against Zionism and opposed the final resolution.[105] The resolution was, however, passed thanks to the efforts of the non-Jewish Zionists.

This early commitment to a Jewish Homeland in Palestine by the American labour movement was not an isolated incident. It marked the beginning of a permanent and most intimate working relationship between Zionism and organized labour. America's foremost labour leaders, William Green (AFL), Philip Murray (CIO), George Meany (AFL-CIO) gave their support to the Zionist cause and used their positions of influence to advance Zionism not only among the labour constituencies but also at government level.

Notes

1. Lecky.
2. As quoted in Louis I. Newman, *Jewish Influence on Christian Reform Movements* (New York, 1966), p. 634. See also Truman Nelson, 'The Puritans of Massachusetts: From Egypt to the Promised Land', *Judaism*, Vol. 16, No. 2, Spring 1967.
3. See Richard B. Morris, 'Civil Liberties and the Jewish Tradition in Early America', *Publications of the American Jewish Historical Society*, Vol. 66, No. 2, September 1956.
4. Samuel H. Levine, 'Palestine in the Literature of the United States to 1867', in Isidore S. Meyer (ed.), *Early History of Zionism in America* (New York, 1958) pp. 21–2.
5. Selig Adler, 'America and the Holy Land: A Colloquim', *American Jewish Historical Quarterly*, Vol. 62, No. 1, September 1972, p. 40.
6. Louis Gasper, *The Fundamentalist Movement* (The Hague, 1963), p. 7.
7. See Chapter Two for a discussion of the Catholic Church's pre-Reformation system of Biblical exegesis.
8. Charles C. Ryrie, *Dispensationalism Today* (Chicago, 1965), pp. 138ff.
9. Clarence B. Bass, *Backgrounds to Dispensationalism* (Grand Rapids, Michigan, 1960), p. 150.
10. Berth M. Lindbert, *A God-Filled Life: the Story of W. E. Blackstone* (American Missionary Society, n.d.); see also *Near East Report*, Vol. 10, No. 4, 23 February 1966, pp. 14–15.
11. W. M. Smith, 'Signs of the Times', *Moody Monthly*, August 1966, p. 5.
12. *America-Israel Bulletin*, Vol. 4, No. 1, October 1965.
13. Reuben Fink, *America and Palestine* (New York, 1945), pp. 20–1.
14. *Near East Report*, Vol. 10, No. 4, 23 February 1966.
15. Fink, op. cit., p. 21.
16. For a complete list of the signatories, see Fink, op. cit., pp. 21–2.
17. This novel was most favourably reviewed by *The Nation*, Vol. 23, 12 October 1876, pp. 230–1. Some parts of this novel were also reprinted in *Harper's Magazine*, Vol. 52, 1876.
18. See, for example, Conder's articles in *Review of Reviews*, Vol. 17, 1898, p. 739; see also his 'Exploration in Palestine', *Literary Digest*, Vol. 60, 22 September 1894, pp. 619–20.
19. 'Present State of the Jewish People in Learning and Culture', *North American Review*, Vol. 83, October 1856, pp. 351–81.
20. Cyrus Adler and Aaron M. Margalith, *With Firmness to the Right: American Diplomatic Action Affecting Jews, 1840–1945* (New York, 1946), pp. 219–20.

21. Wilson to Stephen Wise, Wilson Papers, Library of Congress, Washington D.C., File VI, No. 618.
22. Selig Adler, 'The Palestine Question in the Wilson Era', *Journal of Jewish Social Studies*, Vol. 10, No. 4, 1948, pp. 304–44.
23. Leonard Stein, *The Balfour Declaration*, op. cit.
24. See Josephus Daniels, *The Wilson Era: Years of War and After, 1917–192.* (Chapel Hill, 1946), Chapter 23.
25. Stephen S. Wise, *The Challenging Years: The Autobiography of Stephen Wise* (New York, 1949), pp. 186–7.
26. Ray Stannard Baker, *Woodrow Wilson and World Settlement* (New York 1932), Vol. 2, pp. 205ff.
27. US Department of State, Papers Relating to the Foreign Relations of the United States, *The Lansing Papers, 1914–1920* (Washington, 1940), Vol. 2, p. 71.
28. Stein, op. cit., p. 595.
29. Frankfurter to Lansing, 23 May 1919, General Record of the Department of State, File No. 867 N. 01/75.
30. *New York Times*, 3 March 1919; see also Mack to Lansing, 28 March 1919, General Record of the Department of State, File F.W. 867 N. 00/50.
31. David Hunter Miller, *My Diary at the Conference of Paris: Policy Toward Palestine* (New York, 1924), Vol. 4, pp. 263–4.
32. Ibid.
33. Fink, op. cit., p. 87.
34. Ibid.
35. Ibid., p. 88.
36. Ibid.
37. Hyman B. Grinstein in *America and the Holy Land*, op. cit., p. 17.
38. Goldman to Weizmann, 20 June 1939, Central Zionist Archives, Jerusalem, S 25/237.
39. Quoted in Selig Adler, *America and the Holy Land: A Colloquium*, op. cit., p. 19.
40. 'President on Palestine', *New York Times*, 29 March 1944. Roosevelt was also responsible for stalling in Congress the joint resolution referred to later in this chapter.
41. Nahum Goldmann to the Jewish Agency, 27 April 1944, Central Zionist Archives, Jerusalem, Z 5/388.
42. The Republican Party on 27 June 1944 adopted the following Palestine plank 'calling for the opening of Palestine . . . to unrestricted immigration and land ownership so that in accordance with the full intent and purpose of the Balfour Declaration of 1917 and the resolution of the Republican Congress of 1922, Palestine may be constituted as a free and democratic commonwealth.' See *Jewish Telegraphic Agency Bulletin*, 29 June 1944, p. 3.
43. Ibid., 27 December 1944, Z 5/394.
44. See Herbert Parzen, 'The Roosevelt Palestine Policy, 1943–1945, An Exercise in Dual Diplomacy', *American Jewish Archives*, Vol. 26, No. 1, April 1974, pp. 47–50.
45. Ibid., p. 50. This message was transmitted through Senator Wagner to the 47th annual convention of the Zionist Organization of America. It is also found in the Wagner Papers at the Georgetown University Library, Washington, D.C.

46. Selig Adler, 'Franklin D. Roosevelt and Zionism: The Wartime Record', *Judaism*, Vol. 21, No. 3, Summer 1972, pp. 265–76; see also Irvin Oder, 'The United States in Search of a Policy: Franklin D. Roosevelt and Palestine', *Review of Politics*, Vol. 24, No. 3, July 1962, pp. 320–41.
47. Christopher Sykes, *Two Studies in Virtue* (London, 1953), pp. 199–200.
48. Richard Stevens, *American Zionism and US Foreign Policy, 1942–1947* (Beirut, 1970), p. 45. Until 1923–24 the United States had pursued a free immigration policy. But then the isolationist-controlled Congress under the leadership of Henry Cabot Lodge enacted new immigration laws based on a quota system favouring immigrants from Western and Northern European states over those of Eastern and Southern Europe, a severe blow for Jews who generally came from Eastern Europe. Non-European states were virtually left out of the new quota system.
49. While returning to the United States after the Yalta Conference and his subsequent meeting with Ibn Saud, Roosevelt remarked to Stettinius that '. . . he must have a conference with congressional leaders and re-examine our entire policy in Palestine. He was now convinced, he added, that if nature took its course there would be bloodshed between the Arabs and Jews. Some formula not yet discovered would have to prevent this warfare, he concluded.' See Edward R. Stettinius, *Roosevelt and the Russians* (Garden City, New York, 1949), pp. 289–90.
50. See John Snersinger, *Truman, the Jewish Vote and the Creation of Israel* (Stanford, 1974); see also Nadav Safran, *The United States and Israel* (Cambridge, Mass., 1963), p. 43.
51. H. B. Westerfield, a member of the Anglo-American Committee of Inquiry, was convinced that Truman's decision to recognize Israel was taken in an attempt to secure the 'Jewish vote' for the 1948 elections. See his *Foreign Policy and Party Politics* (New Haven, 1955), pp. 227ff. See also Kermit Roosevelt, 'The Partition of Palestine: A Lesson in Pressure Politics', *Middle East Journal*, January 1948, pp. 1–16, esp. p. 4.
52. Clark M. Clifford, 'Factors Influencing President Truman's Decision to Support Partition and Recognize the State of Israel', American Historical Association, Washington, D.C., 28 December 1976, typescript. Clifford himself was a faithful supporter of Zionism.
53. Press Conference of 16 August 1945, in *Public Papers of the Presidents of the United States: Harry S. Truman, 1945* (Washington, 1961), p. 228.
54. Harry S. Truman, *Memoirs* (Garden City, New York, 1956), Vol II: Years of Trial and Hope, p. 157.
55. Ibid.
56. Public Papers of the Presidents of the United States: Harry S. Truman, op. cit., pp. 467–9.
57. Ibid.
58. Frank E. Manuel, *The Realities of American-Palestine Relations* (New York, 1949), p. 328.
59. Text of Ibn Saud's letter in *Department of State Bulletin*, Vol. 15, No. 384, 10 November 1946, pp. 848ff.
60. Sumner Welles, *We Need Not Fail* (Boston, 1948), p. 63. With regard to American pressure upon Latin American states to vote in favour of partition, see Kermit Roosevelt, op. cit., pp. 1–16.
61. See Zvi Ganin, The Limits of American Jewish Political Power: America's

Retreat from Partition', *Jewish Social Studies*, Vol. 39, Nos. 1–2.
62. Margaret Truman, *Harry S. Truman* (New York, 1973), p. 388. In his ow Memoirs, Truman wrote that 'the trusteeship idea was at odds with m attitude and the policy I had laid down.' Ibid., p. 163.
63. Clark Clifford in his address to the American Historical Association on 2 December 1976 gives a most detailed account of this critical period in Marc 1948. Clifford, himself deeply committed to Zionism, very skilfully re inforced the President's own Zionist predispositions.
64. In the aftermath of the UN Partition vote in the General Assembly th majority in Truman's cabinet became convinced that partition could b carried out only by the use of force, which implied to them the deployment o American forces. This was an unthinkable possibility. First, it was seen t play into the hands of the Soviets and second, the US was logistically unabl to supply the estimated 80,000 to 160,000 men needed to implement parti tion. For a discussion of both objections see Millis (ed.), *The Forresta Diaries* and the *New York Times*, 20 January 1948.
65. Eddie Jacobson's account of his role in making possible Weizmann's meetin with President Truman is reprinted in 'Two Presidents and a Haberdasher 1948', *American Jewish Archives*, Vol. 20, No. 1, April 1968, pp. 4–15.
66. Ibid., p. 5.
67. Ibid., p. 6.
68. Ibid. See also Truman's *Memoirs*, op. cit., Vol. 2, p. 160.
69. As quoted in Ganin, op. cit., p. 8.
70. Clifford, op. cit., p. 19.
71. See, for example, 'Creation of a Jewish State', *Watchman-Examiner*, Vol 36, No. 23, 3 June 1948, p. 567. This was an influential Baptist periodical.
72. Clifford, op. cit., p.20.
73. See Adler, op. cit., pp. 282–3.
74. As recorded in Moshe Davis, *America and the Holy Land* (1978), p. 13.
75. Charles Israel Goldblatt, 'The Impact of the Balfour Declaration i America', *American Jewish Historical Quarterly*, Vol. 57, June 1968, p. 463.
76. Reuben Fink, *The American War Congress and Zionism* (New York, 1919).
77. Statement by the representative of Indiana, William E. Cox, cited in Fink *American War Congress*, op. cit.
78. *Congressional Record*, Vol. 62, Part 6, p. 6240.
79. Henry Cabot Lodge, speech reported in *New Palestine*, Vol. 2, 26 May 1922 p. 330.
80. *Congressional Record*, 30 June 1922, pp. 9794–9820; also 3 May 1922, pp. 6240, 6289 and 18 April 1922, p. 5693.
81. As quoted in Goldblatt, op. cit., p. 495.
82. Senate Resolution 247, introduced by Senator Robert F. Wagner of New York and Senator Robert A. Taft of Ohio on 1 February 1944, 79th Congress, 2nd session, House Resolution 418, introduced by Representative Rassulf Compton of Connecticut and Representative James A. Wright of Pennsylvania on 27 January 1944. See *Congressional Record*, Vol. 90, Part 1, p. 586.
83. Reuben Fink, *America and Palestine*, op. cit., pp. 90–389.
84. Ibid., p. 194.
85. Ibid., p. 212, speech delivered on the floor of the US Senate on 8 February 1944.

86. Ibid., pp. 97–100, speech delivered on the floor of the US Senate, 1 March 1944.
87. Ibid., p. 109, speech delivered on the floor of the US Senate, 28 March 1944.
88. Ibid., p. 284.
89. Letter by Secretary of War, Henry L. Stimson, to the Hon. Sol Bloom, Chairman, Foreign Affairs Committee, House of Representatives, Washington, D.C.
90. Reuben Fink, *America and Palestine*, op. cit., pp. 45–6.
91. As listed in Hadley Cantril (ed.), *Public Opinion, 1935–1936* (Princeton, 1951), p. 386.
92. A. B. Elias, 'Christian Cooperation in the Restoration of Zion', *Pro-Palestine Herald*, Vol. 3, Nos. 3–4, pp. 17–18.
93. Report in *New Palestine*, 4 June 1936, p. 9.
94. Ibid., 18 December 1936, p. 1.
95. Wagner Papers, Georgetown University Library, Washington, D.C., Box 194, Folder 49, 1941, Document No. 13, including a complete list of all the original members of the Committee.
96. Ibid., Document No. 23.
97. See Carl Hermann Voss, 'Christians and Zionism in the United States', *The Palestine Yearbook*, Vol. 2, July 1945–September 1946, pp. 493–500.
98. Reinhold Niebuhr, *The Nation*, 21 February 1942, pp. 214–6 and 28 February 1942, pp. 253–5.
99. Niebuhr testified in 1946 before the Anglo-American Committee of Inquiry in Washington on behalf of the Christian Council on Palestine. See US Department of State, *Hearings of the Anglo-American Committee of Inquiry*, 14 January 1946, p. 147.
100. M. Wakefield, 'Palestine – The Human Side', *Advance*, Vol. 138, No. 9, September 1946, p. 26.
101. See William L. Burton, 'Protestant America and the Rebirth of Israel', *Jewish Social Studies*, Vol. 26, No. 4, October 1964, pp. 203–14; see also Herzl Fishman, *American Protestantism and the Jewish State* (Detroit, 1973).
102. United States Department of State, *Hearings*, op. cit., p. 101.
103. See *Report of the AFL Executive Council concerning American Alliance for Labor and Democracy*, Report of Proceedings of the 37th Annual Convention of the AFL, 1917, p. 100.
104. Ibid.
105. Sheila Stern Polishook, 'The American Federation of Labor, Zionism and the First World War', *American Jewish Historical Quarterly*, Vol. 65, No. 3, March 1976, pp. 228–44.

7. Zionism and the Modern Racisms

When on 10 November 1975 the United Nations General Assembly in its Resolution 3379 (XXX) characterized Zionism as 'a form of racism and racial discrimination' the Western world was most shocked. Surely Zionism stood for just the opposite: a form of nationalism, the national liberation movement of the Jewish people. The noted Middle Eastern scholar, Bernard Lewis, summarized the position:

> Zionism is basically not a racial movement but a form of nationalism or, to use the current nomenclature, a national liberation movement. Like other such movements, it combines various currents, some springing from tradition and necessity, others carried on the winds of international change and fashion. Most important among the former is the Jewish religion itself, with its recurring stress on Zion, Jerusalem and the Holy Land, and with the interwoven and recurring themes of bondage and liberation, of exile and return. The messianism and movements of religious revival which arose among Jews from the seventeenth century also made an important contribution to the genesis of this movement.[1]

Like many other Zionist apologists, Bernard Lewis accepted the Zionist mythology surrounding Israel and perpetuated the idea that secular political Zionism represents the fulfilment of the spiritual beliefs of Judaism.

A clear understanding of the phenomenon of non-Jewish Zionism in its full historical perspective enables us to 'demythologize' Zionism and see it for what it originally was – a product of European racist and colonial philosophies. It was not even in its origins a distinctively Jewish movement, encountering opposition, on the one hand, from religious Jews who repudiated the profane attempt to give geographical dimensions to a spiritual kingdom and, on the other, from Jewish civil rights workers seeking full emancipation and open immigration policies.

Zionist colonization of Palestine was a part of the larger European colonial movement at the turn of this century. Zionism, like anti-Semitism, Nazism and apartheid, was an integral part of Western intellectual and political culture with roots far deeper than the 19th and 20th

Centuries. Zionism in its non-Jewish manifestation unmistakably exposes the close association that binds together Zionism with racism, anti-Semitism, Nazism and apartheid.

Zionism, Anti-Semitism and Racism

Early Zionists like Herzl and Weizmann assumed anti-Semitism to be a natural state of affairs, a normal, almost rational reaction of the non-Jew to the 'abnormal, absurd and perverse situation of the Jewish people in the Diaspora.'[2] And Arnold Toynbee has suggested that non-Jewish Zionism may spring from guilt about sub-conscious anti-Semitism, thus intimately connecting Zionism and anti-Semitism in psychological terms.[3] In fact, as we have seen, the history of non-Jewish Zionism is studded with examples of quite consciously anti-Semitic proponents of Zionism. In Chapter One we quoted Meinertzhagen, the chief political officer for Palestine and Syria on General Allenby's staff, and an ardent Zionist. Here is another example of his openly admitted anti-Semitism:

> I am also imbued with anti-Semitic feelings, and would wish that Zionism could be divorced from Jewish nationality. But it cannot, and I prefer to accept it as it is, than oppose it on grounds of immaterial prejudices.[4]

This is the same man who said:

> My views on Zionism are those of an ardent Zionist. The reasons which induced in me a fascination for Zionism are many and complex, but in the main were governed by the unsatisfactory state of the Jews in the world, the great sentimental attraction of re-establishing a race after banishment of 2,000 years, which is not without its scientific interest, and the conviction that Jewish brains and money could, when backed by such a potent idea as Zionism, give to Palestine that impetus in industrial development which it so sorely needs after lying fallow since the beginning of the world.[5]

This alliance between anti-Semitism and Zionism is not just a matter of psychology, rational or subconscious. In theory as well as in practice, Zionism and anti-Semitism operate on the same plane, complementing and reinforcing each other.

Meinertzhagen was of course aware of the strategic importance of Palestine:

> In fact, it is no exaggeration to say that, for the future, a strong and friendly Palestine is vital to the future strategic security of the British Commonwealth. It can never be strong and healthy under divided control, still less under any form of Arab government.[6]

But the connection between anti-Semitism and non-Jewish Zionism goes deeper than this. It is not a mere balancing of interests against prejudices. Non-Jewish Zionism was based on an almost romantic veneration of the Jews as a race, beneath the surface of which lay more negative attitudes towards the Jews as a people. Non-Jewish Zionists like Balfour, Lloyd George or Meinertzhagen strongly believed in the uniqueness of the Jews as a race. It is this perception of their uniqueness that informed immigration quotas to Britain as strongly as nationalist claims to Palestine.

At the level of practical policies, Theodor Herzl regarded the anti-Semites as his most dependable friends and allies. Rather than attack and denounce anti-Semitism, Herzl declared that 'the anti-Semites will be our most dependable friends, the anti-Semitic countries our allies.'[7] Another Zionist theoretician, Jacob Klatzkin, actually welcomed anti-Semitism and applauded the ghettoization of the Jews in Tsarist Russia.[8]

It is also this theory of the uniqueness of the Jewish race which lies behind the deep suspicion felt by Jewish and non-Jewish Zionists alike for assimilated Jews such as Lord Montagu, Lucien Wolf or Lord Reading. We shall let Meinertzhagen speak for this sentiment as well:

> But if the Jews are going to gain a predominating influence in this country, in professions, in trades, in universities and museums, in finance and as landowners, then of course we shall have to act against them, but it will not take the form of the concentration camp.[9]

Racist tendencies in 19th Century philosophy were based on the central idea that a certain race of people is naturally superior to others. Zionism, because of its essential claim that the Jews make up a 'Chosen Race' which should not be assimilated with other 'inferior races', is thus only one manifestation of this kind of racism.

Racist ideas, including those of Zionism, anti-Semitism and Nazism, did not crop up in a vacuum. They were linked to specific historical forces prevailing in society which demanded legitimization. The development of racism in all its different forms of expression corresponded to the emergence and expansion of European imperialism based on the colonization of the non-European world. Racism and its underlying philosophy were used to legitimize the colonial system and to provide ideological support for the imperial process. 'The White man's burden' was to civilize the 'backward' nations incapable of helping themselves.

Non-Jewish Zionists held a specific racist outlook on the Jews which was deeply rooted in the 19th Century colonial racial myth. The Jews were glorified as a chosen race only outside the non-Jewish Christian environment. Jewish superiority was recognized only in correlation to Arab inferiority, with Jewish virtues commonly lauded as the antithesis of Arab vices. In Meinertzhagen's own words 'intelligence was a Jewish virtue and intrigue was an Arab vice'.[10] He described the Jews as 'virile, brave, determined and intelligent' and the Arabs as 'decadent, stupid, dishonest and producing little beyond eccentrics influenced by the romance and silence of the desert'.[11]

With the advent of British imperialist expansion into the Middle East, the native Arabs offered an inevitable racist target because of their different religion, culture, colour and above all their opposition to foreign intrusion. For Palestine, the Jews therefore meant 'progress' and the 'up-setting of modern government'. The Arab population came to stand for 'stagnation, immorality, rotten government, corrupt and dishonest society'.[12]

Non-Jewish Zionists consistently charged that the Arabs were a retrograde people, responsible for the decline of Palestine and the whole Middle East. This racist view set the stage for colonial settlement in Palestine by the Jews. Once again, Meinertzhagen puts this plainly:

> The Palestine Arab will never reach the Jewish standard of ability in any sense. The Jew will always be on top and he means to be there. He looks forward to a Jewish state in Palestine with sovereign rights, a real National Home and not a sham Jewish-Arab confederation . . . The Jew, however small his voice, however mild his manner, will in the end be heard and he will succeed. The Arab will trumpet and bluster, others in Europe and America will sing his praises if the local orchestra breaks down, but he will remain where he is and has for ever been, an inhabitant of the east, nurturing stagnant ideas and seeing no further than the narrow doctrines of Mohammed.[13]

As we have seen, the same anti-Arab notions and prejudices were also entertained by the American non-Jewish Zionists. Recall how Senator Lodge 'could never accept in patience the thought that Jerusalem and Palestine should be under the control of the Mohammedans', and that Arab control over Palestine seemed to him 'one of the great blots on the face of civilization which ought to be erased'.[14] Clark Clifford, two decades later in a memo to President Truman, urged active support for the partition of Palestine, warning that 'the United States appears in the ridiculous role of trembling before threats of a few nomadic desert tribes.'[15] The Jews, on the other hand, were to be relied upon since their society was 'wholly the product of free enterprise' and a Jewish Palestine 'would have the strongest possible orientation to the United States', representing a strong bulwark against Communism.[16]

With non-Jewish Zionism on the rise, a whole complex of prejudices against the Arabs was systematically fostered in the consciousness of the Western people. Racial and cultural stereotypes were created which are still thriving in the West. The Jews were the embodiment of most of the Western virtues. They were to settle in Palestine on behalf of civilization. Zionism's first task was to 'civilize and modernize Palestine' as an outpost of civilization – in the face of savagery, as Herzl himself once declared.[17]

On the whole, the belief in the Jewish race and its racial distinctiveness had stronger protagonists among non-Jews than among Western Jews themselves. The foremost representative of Anglo-Jewry, Lord Edwin Samuel Montagu, in August 1917, at the time of the deliberations on the Balfour Declaration, submitted a memorandum to the British Cabinet stating his view that 'the policy of His Majesty's Government is anti-Semitic in result and will prove a rallying ground for anti-Semites in every country of the world.'[18] Lord Montagu unequivocally rejected the Zionist idea of a distinct Jewish nation and denounced Zionism as 'a mischievous political creed', a form of anti-Semitism. Indirectly he also accused the British non-Jewish Zionists (Balfour, Lloyd George, Lord Milner, Mark Sykes et al) of being secret anti-Semites who wanted to rid the Jews of their newly acquired emancipated status in the civil and political life of England.

Jews in England working towards the goal of complete emancipation were often directly opposed by non-Jewish Zionists. Thus, we saw that Lord Shaftesbury spoke against the 1858 Emancipation Act on the ground that it would violate so-called religious principles. In 1905 Balfour fought for the passage of the Aliens Act restricting Jewish immigration from Eastern Europe because of the 'undoubted evils that had fallen upon the country from an immigration which was largely Jewish'.[19] Balfour, 12 years later hailed as a great Zionist, came under attack at the 7th Zionist Congress for the unveiled anti-Semitism of his anti-Jewish immigration policy. The English delegate to the Congress, M. Shire, charged him with 'open anti-Semitism against the whole Jewish people'.[20]

Lloyd George, too, was known for his mixed feelings when it came to the role of the Jews in England. For example, some of his speeches in Parliament on the South African War were coloured with ordinary vulgar anti-Semitism. 'Even in the debate in Parliament in 1904 on the East Africa offer to the Zionists he had not been able to resist a gibe at the Jews.'[21] He addressed his Jewish party colleague, Sir Alfred Mond, as 'another notorious member of his race'.[22] His hypocritical dual stance on the Jews was also noticed by Prime Minister Asquith when Lloyd George was Minister of Munitions. In his memoirs Asquith described Lloyd George as the only other partisan of Herbert Samuel's Memorandum on the Future of Palestine 'who I need not say does not care a damn for the Jews or their past or their future . . .'[23]

Anti-Semitism was also a component of Mark Sykes' attraction to Zionism. His 'distaste for Jews' was reflected in his early mistrust of Zionism. Yet once exposed to Zionism's true meaning, this fervent believer in nationalism and imperialism began to see Zionism in a different light.[24] The Zionist exhaltation of the 'real Hebrew' as against the Anglicized assimilated Jew made him especially receptive to this new ideology. Like the other non-Jewish Zionists, he, too, 'had no liking for the hybrid type of assimilating Jew'.[25] Instead he preferred the Jew who, like Chaim Weizmann, asserted his racial distinctiveness and proudly displayed his separate national consciousness. Only after his personal acquaintance with the Jewish Zionist leader did Mark Sykes begin to work for the Zionist goal in Palestine.

The synonymity of Zionism and anti-Semitism also accounts for the often contradictory assessments of Woodrow Wilson's adviser, Colonel House. Some Zionists lauded him as a friend of Zionism and the force behind President Wilson's own Zionist policies. Other Zionists accused him of working against Zionism because of his open anti-Semitic prejudices,[26] as displayed, for instance, in his correspondence with Wilson. And in the 1930s when Hitler turned against the Jews in Germany, House reportedly told the American Ambassador to Berlin: 'They [the Nazis] are clearly wrong and even terrible, but the Jews should not be allowed to dominate the economic and intellectual life in Berlin as they have done for a long time.'[27]

Zionism and Nazism

The affinity between Zionism and anti-Semitism also linked Zionism and Nazism: the ideological and political fathers of Nazism shared the premises with the Zionists. The concept of the 'chosen race' in Nazism differed from the concept of the 'chosen race' in Zionism only in the identity of this race; Aryan or Jewish. Both Jewish and non-Jewish Zionists generally felt no special aversion towards Nazism and its anti-Semitic policies and practices. In fact, Weizmann once asked Richard Meinertzhagen, to explain Zionism and its implications for Hitler whom he believed to be 'not antagonistic to Zionism'.[28] Meinertzhagen himself was most understanding of Nazi anti-Semitism. He wrote:

> My own view is that the German has a perfect right to treat the Jew as an alien and deny him German citizenship. He even has the right to expel him from Germany; but it must be done decently and with justice . . . Jews in Germany are now treated as aliens, as indeed they are in race, tradition, culture and religion.[29]

According to Meinertzhagen, Weizmann 'would sooner see the German Jew go under altogether than see Palestine lost.'[30] Weizmann had commissioned Meinertzhagen to conclude a deal with the Nazis that would assist German Jews in emigrating to Palestine.

Recent studies on the subject of Nazi-Zionist collaboration clearly bring to light the identity of interest between the two parties.[31] The technical modalities of their common transactions within their association are of no special concern to our study, and have been extensively treated elsewhere.[32] But the underlying spirit of this Nazi-Zionist working relationship indicates with stunning clarity the racist character of Zionism. From the Zionist viewpoint, the Nazis were qualified to join the ranks of the non-Jewish Zionists. And, in the end, it was Nazism with its anti-Semitic racism which in 1948 made possible the Zionist enterprise in Palestine.

Before Hitler's appearance on the European political stage, Jewish Palestine was nothing more than a minor settlement project of less than 200,000 Jews. The majority were dependent upon Zionist funds collected throughout the Diaspora. In 1927 Jewish emigration from Palestine actually was greater than immigration. In 1934, only 5% of all the land in Palestine was owned by Jews. While non-Jews were talking of the land as the 'land of milk and honey', the idea of migrating to a 'barren land' in the East had little appeal to world Jewry. Even in the face of violent anti-Semitic persecutions, the majority of the Jews preferred to seek refuge in the United States and England. But restrictive immigration laws in the Anglo-Saxon countries often made this impossible. After the Nazi exter-mination camps, however, the future of a Jewish Palestine was guaranteed.

An illuminating event occurred during the 1947 United Nations General Assembly debate on Palestine. At the same time as partition of Palestine was voted through, another resolution had been put forward asking all member states to admit Jews on a quota system. This resolution was defeated – hardly surprising after the failure of the Evian and Bermuda conferences. Those countries which had voted *for* partition either voted against or abstained on the Jewish immigration resolution. Those countries who had voted *against* the partition of Palestine and against Zionism voted in favour of higher Jewish immigration quotas in Western countries and expressed their willingness to accept more Jewish immigrants into their own countries.[33]

Zionism and Apartheid

The similarity between Zionism and South African apartheid consists in their common appeal to a 'civilizing' influence, invoking Biblical pre-cepts. The Dutch Reformed Church, the church of the Afrikaner settlers, relies on Old Testament passages to demonstrate that the inequality of the races is ordained by God. The black natives of Africa are considered to be the inferior descendants of Ham whereas the white settlers regard themselves as the descendants of Shem whose mission was to civilize these blacks.[34]

Zionism likewise depends upon Old Testament passages to justify the Jewish claim to the possession and colonization of Palestine. Only the Jews are capable of bringing 'civilization' back to Palestine where they are reclaiming only what is rightfully theirs according to the Biblical prophecies.

The close interrelationship between Zionism and apartheid was em-bodied in General Jan Christian Smuts' Zionist convictions. Smuts' attraction to Zionism 'welled up not only from his functional role as a surrogate British imperial presence, but from the racist and misconstrued theology of his own Afrikaner people'.[35] His Zionism sprang from his own personal background and from his conception of Western civilization, modified by his Calvinist religious beliefs. His friendship with the Zionist leader, Chaim Weizmann, was the effect rather than the cause of his Zionism.

Smuts' attitude towards Zionism was a necessary corollary of his belief in the dominant historical role of Western civilization and the place he gave to the Jews as its bearer and defender. Civilization was equated with 'white' civilization. White unity was an absolute necessity, and thus left no room for the traditional Western anti-Semitism. Smuts' black/white racial philosophy classified the Jews as white while the Arabs were ranked with the blacks. The spiritual basis of this racial equation was his belief that the Jews had the same background as his own Afrikaner people.

> They had the same characteristics. Both were sour, bitter people; strictly religious, with their lives based on religion learned from the same Book – from the Old Testament . . . They were the Chosen People – as the Dutch felt themselves to be the chosen people – chosen by God Himself, set apart and better than other men, and every Jew knew that he had been specially chosen to be a Jew.[36]

Smuts on many occasions brought up the deep spiritual connection that bound the white people of South Africa to the Jews of Palestine. Addressing a Zionist audience in 1919 he said:

> I need not remind you that the white people of South Africa, and especially the older Dutch population, has been brought up almost entirely on Jewish tradition. The Old Testament, the most wonderful literature ever thought out by the brain of man, the Old Testament has been the very matrix of Dutch culture here in South Africa.[37]

In the terms of this black and white racial classification, Smuts, like the other non-Jewish Zionists, had no regard for the Arabs as a people nor for their position in Palestine. His biographer, Sarah Gertrude Millin, a South African Jewess herself, succinctly describes this condescending attitude:

> As to Arabs, a Bedouin Arab quite naturally cannot seem so romantically strange to a South African as to a European, for the South African very well knows dark skinned peoples; peoples resembling, indeed, the Arabs – and with reason, since Arab blood is in them.[38]

But the Jewish people, this 'little people' as Smuts used to refer to them, 'has had a mission, a civilizing mission, in the world second, perhaps, to none.'[39] The Jewish people were above all the fountain-head of Western civilization to whom the West owed its very existence. And now they were to awaken the Middle East which 'had been sleeping for centuries', and lead it 'along the paths of progress'.[40]

Smuts' position on Jewish immigration into South Africa during the Nazi era again revealed the fact that Zionism and anti-Semitism were mutually interdependent. In 1947, during a parliamentary debate on the issue of alien immgration, one member of the South African Assembly, Mr Kentridge, proposed to liberalize South Africa's immigration laws in order to allow entry for a larger number of Jewish refugees. Smuts objected to this 'humanitarian' request, on Zionist grounds, arguing that increased Jewish immigration into South Africa would not solve the Jewish problem but would only create anti-Semitism. He proposed instead that South Africa concentrate its efforts in assisting the establishment of a Jewish National Home in Palestine as a solution to the Jewish Problem.

The common theoretical foundations of Zionism and apartheid were to be crowned by the future special relationship between the government of Israel and the racist apartheid regime of South Africa. Extensive links between the two have been maintained since 1948 on all levels – the political, economic and military – in defiance of international sanctions and condemnations of apartheid. South Africa was one of the first countries to recognize the state of Israel on 14 May 1948 under the premiership of Smuts. Two days later, Daniel F. Malan's Nationalist Party defeated Smuts in the general elections. Malan's ascent to the premiership, however, had no adverse effect upon Zionist-South African co-operation.

Malan's perceptions were both anti-Semitic and Zionist. In 1930, it had been Malan who introduced the quota bill restricting Jewish immigration from Eastern Europe. The anti-Jewish policies of Malan's Nationalist Party often bordered on virulent and blatant anti-Semitism. Malan was known as a whole-hearted supporter of Hitler and as a Nazi collaborator. But, notwithstanding this long record of anti-Semitism, the Nationalist Party found reason to modify at least its overt anti-Semitism at approximately the same time as the goal of the political Zionist movement, the creation of a Jewish state in Palestine, was about to become a reality.[42] It was the Nationalist Government under Malan which, immediately after its narrow victory over Smuts on 26 May 1948, extended *de jure* recognition to the Jewish state. The resultant alliance between Zionist Israel and apartheid South Africa was the natural outgrowth of their common political racist philosophy. Malan's concession to the new state meant that he now averred that the race-consciousness of the Jews would condition them to 'more easily understand and respect the same feeling in the case of every other section of the community.'[43] Dr Leslie Rubin, a South African exile and co-founder of the Liberal Party, made the following astute observation:

There was a sense of affinity with the Israelis in having thrown off the British yoke. A psychologist might have called it admiration for the achievement by another of what was for them still a suppressed desire. Then – this is the view which was put to me by a leading Afrikaaner intellectual of genuine feeling – many Nationalists saw the success of the Jews against the Arabs as a victory of White over non-White. Malan himself growing old, displayed a voice with much fervour, a highly emotional people-of-the-book enthusiasm for the restoration of the Jews to their ancient homeland in accordance with Biblical prophecy.[44]

Between July 1961 and June 1967 the cordial state of relations between Israel and South Africa was disturbed by Israel's decision to cast its vote in the United Nations General Assembly in favour of a resolution condemning South Africa's apartheid policy. The Israeli vote was intended to placate the Black African states Israel was courting at the time. The South African Prime Minister, Hendrik F. Verwoerd, publicly exposed the hypocrisy of the Israeli condemnation of apartheid by pointing out the congruency between Zionism and apartheid: 'The Zionists took Israel from the Arabs after the Arabs lived there for a thousand years . . . Israel, like South Africa, is an apartheid state.'[45]

The South African advocates of apartheid were very keenly aware of the community of destiny that bound the future of South Africa to that of Israel, as stated in the official organ of the Nationalist Party, *Die Burger*:

> Israel and South Africa have a common lot. Both are engaged in a struggle for existence, and both are in constant clash with the decisive majorities in the United Nations. Both are reliable foci on strength within the region which would, without them, fall into anti-Western anarchy. It is in South Africa's interest that Israel is successful in containing her enemies, who are among her own most vicious enemies, and Israel would have all the world against it if the navigation route around the Cape of Good Hope should be out of operation because South Africa's control is undermined.[46]

The setback in official relations between the two states that had resulted from Israel's 1961 verbal condemnation of apartheid was in fact very short lived. After the 1967 Arab-Israeli war, the Jewish state again reverted to its earlier open and most cordial relationship with South Africa. The ideological political, economic and military relationships between the two partners were extensively expanded and in 1973 the world community for the first time condemned 'the unholy alliance between Portuguese colonialism, South African racism, Zionism and Israeli imperialism'.[47]

Notes

1. Bernard Lewis, 'The Anti-Zionist Resolution', *Foreign Affairs*, Vol. 55 No. 1, October 1976, p. 55.
2. *The Diaries of Theodor Herzl* (New York, 1956).
3. Arnold Toynbee, *The Study of History* (New York, 1961).
4. Richard Meinertzhagen, *Middle East Diary 1917–1956* (London, 1959), p. 67.
5. Ibid., p. 49.
6. Ibid., p. 203.
7. Herzl, op. cit., Vol. 1, p. 84.
8. See his *Krisis und Entscheidung im Judentum* (Berlin, 1921), pp. 118, 62.
9. Meinertzhagen, op. cit., p. 183.
10. Ibid., p. 81.
11. Ibid., p. 17.
12. Ibid., p. 12.
13. Ibid., pp. 161 and 167.
14. Senator Lodge speaking in 1922 in Boston, *New Palestine*, Vol. 2, 1922, p. 330.
15. Clark Clifford to Truman, 6 March 1948, Clark Clifford Papers, Truman Library, Box 13, pp. 10–11.
16. Ibid., Box 14, 'Summary of Proposals for American Policy in Palestine'.
17. Herzl, Theodor, *The Jewish State* (London, 1934).
18. Great Britain, Public Record Office, Cab. 24/24, 23 August 1917.
19. H.C., 10 July 1905, O.R. col. 155 and H.C., 2 May 1905, O.R. col. 795. See also David V. Lipman, *Social History of the Jews in England* (London, 1954) pp. 141ff.
20. *Protokoll*, 7 Zionisten Kongress, 1905, p. 85.
21. As quoted by Leonard Stein, *The Balfour Declaration* (London, 1961), p. 143.
22. Ibid.
23. Earl of Oxford and Asquith, *Memories and Reflections* (London, 1928), Vol. 2, p. 65.
24. Stein, op. cit., p. 274.
25. Nahum Sokolow, *The History of Zionism* (London, 1919), Vol. 2, p. xxi.
26. Reuben Fink described House as a devoted friend of Zionism in *America and Palestine* (New York, 1945), p. 31. Selig Adler, on the other hand, describes him as 'not only bitterly anti-Zionist, but also deeply anti-Semitic.' See 'The Palestine Question in the Wilson Era', *Journal of Jewish Social Studies*, Vol. 10, No. 4, 1948, p. 306.
27. As quoted in William E. Dodd, Jr. and Martha Dodd (eds), *Ambassador Dodd's Diary* (New York, 1941), p. 10.
28. As quoted in Meinertzhagen, op. cit., p. 152. Between 1934 and 1939 Meinertzhagen had three interviews with Hitler and Ribbentrop, the German Foreign Minister. On each occasion, the subject of Zionism was discussed.
29. Ibid., pp. 158, 152.
30. Ibid.
31. One of the most complete, documented and thus authoritative studies on the Nazi-Zionist complicity is Eliahu Ben Elissar, *La Diplomatie du IIIe Reich et les Juifs* (Paris, 1969).

32. Ibid. See also Klaus Polkehn, 'Secret Contacts: Zionist-Nazi Relations, 1933–1941', *Journal of Palestine Studies*, Vol. 5, Nos. 3/4, Spring/Summer 1967, pp. 54–82. The author discusses the origins and dealings of the Haavara agreement of 1933 which traded German Jewish emigration to Palestine for imports of German goods into Palestine at a time when the Western countries were attempting an economic boycott of Nazi Germany.
33. UN Records, 127th Plenary Session of the General Assembly, 28 November 1947.
34. For a detailed study of the ideological basis underlying South African apartheid see George Jabbour, *Settler Colonialism in Southern Africa and the Middle East* (Beirut, 1970).
35. Richard P. Stevens, 'Israel and Africa' in *Zionism and Racism* (Tripoli, 1977), p. 165.
36. H. C. Armstrong, *Grey Steel: J. C. Smuts, A Study in Arrogance* (London, 1937), p. 300.
37. As quoted in Richard P. Stevens, *Weizmann and Smuts. A Study in Zionist-South African Cooperation* (Beirut, 1975), p. 33.
38. Sarah Gertrude Millin, *General Smuts* (London, 1936), Vol. 2, pp. 112–13.
39. As quoted in Stein, op. cit., p. 483.
40. See Stevens, *Weizmann and Smuts*, op. cit., p. 112.
41. *South African Zionist Record*, 18 April 1947.
42. Richard G. Weisbord, 'Dilemma of South African Jewry', *Journal of Modern African Studies*, Vol. 5, September 1967, p. 239.
43. Ibid., p. 236.
44. Leslie Rubin, 'Afrikaaner Nationalism and the Jews', *Africa South*, Vol. 1, No. 3, April–June 1957, p. 2.
45. *Rand Daily Mail*, 21 November 1961.
46. *Die Burger*, Cape Province, 29 May 1968.
47. General Assembly Resolution 3151 G (XXVIII) of 14 December 1973. See also *Report on the Relations between Israel and South Africa*, adopted by the UN Special Committee against Apartheid on 19 August 1976.

8. Palestine Today: Political Culture and Foreign Policy

A clear grasp of non-Jewish Zionism and its history indicates the depth of Western support for the Zionist state in Palestine. It also counteracts the widely accepted myth that Western support for Israel is largely due to an influential Jewish minority within Western political systems, especially the United States. Zionist pressure politics, the Zionist lobby or the Jewish vote, do not account for the substantial non-Jewish support which Zionism has been able to mobilize in the West.

The Zionist movement was able to enlist supporters among non-Jews throughout the Western world long before it was able to attract large-scale Jewish support as a result of World War II. The political congruence of Zionism and Western culture is of much longer standing than that between Zionism and its seemingly most natural constituency, Judaism and world Jewry.

Today the majority of the non-Jews in the West do not regard Zionism as racism but as a moral force which, conceived first as a religious doctrine, had its roots deep within the history of Western civilization. Its underlying assumptions and main ideas were first conceived and transmitted by non-Jews in various guises, religious, social, economic or strategic.

Applied to the Palestine conflict today, non-Jewish Zionism is still a major element in the foreign policy decision-making process of the Western nations, in particular in the United States and Western Europe. To conclude our study, we shall concentrate on the relationship between political culture and the formulation of Western foreign policy on the Arab–Israeli conflict.

Forming Political Imagery

Political culture is the pattern of individual attitudes towards politics among the members of a given political system. Political culture therefore encompasses the actual performance of this given political system as well as the subjective realm which gives meaning to political actions. A nation's political culture consists of attitudes, beliefs, values and skills

132

which are shared by an entire population or by separate parts thereof, be they regional groups, social classes or ethnic groups.[1] Often taking the form of stereotypes, favourable or unfavourable associations, these attitudes are the product of the historically prevailing political atmosphere. They are present in national customs but also in fairly consistent attitudes towards other peoples and the outside world in general. Altogether, this heritage has produced deeply ingrained prejudices as well as predilections which shape the people's attitudes and also colour the views of political decision-makers.

Modern political scientists have established that political culture and foreign policy decision-making are complementary in that foreign policy expresses behavioural patterns which have been stabilized with the passage of time. Current behaviour is circumscribed and directed by past patterns of behaviour in and throughout history.

In our study of non-Jewish Zionism, we have identified a set of ideas that came to be the underlying assumptions of modern political Zionism and have traced their origin to the beginnings of modern European history in the 16th Century. The notion that the Jews form a nation apart, that they once had been a nation and that they will be a nation again in the most modern sense was developed by non-Jews in conformity with the Protestant concept of the national church. When Medieval Catholic universalism had made room for Protestant particularism, Judaism came to be accepted as the national religion of the 'Jewish nation'.

According to Protestant Biblical exegesis, Palestine came to be thought of as the land of all the Jews. So developed the myth that the Jews outside Palestine in the Christian West were strangers there and exiles from their Homeland. Biblical fundamentalism, as an outgrowth of the Protestant tradition, further developed the myth of Israel's Restoration. What was posited was a supra-rational relationship between the land of Palestine and the Jewish people as the direct descendants of the ancient Biblical Hebrew tribes of Israel. It was Protestant Christian theology which established the unbroken continuity between the two, the land and the people.

The very idea of the Restoration of the Jews to Palestine as a nation has been a popular theme throughout four centuries of modern European history. It was always present in modern Western culture, first in the spiritual realm, but then also in the secular political one. In some periods it was central, in others only peripheral; but it was always present, reinforcing the prevalent mental attitude that connected the Jews to Palestine. The Hon. John J. Dingell, a member of the House of Representatives from the state of Michigan, in 1939 spoke for many other non-Jewish Zionists who based their Zionism simply on their cultural upbringing:

> I have always been taught to believe that Palestine was the ancestral, the historic and the God-given land of the Jews; and I was taught, moreover,

that it was ordained by God that some day the Jews of the world would return to their homeland.[2]

Long before Theodor Herzl accepted 'the mighty legend' of Palestine this legend had been made an intrinsic component of Western culture. The legend of Palestine as the ancestral home of all Jews vividly lived in the imagination of most Christians at the turn of the century, and continues to be felt today in the West's unequivocal support for Israel.

People view reality through a set of images which may or may not correspond to empirical reality. This also holds true for foreign policy. This set of images is the product of a certain political culture and is transmitted from generation to generation through the process of socialization. The Zionist image matrix that evolved in the West over four centuries and which accounts today for the widespread Western pro-Israeli attitudes and policies is very complex but can be looked upon as the sum of the following images: the Biblical image, the image of self-identification and the moral image.

The Biblical Image

Very few people actually have a highly accurate knowledge of the history and issues underlying the Arab-Israeli conflict. Yet most people have been exposed at one time or another in their lives to Biblical stories dealing with the ancient Israelites. Therefore modern Israel becomes the present-day extension of Biblical Israel, an image construction which the Zionist movement utilized most effectively for its own ends.

Once the modern setting is linked with the Biblical past, the scenario of the past finds contemporary application. The Arab-Israeli conflict becomes in the general imagination the extension of the Biblical conflict between David and Goliath, with Israel in the role of the poor David: 'Little Israel, coming on like little David of the Old Testament, with its aerial slingshot thoroughly trounced the burnoosed Arab Goliath in 1967.'[3] This Biblical analogy did not come from the mouth of a fundamentalist preacher but from the pen of the editor of the noted *Los Angeles Herald Examiner*.

The same sentiment was voiced by Senator Joseph Montoya of New Mexico on the Senate floor: 'It is a little hard to believe that David [Israel] is the real aggressor against Goliath.'[4] Again Senator Montoya was neither a fundamentalist nor did he have to take into account 'the Jewish vote' since his State had hardly any Jews residing in it. And still he, like many others of his colleagues in the Senate, perceived the Arab-Israeli conflict through the Biblical image. This is but one more testimony to the organic connection between the Bible and American culture.

In the American tradition, the Bible is the source of the common faith, a cohesive force in national aspiration. Its language and imagery, moral directives and human strivings are embedded in the American character. In both glorious and trying times of American history, prophets and idolators, Kings and commoners who lived centuries ago in ancient Israel rose to play contemporary roles.[5]

The Image of Self-Identification

Biblical imagery as a cohesive force within Western culture indirectly gave rise to the second image, self-identification with the Zionists in Palestine. The Israelis are perceived as hard-working, pioneering, egalitarian and audacious – all the qualities that characterized the early American pioneers and settlers. According to this popular image the Zionist settlement in Palestine is comparable to the modern Christian pioneer settlements which became the United States or South Africa. The Protestant minister John Haynes most fittingly expressed this image during a visit to Palestine in 1929:

> As I met and talked with these toilers on the land, I could think of nothing but the early English settlers who came to the bleak shores of Massachusetts, and there amid winter's cold in an untilled soil, among an unfriendly native population, laid firm and sure the foundations of our American Republic. For this reason I was not surprised later, when I read Josiah Wedgewood's 'The Seventh Dominion' to find this distinguished Gentile Zionist of Britain speaking of these Jewish pioneers as 'the Pilgrim Fathers of Palestine'. Here is the same heroism dedicated to the same ends . . . It is obvious that the native Arabs while no less stubborn and savage than the American Indians, cannot be removed from the scene.[6]

The same idea was also in President Truman's mind when, on 28 October 1948, he outlined his policy towards Israel, pledging American support for a strong and free state: 'What we need now is to help the people in Israel, and they've proved themselves in the best traditions of pioneers. They have created out of a barren desert a modern and efficient state with the highest standard of Western civilization.'[7] More recently President Jimmy Carter struck the same chord in a speech before the Israeli Knesset in March 1979:

> Seven Presidents have believed and demonstrated that America's relationship with Israel is more than just a special relationship. It has been and it is a unique relationship. And it is a relationship which is indestructible, because it is rooted in the consciousness and the morals and the religion and the beliefs of the American people themselves . . . .
>
> Israel and the United States were shaped by pioneers – my nation is also a nation of immigrants and refugees – by peoples gathered in both nations from many lands . . . We share the heritage of the Bible . . . .[8]

On a more extended level, this image of personal self-identification with the Israelis includes the whole of Israel as 'the product of free enterprise',[9] and a 'bastion of democracy',[10] an 'oasis of freedom in the midst of a desert of authoritarian regimes',[11] or the bulwark against communism and radical Arab nationalism. The Middle East conflict is conceived by the general Western public as part of the larger and more important struggle between the democratic West and the Communist world.

The Moral Image

This finally leads us to the image of the mutual interests between Israel and the West as based on bonds of culture and moral sentiment. In the United States today, American support for Israel is often an issue of national self-interest. Even Senator Fulbright, by no means known as a friend of Zionism, called for a United States guarantee of Israeli security on the grounds that American interests are linked to Israel 'by bonds of culture and sentiments'.[12] The American relationship with Israel is expressed in the identity of their basic values, or in the words of Senator Dole of Kansas:

> American-Israeli friendship is no accident. It is a product of our shared values. We are both democracies. We are both pioneer states. We have both opened our doors to the oppressed. We have both shown a passion for freedom and we have both gone to war to protect it.[13]

Today the majority of Americans, both in and out of the political decision-making process, still find an echo of their own image in Israel's existence. They regard the question of Israel as a moral and religious matter of deep personal concern. They believe not only that Israel must exist, but that it must exist as a Jewish state. Former President Jimmy Carter is one representative of this trend in contemporary American attitudes to Zionism and Israel. His own fundamentalist background and religious views were related to his Middle East policy. As President he saw the state of Israel first and foremost as 'a return at last, to the Biblical land from which the Jews were driven so many hundred of years ago . . . The establishment of the nation of Israel is the fulfilment of Biblical prophecy and the very essence of its fulfilment.'[14] As a result Carter's policy towards Israel was influenced by his own perception of the state of Israel as truly the land God had promised to the Jews and to which he himself confessed to have 'an absolute and total commitment as a human being, as an American, as a religious person.'[15] Consequently Carter's conception of peace in the Middle East revolved around 'the permanent and secure existence of the Jewish state of Israel.'[16]

Congressional Zionism and the 'Jewish Factor'

Traditionally it has been argued that the bastion of Zionist and pro-Israel sentiment in the United States is in Congress. It is true that there has been consistent Congressional support for a Jewish state in Palestine since the 1922 Joint Congressional Resolution in favour of the Balfour Declaration. Israel's Congressional supporters often number more than 70 in the Senate and a clear majority in the House of Representatives. Such support is clearly identifiable in Congressional voting patterns on resolutions on the Middle East as well as in such independent activities as petitions or letters to the Executive attempting to influence policy.

American foreign policy analysts are convinced that the intimate American-Israeli relationship is substantially influenced by the United States Congress, and tend to blame Congress for the pro-Israeli American policy. While being aware that Congress' foreign policy role is only marginal, they maintain that American-Israeli relations are an exception in this respect.

Many scholars have already studied and analysed the various factors involved in Congressional support for Israel.[17] They have also identified the independent and dependent variables which explain Congressional voting behaviour on issues related to Israel and the Arab-Israeli conflict. They distinguish the following factors as the most significant: the 'Jewish vote', Jewish financial support for Senators and members of the House of Representatives, the presence of an effective Jewish lobby on Capitol Hill and certain ideological factors. There is a vast body of literature on each of these causal factors.

Most analysts generally agree in concluding that, while all factors appear to have at least some factual basis, there is no single cause that can account for the strong Congressional support for Israel. Even the multi-causal explanation is often unsatisfactory. 'The pro-Israel sentiments of major non-Jewish segments of the articulate public are probably at least as important in determining congressional support as the electoral and financial strength of the Jewish community in the United States.'[18] With these observations Robert H. Trice hints at the importance of the all-pervasive presence of non-Jewish Zionist thinking within American culture:

> . . . we must first fully understand the complex reasons that underlie the apparent affinities of diverse segments of American society for the state of Israel if we are ever to fully understand congressional support for Israel. For to the extent that congressmen are the primary media through which most domestic forces make their imprint on foreign policy, we should expect congressmen to reflect and be sensitive to broader and deeper currents of opinion within the general populations.[19]

The underlying Zionist predispositions of members of Congress are merely a reflection of those of the general American public. The Zionist lobby does not *create* pro-Israel attitudes but only serves to strengthen already existing attitudes and tendencies, especially since the opposing viewpoint is not represented effectively.

To explain non-Jewish support for Zionism by asserting that Congress, the mass media or the universities are all owned or controlled by Jews is not only factually incorrect, but tends to obscure the real strength of Zionism, namely its fusion with Western and American culture. Aaron Wildavsky, the Jewish political scientist, is one of the few who look to American-Israeli relations within the matrix of Zionism:

> Whether anyone likes it or not, Israel is of, by, and for the West. By deciding for development, Israel feels, smells, and looks like a Western country. Unlike Vietnam . . . Israel is not part of the periphery but contains the core of the West. For better or for worse Israel is us . . .
>
> By acting as if there were no American national interest in Israel, the United States would simultaneously be rejecting its own religious, moral, political, and cultural identity.[20]

The authenticity of the American commitment to Israel derives not from the 'Jewish factor', but from the nature of American society as it has evolved over the past centuries. The record of non-Jewish Zionism indicates that so-called 'Christian Zionist sentiments' are both genuine and indigenous to the American culture. Non-Jewish concern for Palestine is not simply a commodity to be produced whenever it serves the purposes of the Zionist and Israeli leadership. Much of non-Jewish Zionist attitudes and activities are self-generating and not mere responses to Zionist or Israeli pressures.[21]

Palestine's Future Vs. America's Past

Viewing American support for Israel from the vantage point of the long history and tradition of non-Jewish Zionism, it is evident that the only constant factor in American policy towards the Middle East is support for the Jewish state. Given the constellation of all the political factors at play within the United States, there is no reasonable and foreseeable way in which a shift in this policy may be brought about.

It is, furthermore, evident that American attitudes towards the Middle East reflect not only a strong emotional pro-Israel bias, but that this bias is accompanied by an equally pervasive dislike and distrust of the Arabs. A common denominator between Jewish and non-Jewish Zionists is their mutual representation of the Arabs as deficient in the desirable qualities of Westerners.

Zionism not only set the stage for the colonial settlement in Palestine, but it also brought in its train a negative attitude towards the native Arabs in Palestine. There exists a long historical tradition of anti-Arab prejudice going back to the early 19th Century, and a consistent disinclination on the part of Western scholars to acknowledge the contributions of Islamic civilization to the West.[22] Today popular culture is used to portray the

Arabs as the villains of the world and as the number one enemy of Western civilization and all its values. The growth of non-Jewish Zionism is inseparable from the mass inculcation of a whole complex of anti-Arab prejudices.

As we have shown in the previous chapters, Arab society gradually became synonymous with backwardness, and the Arabs of Palestine were presented as intellectually and psychologically inferior to the newly immigrating Jews. The novel *Exodus* presented the Arabs of Palestine as 'the dregs of humanity, thieves, murderers, highway robbers, dope runners and white slavers.'[23] The film version fixed this image in living colour. More recently such novels and current best-sellers as *The Odessa File*, *The Pirate* or *Black Sunday* continue to reinforce this conventional Western perception of the Arab world.

In many cases the problem is more one of ignorance rather than outright prejudice. Several studies have already dealt with the way in which anti-Arab/pro-Israel attitudes pervade American secondary school textbooks. One such analysis concluded that none of the 20 books examined presented the Arab people in a favourable light, though many were pro-Israel.[24]

The resulting configuration of attitudes held by the American public comes to establish the policy parameters limiting and defining American foreign policy towards the Middle East. For, in the end, a political system forms its foreign policy, not so much to maximize its national interests as such, but more so its perception of these interests. This is why some concerned Americans have urged the Arab world to take the indirect road to policy changes by strengthening its own imagery within the United States.

But this can be done successfully only if the West finally comes to grips with its own Zionist leanings. On the rudimentary level we have first to examine our own pro-Israeli attitudes and predispositions and to recognize them as the outcome of a centuries long process of socialization and spiritual innoculation. We will then discover that as a result of non-Jewish Zionism a whole complex of prejudices against the Arabs, their culture and their religion, have been systematically inculcated into our own consciousness and have thus directly or indirectly influenced our views on Palestine, the Palestine problem and the Palestinian people.

Fortunately the present political realities in the Middle East, and particularly in Lebanon, create a new opportunity for us in the West to re-evaluate Zionism and all that it stood and continues to stand for in the Middle East. We can no longer afford to look at Israel and its policies through the Zionist prism and the coloured spectacles of our own mythological history or fundamentalist theology. Today, with the Israeli army occupying Lebanon, the facts speak for themselves more clearly than ever before. Israel rationalized its aggression against Lebanon as an action for 'peace' and its land-grabbing of territories belonging to others as a 'strategy for security'. The recent events in Lebanon, and Israel's air raid on the Iraqi nuclear installation indeed make a mockery of Israel's 'security policy' and its underlying Zionist semantics.

The popular imagery and biblical analogy of David and Goliath cannot justifiably be applied to Israel and its Arab neighbours. It was merely another myth created and perpetuated by Zionism in order to rally world public opinion and support for its geo-political cause, namely the expansion and consolidation of the Jewish state. Again and again during its short history of existence as an independent state, Israel has demonstrated its military might and superiority over its Arab neighbours. It is Israel's superior military strength, carefully nurtured by its Western allies, that threatens its neighbours, not the reverse, as Israel wants us to believe. Never has this fact been as clear to so many as it is now. The events in Lebanon in 1982 provided a decisive and authoritative contribution to the demystification of the myth of Israel as the brave, helpless, little David, surrounded by millions of vengeful Arabs. Yet, due to their political disunity and military weakness, the Arabs have never even come close to being a 'Goliath'. President Reagan himself recognized this and stated it during a National Security Council meeting: 'Israel is no longer David. It's Goliath.'[25]

Finally, we have to recognize that Israel is not the embodiment of Western virtues, but is pursuing its own adventurist, single-minded policies, which often run counter to Western interests themselves.

Notes

1. The following studies introduce the reader to the modern political theory of political culture: Gabriel A. Almond and G. Bingham Powell, Jr., *Comparative Politics. A Developmental Approach* (Boston, 1966), Chapter 3; Lucian W. Pye, 'Introduction: Political Culture and Political Development' in Lucian W. Pye and Sidney Verba (eds.), *Political Culture and Political Development* (Princeton, 1965).
2. Reuben Fink, *Palestine and America* (New York, 1945).
3. Editorial by William Randolph Hearst, Jr. in *Los Angeles Herald-Examiner*, 21 March 1971.
4. See United States Senate, 92nd Congress, 1st Session, *Congressional Record*, 24 March 1971, p. 3805.
5. Moshe Davis, *America and the Holy Land*, op. cit., p. 5.
6. John Haynes Holmes, *Palestine. Today and Tomorrow* (London, 1930), pp. 89, 248.
7. As quoted in Louis W. Koenig (ed.), *The Truman Administration: Its Principles and Practice* (New York, 1956), pp. 323–4.
8. *Jerusalem Post*, March 1979.
9. Clark Clifford dwelt on this theme in his recommendations for an American policy towards Palestine in 1947; see Clark Clifford Papers, Truman Library, Box 14.
10. 'Humphrey, A Friend of Israel', *Jerusalem Post*, 15 January 1978, p. 4.

11. Speech by Senator Frank Church of Idaho on 25 April 1977, printed in *Near East Record* (Washington), Vol. 21, No. 19, 11 May 1977, p. 74.
12. Speech by Senator J. W. Fulbright, United States Senate, 91st Congress, 2nd session, *Congressional Record*, 24 August 1970, pp. S 14022–14039. See also Michael Novak, 'The Moral Meaning of Israel', *Commonwealth*, 14 March 1975.
13. *Near East Report*, Vol. 21, No. 20, 18 May 1977, p. 78.
14. Speech by President Jimmy Carter on 1 May 1978, *Department of State Bulletin*, Vol. 78, No. 2015, p. 4.
15. Ibid.
16. Ibid.
17. See, for example, the following studies: Mary A. Barberis, 'The Arab-Israeli Battle on Capitol Hill', *The Virginia Quarterly Review*, Vol. 52, No. 1, 1976, pp. 203–23; David Garnham, 'Factors Influencing Congressional Support for Israel during the 93rd Congress', *The Jerusalem Journal of International Relations*, Vol. 2, No. 3, 1977, pp. 23–45; Robert H. Trice, 'Congress and the Arab-Israeli Conflict: Support for Israel in the U.S. Senate, 1970–1973', *Political Science Quarterly*, Vol. 92, No. 3, 1977, pp. 443–63; Marvin C. Feuerwerger, 'Congress and the Middle East', *Middle East Review*, Winter, 1977/1978, pp. 43–6.
18. Trice, op. cit., p. 463.
19. Ibid.
20. Aaron Wildavsky, 'What's In It For Us? America's National Interest in Israel', *Middle East Review*, Vol. 10, No. 1, Fall 1977, pp. 12–13.
21. Samuel Halperin, *The Political World of American Zionism* (Detroit, 1961), p. 187.
22. For example, Edward W. Said, *Orientalism* (New York, 1978). This work represents one of the most comprehensive studies of the West's biased and prejudiced approach to Arab-Islamic civilization. See also Philip K. Hitti, *Islam and the West* (Princeton, 1962).
23. Committee on the Image of the Middle East, *The Image of the Middle East in Secondary Textbooks* (New York, 1975), p. 25.
24. See Committee on the Image of the Middle East, op. cit., and Ayad al-Qazzas, Ruth Afiyo et al., *The Arabs in American Textbooks* (Garden City, 1975).
25. *Newsweek*, No. 40, 4 October 1982, p. 8.

Selected Bibliography

Books, Government Publications and Special Studies

Adelson, Roger, *Mark Sykes. Portrait of an Amateur* (London, Jonathan Cape, 1975).

Adler, Cyrus and Margolith, Aaron M., *American Intercession on Behalf of Jews in the Diplomatic Correspondence of the United States, 1848–1939* (New York, American Jewish Historical Society, 1943).

Adler, Cyrus and Margolith, Aaron M., *With Firmness in the Right: American Diplomatic Action Affecting Jews, 1840–1945* (New York, American Jewish Committee, 1946).

Adler, Selig; Davis, Moshe, and Handy, Robert T., *America and the Holy Land: A Colloquium* (Jerusalem, Institute of Contemporary Jewry of the Hebrew University, 1972).

Almessiri, Abdelwahab M., *The Land of Promise. A Critique of Political Zionism* (New Brunswick, North American Publisher, 1978).

Amery, Julian, *Life of Joseph Chamberlain* (London, Macmillan, 1951).

Badi, Joseph, *Fundamental Laws of the State of Israel* (New York, Twayne Publishers, 1960).

Baker, Ray S., *Woodrow Wilson and World Settlement* (Garden City, Doubleday, 1922).

Balfour, James Arthur, *First Earl of Balfour. Retrospect, An Unfinished Autobiography, 1848–1886* (Boston, Houghton Mifflin Co. 1930).

Baron, Salo W., *A Social and Religious History of the Jews* (New York, Columbia University Press, 1937).

Baron, Salo W. and Jeanette M., *Palestinian Messengers in America, 1849–79* (New York, Arno Press, 1943).

Beling, Willard A., (ed.) *The Middle East: Quest for an American Policy* (Albany, Suny Press, 1973).

Ben-Gurion, David, *The Rebirth and Destiny of Israel* (New York, Philosophical Library, 1954).

Ben-Jacob, Jeremiah, *Great Britain and the Jews* (London, Carmel Publishers, 1946).

Bentwich, Norman, *Fulfilment in the Promised Land, 1917–1937* (London, Soncino Press, 1938).

Berle, Adolph A., *The World Significance of a Jewish State* (New York, Mitchell Kennerley, 1918).

Berlin, Liebermann J., *Robert Browning and Hebraism. A Study of the Poems of Browning which are based on Rabbinical Writings and other Sources in Jewish Literature* (Zurich, 1934).

Berman, Myron, *The Attitude of American Jewry towards East European Jewish Immigration, 1881–1914.* (Thesis submitted to Columbia University, New York, 1963).

Berthold, Fred, Jr., and Carsten, W. Alan and Penzel, Klaus and Ross, James F., (eds.) *Basic Sources of the Judeo-Christian Tradition* (Englewood Cliffs, N.J., Prentice Hall Inc. 1962).

Bevan, Edwyn R. and Singer, Charles, *The Legacy of Israel* (Oxford, Clarendon Press, 1944).

Blackstone, William E., *Jesus is Coming* (Chicago, Fleming H. Revell Co. 1908).

Carlyle, Thomas, *Oliver Cromwell's Letters and Speeches*, 3 vols. (London, J. M. Dent & Sons Ltd. 1908).

Cavro-Demars, Lucien, *Aux sources du Sionisme* (Beirut, Librairie du Liban, 1971).

Cohen, Israel, (ed.) *Speeches on Zionism* (London, Arrowsmith, 1928).

Cohen, Israel, *The Zionist Movement* (New York, Zionist Organization of America, 1946).

Cohen, Morris S., *The Faith of a Liberal* (New York, 1946).

Cohn, Josef, *England und Palestina* (Berlin, Vowinckel Verlag, 1931).

Crum, Bartley C., *Behind the Silken Curtain. A Personal Account of Anglo-American Diplomacy in Palestine and the Middle East* (New York, Simon & Schuster, 1947).

Davis, Moshe, (ed.) *Israel: Its Role in Civilization* (New York, Harper & Row, 1956).

Davis, Moshe, (ed.) *With Eyes Toward Zion* (New York, Arno Press, 1977).

Davis, Moshe, (ed.) *World Jewry and the State of Israel* (New York, Arno Press, 1977).

de Novo, John A., *American Interests and Policies in the Near East, 1900–1939* (Minneapolis, University of Minnesota Press, 1963).

Dubnow, Simon, *Weltgeschichte des Juedischen Volkes* (Jerusalem, The Jewish Publishing House, 1971).

Elath, Eliahu, *Zionism at the United Nations: A Diary of the First Days* (Philadelphia, Jewish Publication Society of America, 1976).

Ellern, Hermann and Bessi, *Herzl, Hechter, and Grand Duke of Baden and the German Emperor, 1896–1904* (Tel Aviv, 1961).

Evans, Laurence, *United States Policy and the Partition of Turkey, 1914–24* (Baltimore, The Johns Hopkins Press, 1965).

Feingold, Henry L., *Zion in America* (New York, Twayne Publishers Inc. n.d.).

Fink, Reuben, (ed.) *America and Palestine* (New York, American Zionist Emergency Council, 1945).

Fisch, Harold, *The Dual Image: The Figure of the Jews in English and American Literature* (London, World Jewish Library, 1971).

Fishman, Hertzel, *American Protestantism and a Jewish State* (Detroit, Wayne State University Press, 1973).

Fosdick, Harry Emerson, *A Pilgrimage to Palestine* (New York, Macmillan, 1927).

Friedman, I., *Germany, Turkey and Zionism, 1897–1918* (Oxford, Clarendon Press, 1977).

Friedrich, Carl J., *American Policy Toward Palestine* (Westport, Greenwood Press, 1944).

Ganin, Zvi, *Truman, American Jewry, and Israel, 1945—1948* (New York, Homes and Meier, 1979).

Garraty, John A., *Henry Cabot Lodge. A Biography* (New York, Alfred A. Knopf, 1953).

Gelber, Nathan M., *Vorgeschichte des Zionismus. Judenstaatsprojekte in den Jahren 1645—1845* (Vienna, Phaidon Verlag, 1927).

Gerson, Louis L., *The Hyphenate in Recent American Politics and Diplomacy* (Lawrence, Kansas, University of Kansas Press, 1964).

Gilbert, Martin, *Churchill and Zionism* (London, World Jewish Congress, 1974).

Glick, Edward Bernard, *The Triangular Connection. America, Israel and American Jews* (London, George Allen & Unwin, 1982).

Goldston, Robert C., *Next Year in Jerusalem* (Boston, Little Brown, 1978).

Gottheil, Richard J. H., *Zionism* (Philadelphia, Jewish Publication Society of America, 1914).

Guelherter, Menajem, *Precursores Cristianos del Estado Judio* (Buenos Aires, Latin American Jewish Congress, 1972).

Halperin, Samuel, *The Political World of American Zionism* (Detroit, Wayne State University Press, 1961).

Hanna, Paul L., *British Policy in Palestine* (Washington, D.C., American Council on Public Affairs, 1942).

Hedenquist, Gote, (ed.) *The Church and the Jewish People* (London, Edinburgh House, 1954).

Heller, Joseph Elias, *The Zionist Idea* (London, Joint Zionist Publications Committee, 1947).

Henderson, Philip, *The Life of Laurence Oliphant* (London, Hale, 1956).

Hertzberg, Arthur, (ed.) *The Zionist Idea: A Historical Analysis and Reader* (New York, Athenum, 1969).

Herzl, Theodor, *The Jewish State* (London, Central Office of the Zionist Organization, 1934).

Hess, Moses, *Rome and Jerusalem. A Study in Jewish Nationalism* (New York, Bloch Publishing House, 1945).

Holmes, John H., *Palestine Today and Tomorrow: A Gentile's Survey of Zionism* (New York, Macmillan, 1929).

Hollingsworth, Arthur George, *The Holy Land Restored* (London, Seeleys, 1849).

Hyamson, Albert M., *Palestine. The Rebirth of an Ancient People* (London, Sidgwick & Jackson, 1917).

Hyamson, Albert M., *British Projects for the Restoration of the Jews* (London, 1917).

Isaacs, Stephen D., *Jews and American Politics* (Garden City, New York, Doubleday, 1974).

Jeffries, J. M. N., *Palestine: The Reality* (London, Longmans, Green & Co. 1939).

Kallen, Horace Meyer, *Zionism and World Politics. A Study in History and Social Psychology* (Garden City, Doubleday, 1921).

Kennedy, John F., *John F. Kennedy on Israel, Zionism and Jewish Issues* (New York, The Herzl Press, 1965).

Kimche, Jon and David, *The Secret Roads: The Illegal Migration of a People, 1938—1948)* (London, 1954).

Kobler, Franz, *Napoleon and the Jews* (New York, Schocken Books, 1976).

Kobler, Franz, *The Vision Was There* (London, Lincolns Prager Ltd. 1956).

Koestler, Arthur, *Promise and Fulfilment* (London, Macmillan & Co. 1949).

Laqueur, Walter Z., *A History of Zionism* (London, Weidenfeld & Nicolson, 1972).

Levine, Samuel H., *Changing Concepts of Palestine in American Literature to 1867*. (Thesis submitted to New York University, 1953).

Lipsky, Louis, *A Gallery of Zionist Profiles* (New York, Farrar, Strauss & Cudahy, 1956).

Littell, Franklin H., *The Crucifixion of the Jews* (New York, Harper & Row, 1975).

Lowdermilk, Walter Clay, *Palestine, Land of Promise* (New York, Harper Bros. 1944).

Malachy, Yona, *American Fundamentalism and Israel* (Jerusalem, The Hebrew University Press, 1978).

Manuel, Frank E., *The Realities of American Palestine Relations* (Washington, Public Affairs Press, 1949).

Meyer, Isadore S., (ed.) *Early History of Zionism in America* (New York, American Jewish Historical Society, 1958).

Meinertzhagen, Richard, *Middle East Diary, 1917–1956* (London, Cresset Press, 1960).

Mendenhall, George E., *The Tenth Generation: The Origins of the Biblical Tradition* (Baltimore, Johns Hopkins University Press, 1975).

Newman, Chaim, *Gentile and Jew* (London, Alliance Press Ltd. n.d.).

Newman, Louis I., *Jewish Influence on Christian Reform Movements* (New York, AMS Press Inc. 1966).

Perkins, Frances, *The Roosevelt I Knew* (New York, Viking Press, 1946).

Poliakov, Leon, *The History of Anti-Semitism* (New York, Vanguard Press, 1965).

Poppel, Stephen M., *Zionism In Germany, 1897–1933* (Philadelphia, Jewish Publication Society of America, 1976).

Rabinowicz, Oskar K., *Winston Churchill on Jewish Problems* (London, Lincoln Prager Ltd. 1956).

Rengstorf, Karl H., and Kortzfleisch, Siegfried, *Kirche und Synagogue* (Stuttgart, Klett Verlag, 1970).

Rose, N. A., *The Gentile Zionists* (London, 1973).

Roth, Cecil, *England in Jewish History* (London, Jewish Historical Society of England, 1949).

Roth, Cecil, *Essays and Portraits in Anglo-Jewish History* (Philadelphia, Jewish Publication Society of America, 1962).

Roth, Cecil, *The Jews in the Renaissance* (New York, Harper & Row, 1959).

Roth, Cecil, (ed.) *Magna Bibliotheca Anglo Judaica: A Bibliographical Guide to Anglo-Jewish History* (London, 1937).

Roth, Cecil, *The Nephew of the Almighty. An Experimental Account of the Life and Aftermath of Richard Brothers* (London, Edward Goldston Ltd. 1933).

Rubinstein, Arieh, (ed.) *The Return to Zion* (Jerusalem, Keter Publishing House, 1974).

Sachar, Howard M., *A History of Israel From the Rise of Zionism to Our Time* (New York, Knopf, 1976).

Said, Edward W., *Orientalism* (New York, Vintage Books, 1978).

Schwarzfuchs, Simon, *Napoleon, the Jews and the Sanhedrin* (London, Routledge & Kegan Paul, 1979).

Seiferth, Wolfgang, *Synagogue und Kirche im Mittelalter* (Munchen, Koesel, 1964).

Short, Wilfrit M., *The Mind of A. J. Balfour. Selections from his non-political Writings, Speeches and Addresses* (New York, Georg H. Doran Co. 1918).

Sidebotham, Herbert, *England and Palestine. Essays Towards the Restoration of the Jewish State* (London, Constable & Co. Ltd. 1918).

Silverberg, Robert, *If I Forget Thee O Jerusalem: American Jews and the State of Israel* (New York, William Morrow, 1970).

Snetsinger, John, *Truman, The Jewish Vote and the Creation of Israel* (Stanford, Hoover Institution Press, 1974).

Sokolow, Nahum, *History of Zionism, 1600–1918*, 2 vols. (London, Longmans, Green & Co. 1919).

Sokolow, Nahum, *Zionism in the Bible* (London, Zionist Organization Publications, 1918).

Stein, Leonard, *Zionism* (London, E. Denim Ltd. 1925).

Stein, Leonard, *The Balfour Declaration* (London, Vallentine, Mitchell, 1961).

Stember, Charles Herbert et al., *Jews in the Mind of America* (New York, Basic Books, 1966).

Stevens, Richard P., *American Zionism and US Foreign Policy* (Beirut, Institute for Palestine Studies, 1970).

Stevens, Richard P., *Weizmann and Smuts: A Study in Zionist-South African Cooperation* (Beirut, Institute for Palestine Studies, 1975).

Sykes, Christopher, *Two Studies in Virtue* (London, Collins, 1958).

Tibawi, A. L., *Anglo-Arab Relations and the Question of Palestine 1914–1921* (London, Luzac, 1978).

Truman, Harry S., *Memoirs – Years of Trial and Hope, 1946–1952* (New York, New American Library, 1962).

Tuchman, Barbara W., *Bible and Sword. England and Palestine from the Bronze Age to Balfour* (London, Alvin Redman Ltd. 1957).

Welles, Sumner, *We Need not Fail* (Boston, Houghton Mifflin Co. 1948).

Wilson, Evan M. *Decision on Palestine* (Stanford, Hoover Institution Press, 1980).

Wise, Stephen S., *Challenging Years* (New York, G. P. Putman Sons, 1949).

Wolf, Lucien, *The Jewish National Movement* (London, St. Clements Press, 1917).

Wyman, David S., *Paper Walls: America and the Refugee Crisis, 1938–1941* (Amherst, Mass., 1968).

Zebel, Sydney, *Balfour: A Political Biography* (Cambridge, Cambridge University Press, 1973).

Zweig, Ferdinand, *Israel: The Sword and the Harp* (London, Heinemann, 1969).

Articles

Abu-Jaber, Faiz, 'American-Arab Relations from the Balfour Declaration to the Creation of the State of Israel, 1917–1948', *Middle East Forum*, Vol. XLIV, no. 4 (1968), pp. 5–20.

Adler, Selig, 'Franklin D. Roosevelt and Zionism. The Wartime Record',

Judaism, Vol. XXI (Summer 1972), pp. 265–76.

Adler, Selig, 'The Palestine Question in the Wilson Era', *Jewish Social Studies*, Vol. X (October 1948), pp. 303–34.

Adler, Selig, 'The United States and the Holocaust', *American Jewish Historical Quarterly*, Vol. LXIV, no. 1 (September 1974), pp. 14–23.

Agus, Jacob, 'Israel and the Jewish-Christian Dialogue', *Journal of Ecumenical Studies*, Vol. VI, no. 1 (1969), pp. 18–36.

Avineri, Shlomo, 'The Reemergence of Anti-Semitism', *Congress Monthly*, Vol. 43, no. 1 (December 1975 – January 1976), pp. 14–16.

Balboni, Alan, 'The American Zionist Lobby – Basic Patterns and Recent Trends', *Middle East Forum*, Vol. XLVIII, nos. 3 & 4 (1972), pp. 83–100.

Barberis, Mary A., 'The Arab-Israeli Battle on Capitol Hill', *The Virginia Quarterly Review*, Vol. 52, no. 1 (Winter 1976), pp. 203–23.

Barnes, James J., 'Mein Kampf in Britain, 1930–39', *The Wiener Library Bulletin*, Vol. XXVII, no. 32 (1974), pp. 2–10.

Barzilay, E., 'The Jew in the Literature of the Enlightenment', *Jewish Social Studies*, Vol. XVIII (1956), pp. 243–61.

Berkhof, H., 'Israel as a Theological Problem in the Christian Church', *Journal of Ecumenical Studies*, Vol. VI, no. 3 (1969), pp. 329–47.

Brecher, Michael, 'American Jewry's Influence on Israeli-US Relations, Reality and Images', *The Wiener Library Bulletin*, Vol. XXV, no. 1 & 2 (1971), pp. 2–7.

Burton, William, 'Protestant America and the Rebirth of Israel', *Jewish Social Studies*, Vol. XXVI, no. 4 (October 1964), pp. 203–14.

Cohn, Henry J., 'The Jews in the Reformation Era', *Jewish Quarterly*, Vol. 19, no. 3 (Autumn 1971), pp. 4–7.

Crossman, R. H. S., 'Gentile Zionism and the Balfour Declaration', in Norman Podhoretz (ed.) *The Commentary Reader* (New York, Athenum, 1966), pp. 284–94.

Davies, Alan T., 'Anti-Zionism, Anti-Semitism, and the Christian Mind', *The Christian Century* (19 August 1970).

Dawson, W. H., 'Cromwell and the Jews', *The Quarterly Review*, Vol. CCLXIII (1934), pp. 269–86.

Dow, J. G. 'Hebrew and Puritan', *Jewish Quarterly Review*, Vol. III (1891), pp. 52–84.

Duvernoy, Claude, 'A Messianic Light on Zionism', *The Jerusalem Post* (2 March 1977), p. 8.

Edelsberg, Herman, 'Harry Truman and Israel', *The National Jewish Monthly*, Vol. 87, no. 6 (February 1973), pp. 23–9.

Elias, A. B., 'Christian Cooperation in the Restoration of Zion', *Pro-Palestine Herald*, Vol. 3, nos. 3–4 (1934), pp. 17–18.

Feingold, Henry L., 'Roosevelt and the Holocaust: Reflections on New Deal Humanitarianism', *Judaism*, Vol. XVIII (Summer 1969), pp. 259–76.

Feldblum, Esther, 'On the Eve of a Jewish State, American Catholic Responses', *American Jewish Historical Quarterly*, Vol. 64, no. 2 (December 1974), pp. 99–119.

Feuer, Leon I., 'The Birth of the "Jewish Lobby" ', *Jewish Digest*, Vol. XXII, no. 11 (July–August 1977), pp. 51–6.

Fitzsimons, M. A., 'Britain and the Middle East, 1944–1950', *The Review of Politics*, Vol. XXIII, no. 1 (January 1959), pp. 21–30.

Flamery, Edward H., 'Anti-Zionism and the Christian Psyche', *Journal of Ecumenical Studies*, Vol. XI, no. 2 (1969), pp. 173–84.

Friedman, Isaiah, 'The Response to the Balfour Declaration', *Jewish Social Studies*, Vol. XXXV, no. 2 (1973), pp. 105–24.

Ganin, Zvi, 'The Limits of American Jewish Political Power: America's Retreat from Partition, November 1947–March 1949', *Jewish Social Studies*, Vol. XXXIX, nos. 1 & 2 (1977), pp. 1–36.

Garnham, David, 'Factors Influencing Congressional Support for Israel during the 93rd Congress', *The Jerusalem Journal of International Relations*, Vol. 2, no. 3 (Spring 1977), pp. 23–45.

Gessman, Albert M., 'Our Judeo-Christian Heritage', *Issues*, Vol. XXII, nos. 3–4 (Winter 1969), pp. 1–9.

Goldblatt, Chas. I., 'The Impact of the Balfour Declaration in America', *American Jewish Historical Quarterly*, Vol. LVII (June 1968), pp. 455–515.

Gottgetreu, Eric, 'When Napoleon Planned a Jewish State', *The Jewish Digest*, Vol. XX, no. 8 (May 1975).

Haddad, H. S., 'The Biblical Bases of Zionist Colonialism', *Journal of Palestine Studies*, Vol. III, no. 4 (Summer 1974), pp. 97–113.

Halperin, Samuel and Oder, Irvin, 'The U.S. in Search of a Policy. Franklin D. Roosevelt and Palestine', *Review of Politics*, Vol. XXIV (July 1962).

Huff, Earl D., 'A Study of a Successful Interest Group: The American Zionist Movement', *Western Political Science Quarterly*, Vol. XXV (March 1972), pp. 109–23.

Laytner, Anson, 'Israel Through the Third World Looking Glass', *The Jewish Spectator*, Vol. 43, no. 4 (Winter 1978), pp. 45–8.

Lewis, Bernard, 'The anti-Zionist Resolution', *Foreign Affairs*, Vol. 55, no. 1 (October 1976), pp. 56–64.

Lichtheim, Georg, 'Winston Churchill and Zionism', *Midstream*, Vol. 5, no. 2 (Spring 1959), pp. 19–29.

Machover, Moshe and Offenberg, Mario, 'Zionism and its Scarecrows', *Khamsin*, no. 6 (1978), pp. 33–59.

Nelson, Truman, 'The Puritans of Massachusetts: From Egypt to the Promised Land', *Judaism*, Vol. XVI, (1967), pp. 193–206.

Newman, Aubrey, 'Napoleon and the Jews', *European Judaism*, Vol. 2, no. 2 (Winter 1967), pp. 25–32.

Nicholls, David, 'Few are Chosen: Some Reflections on the Politics of A. J. Balfour', *The Review of Politics*, Vol. 30, no. 1 (January 1968), pp. 33–41.

Parzen, Herbert, 'President Truman and the Palestine Quandary: His Initial Experience', *Jewish Social Studies*, Vol. 35, no. 1 (January 1973), pp. 42–72.

Patinkin, D., 'Mercantilism and the Readmission of the Jews to England', *Jewish Social Studies*, Vol. 8, (1946), pp. 161–78.

Pfaff, Richard, 'Perceptions, Politicians and Foreign Policy: The U.S. Senate and the Arab-Israeli Conflict', *Middle East Forum* (Summer 1971), pp. 39–49.

Polishook, Sheila Stern, 'The American Federation of Labor Zionism and the First World War', *American Jewish Historical Quarterly*, Vol. LXV, no. 3 (March 1976), pp. 228–44.

Polkehn, Klaus, 'Secret Contacts: Zionism and Nazi Germany, 1933–1941', *Journal of Palestine Studies*, Vol. V, nos. 3–4 (Spring–Summer 1976), pp. 54–82.

Rabinovich, Abraham, 'Evangelicals to gather in Capital to Support Israel', *The Jerusalem Post* (11 January 1978).

Rosen, Jane, 'U.S. Middle East Policy Courtesy of the Jewish Lobby', *The Guardian* (25 September 1977).

Rotenstreich, Nathan, 'Toynbee and Jewish Nationalism', *Jewish Social Studies*, Vol. XXIV, no. 3 (1962), pp. 131–43.

Rodkey, Frederick Stanley, 'Lord Palmerston and the Rejuvenation of Turkey, 1830–1841', *Journal of Modern History*, Vols. 1 & 2, nos. 4 & 2 (December 1929 & January 1930), pp. 570–93, 193–225.

Scult, Mel, 'English Missions to the Jews – Conversion in the Age of Emancipation', *Jewish Social Studies*, Vol. XXXV, no. 1 (1973), pp. 3–17.

Sewell, Arthur, 'Milton and the Mosaic Law', *The Modern Language Review*, Vol. XXX, no. 1 (January 1935), pp. 13–18.

Shimoni, Gideon, 'Jan Christian Smuts and Zionism', *Jewish Social Studies*, Vol. XXXIX, no. 4 (1977), pp. 269–98.

Shulim, Joseph, 'Napoleon I As the Jewish Messiah: Some Contemporary Conceptions in Virginia', *Jewish Social Studies*, Vol. 7 (1945), pp. 275–80.

Singer, Sholom A., 'The Expulsion of the Jews from England in 1290', *The Jewish Quarterly Review*, Vol. LV, no. 1 (1964/65), pp. 117–35.

Strober, G. S., 'American Jews and the Protestant Community', *Midstream*, Vol. XX (August – September 1974), pp. 47–66.

Stone, Elihu D., 'The Zionist Outlook in Washington', *New Palestine*, Vol. XXXIV (17 March 1944).

Stookey, Robert W., 'The Holy Land: The American Experience', *Middle East Journal*, Vol. XXX, no. 3 (Summer 1976), pp. 351–405.

Trice, Robert H., 'Congress and the Arab-Israeli Conflict: Support for Israel in the U.S. Senate, 1970–73', *Political Science Quarterly*, Vol. 92, no. 3 (February 1977), pp. 443–63.

Verete, Mayir, 'The Restoration of the Jews in English Protestant Thought, 1790–1840', *Middle Eastern Studies*, Vol. 8, no. 1 (January 1972), pp. 3–50.

Wilensky, Mordecai L., 'Thomas Barlow's and John Dury's Attitude Towards the Readmission of the Jews to England', *The Jewish Quarterly Review*, Vol. L, no. 2 (October 1959), pp. 167–268.

Index